T0184006

Lecture Notes in Computer Science   11387

Commenced Publication in 1973
Founding and Former Series Editors:
Gerhard Goos, Juris Hartmanis, and Jan van Leeuwen

Editorial Board

David Hutchison
  Lancaster University, Lancaster, UK
Takeo Kanade
  Carnegie Mellon University, Pittsburgh, PA, USA
Josef Kittler
  University of Surrey, Guildford, UK
Jon M. Kleinberg
  Cornell University, Ithaca, NY, USA
Friedemann Mattern
  ETH Zurich, Zurich, Switzerland
John C. Mitchell
  Stanford University, Stanford, CA, USA
Moni Naor
  Weizmann Institute of Science, Rehovot, Israel
C. Pandu Rangan
  Indian Institute of Technology Madras, Chennai, India
Bernhard Steffen
  TU Dortmund University, Dortmund, Germany
Demetri Terzopoulos
  University of California, Los Angeles, CA, USA
Doug Tygar
  University of California, Berkeley, CA, USA

More information about this series at http://www.springer.com/series/7410

Sokratis K. Katsikas · Frédéric Cuppens
Nora Cuppens · Costas Lambrinoudakis
Annie Antón · Stefanos Gritzalis
John Mylopoulos · Christos Kalloniatis (Eds.)

Computer Security

ESORICS 2018 International Workshops,
CyberICPS 2018 and SECPRE 2018
Barcelona, Spain, September 6–7, 2018
Revised Selected Papers

 Springer

Editors
Sokratis K. Katsikas [iD]
Norwegian University of Science and
Technology
Gjøvik, Norway

Frédéric Cuppens
IMT Atlantique
Cesson-Sévigné, France

Nora Cuppens
IMT Atlantique
Cesson-Sévigné, France

Costas Lambrinoudakis
University of Piraeus
Piraeus, Greece

Annie Antón
Georgia Institute of Technology
Atlanta, GA, USA

Stefanos Gritzalis
University of the Aegean
Karlovasi, Greece

John Mylopoulos
University of Toronto
Toronto, ON, Canada

Christos Kalloniatis [iD]
University of the Aegean
Mytilene, Greece

ISSN 0302-9743   ISSN 1611-3349   (electronic)
Lecture Notes in Computer Science
ISBN 978-3-030-12785-5   ISBN 978-3-030-12786-2   (eBook)
https://doi.org/10.1007/978-3-030-12786-2

Library of Congress Control Number: 2019930854

LNCS Sublibrary: SL4 – Security and Cryptology

This Springer imprint is published by the registered company Springer Nature Switzerland AG
The registered company address is: Gewerbestrasse 11, 6330 Cham, Switzerland

Preface

This book contains revised versions of the papers presented at the Fourth Workshop on the Security of Industrial Control Systems and Cyber-Physical Systems (CyberICPS 2018), and the Second International Workshop on Security and Privacy Requirements Engineering (SECPRE 2018). Both workshops were co-located with the 23rd European Symposium on Research in Computer Security (ESORICS 2018) and were held in Barcelona, Spain, during September 6–7, 2018.

CyberICPS aims to bring together researchers, engineers, and government actors with an interest in the security of industrial control systems and cyber-physical systems in the context of their increasing exposure to cyber-space, by offering a forum for discussion on all issues related to their cyber-security. Cyber-physical systems range in size, complexity, and criticality, from embedded systems used in smart vehicles, to SCADA and industrial control systems such as energy and water distribution systems, smart transportation systems, etc.

CyberICPS 2018 attracted 15 high-quality submissions, each of which was assigned to three referees for review; the review process resulted in accepting eight full papers to be presented and included in the proceedings. These cover topics related to threats, vulnerabilities, and risks that cyber-physical systems and industrial control systems face; cyber-attacks that may be launched against such systems; and ways of detecting and responding to such attacks.

For many years, software engineers have focused on the development of new software thus considering security and privacy mainly during the development stage as an adhoc process rather than an integrated one initiated during the system design stage. However, the data protection regulations, the complexity of modern environments such as IoT, IoE, cloud computing, big data, cyber-physical systems, etc. and the increased level of users' awareness in IT have forced software engineers to identify security and privacy as fundamental design aspects leading to the implementation of more trusted software systems and services. Researchers have addressed the necessity and importance of implementing design methods for security and privacy requirements elicitation, modeling, and implementation in the past few decades in various innovative research domains. Today, security by design (SbD) and privacy by design (PbD) are established research areas that focus on these directions. SECPRE aimed to provide researchers and professionals with the opportunity to present novel and cutting-edge research on these topics.

SECPRE 2018 attracted 11 high-quality submissions, each of which was assigned to three referees for review; the review process resulted in accepting five papers to be presented and included in the proceedings. These cover topics related to security and privacy requirements assurance and evaluation; and to security requirements elicitation and modeling.

We would like to express our thanks to all those who assisted us in organizing the events and putting together the programs. We are very grateful to the members of the

Program Committees for their timely and rigorous reviews. Thanks are also due to the Organizing Committees of the events. Last, but by no means least, we would like to thank all the authors who submitted their work to the workshops and contributed to an interesting set of proceedings.

November 2018

Sokratis K. Katsikas
Frédéric Cuppens
Nora Cuppens
Costas Lambrinoudakis
Annie Antón
Stefanos Gritzalis
John Mylopoulos
Christos Kalloniatis

Organization

Fourth Workshop on the Security of Industrial Control Systems and of Cyber-Physical Systems (CyberICPS 2018)

General Chairs

Sokratis K. Katsikas	Center for Cyber and Information Security, Norwegian University of Science and Technology, Norway and Open University of Cyprus, Cyprus
Frédéric Cuppens	IMT Atlantique, Cybersecurity and Digital Law, France

Program Committee Co-chairs

Nora Cuppens	IMT Atlantique, Cybersecurity and Digital Law, France
Costas Lambrinoudakis	University of Piraeus, Greece

International Program Committee

Alcaraz Cristina	University of Malaga, Spain
Ayed Samiha	IMT-Telecom Bretagne, France
Conti Mauro	University of Padua, Italy
Espes David	University of Brest, France
Garcia-Alfaro Joaquin	Telecom SudParis, France
Gkioulos Vasileios	Norwegian University of Science and Technology, Norway
Gollmann Dieter	Hamburg University of Technology, Germany
Laarouchi Youssef	EDF R&D, France
Mambo Masahiro	Kanazawa University, Japan
Mauw Sjouke	University of Luxembourg, Luxembourg
Meng Weizhi	Institute for Infocomm Research, Singapore
Mitchell Chris	Royal Holloway, University of London, UK
Pandey Pankaj	Norwegian University of Science and Technology, Norway
Roudier Yves	EURECOM, France
Song Houbling	Embry-Riddle Aeronautical University, USA
Spathoulas Georgios	University of Thessaly, Greece
State Radu	University of Luxembourg, Luxembourg
Wahid Khan Ferdous	Airbus Defence and Space GmbH, Germany
Yaich Reda	IRT SystemX, France
Zanero Stefano	Politecnico di Milano, Italy

Second International Workshop on Security and Privacy Requirements Engineering (SECPRE 2018)

General Chairs

Annie Antón	Georgia Institute of Technology, College of Computing, School of Interactive Computing, USA
Stefanos Gritzalis	University of the Aegean, School of Engineering, Greece

Program Committee Co-chairs

John Mylopoulos	University of Toronto, Department of Computer Science, Canada
Christos Kalloniatis	University of the Aegean, School of Social Sciences, Greece

International Program Committee

Cuppens Frederic	Telecom Bretange, France
De Capitani di Vimercati Sabrina	Università degli Studi di Milano, Italy
Dimitrakos Theo	University of Kent, UK
Dubois Eric	Luxembourg Institute of Science and Technology, Luxembourg
Fernandez-Gago Carmen	University of Malaga, Spain
Fernandez-Medina Eduardo	University of Castilla-La Mancha, Spain
Gharib Mohamad	University of Florence, Italy
Giorgini Paolo	University of Trento, Italy
Heisel Maritta	University of Duisburg-Essen, Germany
Juerjens Jan	University of Koblenz-Landau, Germany
Lambrinoudakis Costas	University of Pireus, Greece
Li Tong	Beijing University of Technology, China
Martinelli Fabio	National Research Council, CNR, Italy
Massey Aaron	University of Maryland, USA
Mouratidis Haralambos	University of Brighton, UK
Pavlidis Michalis	University of Brighton, UK
Rosado David Garcia	University of Castilla-La Manca, Spain
Salnitri Mattia	University of Trento, Italy
Samarati Pierangela	Università degli Studi di Milano, Italy
Staddon Jessica	North Carolina State University, USA
Zannone Nicola	Eindhoven University of Technology, The Netherlands

Contents

Security of Industrial Control Systems and Cyber-Physical Systems (CyberICPS 2018)

Improving SIEM for Critical SCADA Water Infrastructures Using Machine Learning

Hanan Hindy[1]([⊠]) [iD], David Brosset[2] [iD], Ethan Bayne[1] [iD], Amar Seeam[3] [iD], and Xavier Bellekens[1] [iD]

[1] Division of Cyber Security, Abertay University, Dundee, Scotland, UK
{1704847,e.bayne,x.bellekens}@abertay.ac.uk
[2] Naval Academy Research Institute, Brest, France
david.brosset@ecole-navale.fr
[3] Department of Computer Science, Middlesex University, Flic-en-Flac, Mauritius
a.seeam@mdx.ac.mu

Abstract. Network Control Systems (NAC) have been used in many industrial processes. They aim to reduce the human factor burden and efficiently handle the complex process and communication of those systems. Supervisory control and data acquisition (SCADA) systems are used in industrial, infrastructure and facility processes (e.g. manufacturing, fabrication, oil and water pipelines, building ventilation, etc.) Like other Internet of Things (IoT) implementations, SCADA systems are vulnerable to cyber-attacks, therefore, a robust anomaly detection is a major requirement. However, having an accurate anomaly detection system is not an easy task, due to the difficulty to differentiate between cyber-attacks and system internal failures (e.g. hardware failures). In this paper, we present a model that detects anomaly events in a water system controlled by SCADA. Six Machine Learning techniques have been used in building and evaluating the model. The model classifies different anomaly events including hardware failures (e.g. sensor failures), sabotage and cyber-attacks (e.g. DoS and Spoofing). Unlike other detection systems, our proposed work helps in accelerating the mitigation process by notifying the operator with additional information when an anomaly occurs. This additional information includes the probability and confidence level of event(s) occurring. The model is trained and tested using a real-world dataset.

Keywords: Cyber-physical systems · Machine learning · SCADA · SIEM

1 Introduction

An increasing number of networked control systems are being deployed for the monitoring, control and response of physical infrastructure. Deprecated infrastructure is being replaced by SCADA systems that are compatible with IoT

© Springer Nature Switzerland AG 2019
S. K. Katsikas et al. (Eds.): CyberICPS 2018/SECPRE 2018, LNCS 11387, pp. 3–19, 2019.
https://doi.org/10.1007/978-3-030-12786-2_1

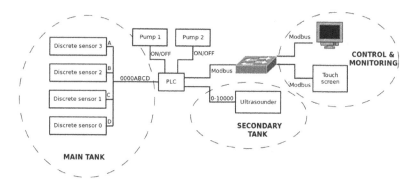

Fig. 1. Network architecture

devices, enabling remote monitoring and control of previously isolated systems. Through this upgrade, industries are able to achieve higher reliability and flexibility of deployed systems. However, by enabling external internet access, industries are introducing the increased risk of cyber-attacks to potentially critical infrastructure [28].

Vulnerabilities in critical infrastructure protection (CIP) is due to five factors. The first is the *lack of open protocols*. Current programmable logic controllers (PLCs) are often controlled through proprietary network protocols that have not been scrutinized by security professionals and act as a black box, hence increasing the attack surface [9]. The second is due to the *lack of segmentation* in network infrastructure [17]. Current PLCs are connected to control networks for the data to be analysed in real time by higher management. Whilst this may increase profit margins and decrease the reaction time to market changes, the lack of segmentation allows for transversal network attacks. The third one is due to the *number of off-the-shelf equipment* being set up in the network [8]. By including off-the-shelf hardware, the attack surface increases, and introduces other potentially weak links (i.e. Entry points). The fourth one is due to the *lack of training received* by the operators and the inability of the operator to distinguish between incidents and cyber-attacks [2,6]. Finally, the fifth one is due to the *exponential growth of organized cyber-crime* and nation state-sponsored cyber-warfare to destabilize countries [16,27].

Critical infrastructure network security is intrinsically different from computer networks as the interaction between the nodes is done in real time at a physical level. Threats affecting computer networks and their associated intrusion detection systems (IDS) are discussed in [13,14]. Numerous efforts have been made to apply current cyber-security solutions to CIP networks, however, the solutions proposed are often not suited for the infrastructure and do not consider the underlying risks posed by compromised sensor data [12]. As a results, despite the advances made in the design and implementation of cyber-security solutions, there is little research being made with the goal of improving SIEM and increase the resilience of CIP against cyber-incidents. In recent years, the number of attacks against critical infrastructure has significantly increased. The Stuxnet malware is an example of a high-profile SCADA attack, which was first discovered in an Iranian power plant in 2010. Stuxnet was used to infect and reprogramme the PLCs while hiding the changes made using a custom-made PLC rootkit [19]. Another example is the Maroochy attack against a sewage system, causing 800.000 L of sewer waste to be released in waterways and parks. The Maroochy attack was perpetrated by an insider, taking advantage of insecure communication between the pumping station and the central SCADA control system [7]. The Ukrainian power grid attack is another example of a large SCADA attack, where 225,000 people were affected by the loss of power. The attacker managed to switch off 30 substations for over 6 hours. In total, over 74 MWh of electricity was not supplied to the energy grid, representing a total of 0.015% of the daily electricity consumption of the country. The attack was later attributed to "Sandworm", a Russian group of hackers known for advanced persistent threats [22]. These attacks demonstrate that when attacking a CIP, attackers often study the system extensively to perpetrate the attack as stealthily as possible, tailoring their strategies towards the particular system.

In this manuscript, we aim at improving Security Information and Event Management (SIEM) for critical infrastructure using machine learning to identify patterns in the data reported by PLCs in a water system controlled by SCADA. The contributions of this paper are as follows:

– We provide a new SIEM methodology that leverage sensor data and the event-driven nature of cyber-physical systems.
– We categorize the attacks in 14 categories, based on the data emerging from the dataset. Out prototype features 3 experiments using machine learning algorithms for the detection of the said anomalies.
– We propose the usage of probabilistic model to decrease the mitigation time.
– We conduct a thorough evaluation of SIEM performances through a operational scenarios in the third experiment. The two best predictions are proposed to the operator allowing him to alleviate cyber-attacks when an event is detected. The anomaly detection provides an accuracy of 95.64% with an 85% confidence.

The remainder of this paper is organized as follows; Sect. 2 discusses equipment used to generate the dataset. Section 3 provides an overview of the dataset, the scenarios and the features, while Sect. 4 presents the results obtained by applying machine learning technique to differentiate between different scenarios. Section 5 discusses the results and limitations discovered. Section 6 presents related work in this field. The paper ends by concluding our findings in Sect. 7.

2   Experimental Set-Up

In this section we describe the architecture of SCADA controlled critical infrastructure (CI) used to gather the dataset described in Sect. 3. Current CI systems are interconnected and are increasingly prone to faulty operations and cyber-attacks. Risks present are caused by the fragmentation of technology incorporated into the CI, vulnerabilities within hardware and software components and through physical tampering of equipment by malicious actors. The design of the CI presented in this research represents a real world, real-time system that is capable of working under normal and abnormal conditions. Additionally, the presented system can be exposed to the aforementioned vulnerabilities.

Figure 1 provides a high level overview of the network of the system. The system is composed of two tanks—the main tank and a secondary tank. Each tank can contain either fuel or water and can be set to two distinct modes—acting either as a distributor or as storage. The main and secondary tank has a capacity of 9 and 7 litres respectively. The main tank is composed of four sensors connected to a PLC. The sensors are then connected to both Pump1 and Pump2. Both pumps control the flow of water between the main tank and the secondary tank. The main tank utilizes the four sensors to measure the level of liquid, whilst the secondary tank monitors fluid volume with an ultrasound sensor. Data gathered from the sensors are transferred to the control and monitoring network using the Modbus protocol.

2.1 Modbus Protocol

The Modbus protocol operates at the application layer of the open systems interconnection (OSI) model. It enables communication between interconnected network nodes based on a request and reply methodology. The protocol requires little processing overhead, which makes it a sensible candidate for communications between PLCs, Sensors, or Remote Terminal Units (RTUs).

The Modbus protocol works independently of protocols implemented in other layers of the OSI model, hence, it can be used both on routable network or used for serial communications [15].

The data being stored by the Modbus protocol in slave devices can be categorized in four different ways as listed below:

- **Discrete Input** Read-Only Access, it provides Physical I/O
- **Input Register** Read-Only Access, it provides Physical I/O
- **Holding Register** Read-Only Access, it provides Read-Write Data
- **Coil** Read-Write Access, it provides application data

Each table can contain up to 9,999 values, however, some devices can allow up to 65,536 addresses across all tables. Each vendor has its own specification of the Modbus data tables, and the set-up often requires the operator to read the vendor-specific documentation.

2.2 Sensors and PLC

As shown in Fig. 1 the system is composed of a single PLC. The PLC is a compact Base Twido PLC, with 40 discrete I/O, 24 discrete inputs, and 14 relays. The system is also composed of a Modicon M238 logic controller. The system can be sent instructions through the touch screen or via a remote system connected to the network.

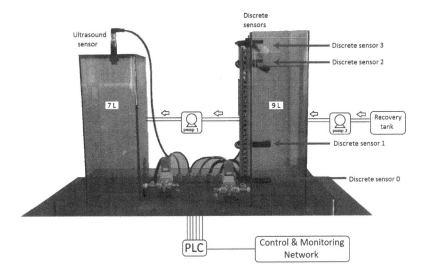

Fig. 2. System architecture

The system is also composed of five sensors as shown in Fig. 1. Four discrete level sensors are located in the main tank. The first sensor (S0) indicates a low level in the tank (1.25 L), the second sensor (S1) indicates a measure of less than 3.35 L, the third sensor (S2), indicates a level of 8 L while the last sensor (S3) indicates a full tank measure (9 L).

The secondary tank is fitted with a single ultrasound sensor. The ultrasound sensor is a Schneider-Electric cylindrical M18 ultrasonic sensor. The sensor is fitted at the top of the tank and is used to measure the distance of the liquid surface to the top of the tank. The sensor can also be used to detect the presence or absence of liquid in the tank.

2.3   Operation Mode

The system is controlled automatically through the PLC to avoid the spillage of liquid stored in tanks. Figure 2 illustrates the physical system. For the purpose of this research, the primary tank is filled from a recovery tank, however, the recovery tank in our system can be substituted by other liquid source, such as a river, a fuel line, etc.

Once the primary tank is filled from the recovery tank using pump 2, the PLC activates Pump 1 to transfer liquid to the secondary tank to avoid spillage.

To simulate a constant liquid consumption from the tanks, valves at the bottom of both the primary and the secondary tanks can be opened. The PLC monitors tank volumes by reading all sensor data registers at 0.1 s intervals. The PLC will automatically refuel the primary tank using Pump 2 when the volume of liquid goes below 1.25 L. Similarly, Pump 2 will be instructed to stop when a total volume of 9 L is reached. The secondary tank will be refuelled when

Table 1. Registers extracted bits representation

Reg. No.	Bit No.	Value
2	4	Discrete Sensor 3
	5	Discrete Sensor 2
	6	Discrete Sensor 1
	7	Discrete Sensor 0
4	16-bits	Depth Sensor

Reg. No.	Bit No.	Value
3	0	Pump 2
	1	Pump 1
	5	Pump 2 Valve
	4	Pump 1 Valve

ultrasound sensors detect the liquid level to be below 2.1 L. Furthermore, the PLC will only deactivate pump 1 once the ultrasound sensor detects that the secondary tank has reached a level of 6.3 L.

3   Dataset

This section describes the dataset gathered by the IC and the scenarios recorded. The dataset used in this manuscript has been published separately in a dataset publication [21].

The CI presented in Sect. 2 was used to gather data for the dataset and outputted into CSV format. The dataset comprises actuator and sensor readings that the PLC recorded periodically at 0.1 s intervals. Within the data collected, PLC registers 2 through 4 provided output data describing the state of the system that was used for analysis.

Table 1 provides an overview of the different registers used by the PLC. As shown, Register 2, provides the bits indicating the binary state of the discrete sensors. A population count can be done on the register to retrieve the state of each sensor separately. Register 3 contains the state of the pump, either as active or inactive, while Register 4 contains the step value from 0 to 10,000 of the ultrasound sensors (e.g. Step 3,000 represents 2.1 L of liquid in the tank).

3.1   Scenarios

The dataset consists of 14 different scenarios as shown in Table 2. Each scenario covers one of 5 operational scenarios representing the potential threat (i.e. sabotage, accident, breakdown, or cyber-attack) as well as 6 affected components. The affected components are system components that are directly affected by the anomaly.

The recorded data is organized in 15 different CSV files of variable duration based on the type of incident recorded (i.e. a sabotage incident may take less time than a distributed denial of service).

3.2   Pre-processing

This subsection highlights the pre-processing of the data obtained. The pre-processing is composed of six steps.

Table 2. Dataset scenarios, operational scenarios and affected components

	Scenario	Affected component	Operational scenario	No. of instances
1	Normal	None	Normal	5519
2	Plastic bag	Ultrasound sensor	Accident/sabotage	10549
3	Blocked measure 1		Breakdown/sabotage	226
4	Blocked measure 2			144
5	Floating objects in main tank (2 objects)		Accident/sabotage	854
6	Floating objects in main tank (7 objects)			733
7	Humidity		Breakdown	157
8	Discrete sensor failure	Discrete sensor 1		1920
9	Discrete sensor failure	Discrete sensor 2		5701
10	Denial of service attack	Network	Cyber-attack	307
11	Spoofing			10130
12	Wrong connection		Breakdown/sabotage	6228
13	Person hitting the tanks (low intensity)	Whole subsystem	Sabotage	347
14	Person hitting the tanks (medium intensity)			281
15	Person hitting the tanks (high intensity)			292

1. Extract Instances

Firstly, each scenario instances are extracted from the log file. An instance is represented by the recording of the register values at a specific time. Each log file has 10 rows per instance. Each row contains The Date, Time, the Register Number, and the Register Value of the PLC.

2. Calculate rate of change of Register 4

The value of Register 4 is the most significant. However, the significance is not in its single value but in how the value changes over time. This significance can be formulated in the rate of change over time. Figure 3 shows the rate change in Register 4 value over 15 different scenarios.

For each instances, the rate of change is calculated over 10 time frames as expressed in Eq. 1.

$$Rate \ of \ change_i = \frac{reg4_i - reg4_{i-10}}{time_i - time_{i-10}} \qquad (1)$$

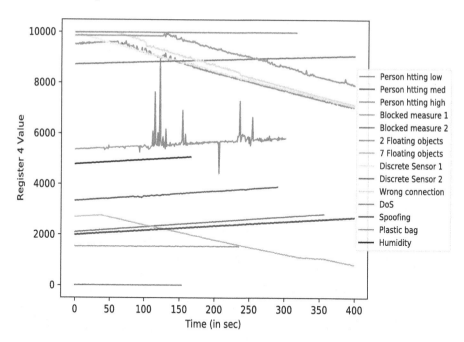

Fig. 3. Rate of change of register 4 value over different scenarios

3. Apply Threshold

Table 2 shows the number of recorded instances per scenario. As shown in the table, the events are not statistically distributed over the scenarios. Therefore, the most instances scenario will bias the classification model output. A threshold is applied to take only the first N instances of each file. N should satisfy two conditions (a) reduce the gap between instances count per scenario, (b) keep the variation of instances count per scenario.

4. Serialization
   . A single file is needed for the training process. All Instances are, therefore, serialized.
5. Normalization
6. Split

Finally, the data is normalized and split into 80% training and 20% testing sets.

4   Experiments and Results

This section outlines three experiments conducted and how accurately threats could be identified. Note that the code (pre-processing and experiments) is available in a Github repository[1].

---

[1] https://github.com/AbertayMachineLearningGroup/machine-learning-SIEM-water-infrastructure.

The aim of the experiments is to alert, and provide the operator with the most likely affected components, in order to decrease the time to apply the corrective action.

Six machine learning techniques are used for the classification models, namely, Logistic Regression (LR) Gaussian Naïve Bayes (NB), k-Nearest Neighbours (k-NN), Support Vector Machine (SVM), Decision Trees (DT) and Random Forests (RF) [5, 18, 20, 23, 26, 29].

4.1 Parameters

All experiments are conducted using the following computation parameters:

– Training Set : Testing Set = 80% : 20%
– Evaluation: The overall accuracy is calculated as follows:

$$Overall Accuracy = \frac{TP + TN}{TP + TN + FP + FN}$$

Where:
- True Positive (TP): Number of anomaly instances which scenario is correctly detected
- True Negative (TN): Number of normal instances which are correctly detected
- False Positive (FP): Number of normal instances which are detected as one of the anomaly scenarios
- False Negative (FN): Number of anomaly instances which are detected as normal scenarios

4.2 First Experiment

The aim of the first experiment is to alert the user when an anomaly occurs without specifying the associated scenario. The aim is to provide the operator of the CI with a binary output.

Figure 4 shows the classification results of the six machine learning algorithms applied to data. The algorithms provide a binary output. As shown, the highest accuracies reached are 93.42%, 93.48% and 94% using DT, RF and k-NN respectively.

Providing an alert that an anomaly exists in the data recorded by the sensors is considered important, however, as the alert is provided in a binary fashion, the operator is – in this case – unable to identify the anomaly at first sight and take corrective action. To this end, a second experiment was established with the aim of proving more information to the operator.

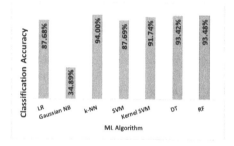

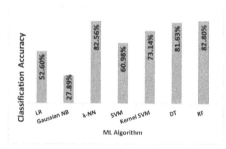

Fig. 4. Anomaly classification accuracy

Fig. 5. Affected component classification accuracy

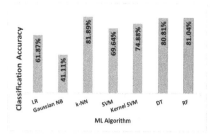

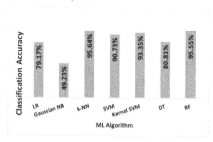

Fig. 6. Scenarios classification accuracy. Trial one (Single scenario reported)

Fig. 7. Scenarios classification accuracy (Alerting with two probable scenarios)

4.3 Second Experiment

The second experiment aims at giving the operator capital information about the anomaly. The alert in this case includes the affected component. The model classifies what components are affected by the five components present in the CI (i.e. Network, Discrete Sensor 1, Discrete Sensor 2, Ultrasound Sensor and Whole System) as well as the 'None' affected case.

Figure 5 shows the classification results of the different machine learning algorithms. The highest accuracies reached are 82.56% and 82.8% using k-NN and RF respectively. The result shows a trade-off between the binary classification offered in the first experiment and by providing the operator with more detailed information. As shown trade-off limits, the accuracy of the system accounts for a large number of false positive, potentially misleading the operator during normal operations.

4.4 Third Experiment

The third experiment aims at notifying the operator with an occurring scenario. To this end, the third experiment is divided in three operational trials.

Table 3. Distribution of probabilistic classification of scenarios

Algorithm	Maximum number of probable scenarios per instance	Number of instance with **1** probable scenario	Number of instance with **2** probable scenarios	Number of instance with **3** probable scenarios	Number of instance with **4** probable scenarios
DT	1	3053	-	-	-
		100%	-	-	-
k-NN	3	1882	962	209	-
		61.64%	31.51%	6.85%	-
RF	4	1737	1004	297	15
		56.9%	32.89%	9.71%	0.5%

Trial One

In the first trial, models are trained to classify the different scenarios. The operator is notified with the scenario occurring. Figure 6 shows the results of these trial. As shown, the accuracy is reduced and demonstrate a high false negative rate, with the highest accuracy only reaching 81.89%.

To overcome this high false positive rate, the scenarios were reviewed and the following conclusions were made: (a) The scenarios are co-related. (b) When models are trained to output the probability of an event belonging to another of the 14 scenarios, a maximum of 4 scenarios have non-zero probabilities. For example, Table 3 shows the count of instances having 1, 2, 3 or 4 probable scenarios. In the second row of Table 3, 61.64% of the instances are classified to a single scenario, 31.51% are classified to be one of 2 possible scenarios and only 6.85% are classified to be one of 3 possible scenarios.

As a result of this analysis, trial two to four are based on reporting two probable scenarios to the operator, reducing the uncertainty of our approach.

Trial Two

In the second trial, the operator is notified with two potential attack scenarios instead of a single one. The two scenarios are the highest probabilities provided by the algorithms. Figure 7 demonstrates that this technique increased the accuracy to reach 95.55% and 95.64% using RF and k-NN receptively. By providing the operator with a probability in the attack scenario he is able to act accordingly and alleviate the attack, hence reducing the overall response time needed.

Table 4 shows an example of correctly classified instances when two probable scenarios are considered. The numbers are calculated in reference to the k-NN classifier. For example, in the first row, '2 Floating Objects' scenario misclassified instances are shown. 53 are misclassified as 'Plastic Bag' sabotage. However, 48 of them can be correctly classified by considering the second probable scenario. In the same manner, in Table 4 row 4, 85 instances of the 'Plastic Bag' scenario

Table 4. Co-relation of scenarios that are misclassified based on highest probable scenario and correct with the second probable one (Calculated based on k-NN experiment)

Scenario (X)	Instances count where X Is Not 1st Scenario	Scenario (Y) The count of instances classified as Y while the correct is X							
		Is 2nd Scenario	2 Floating Objects	7 Floating Objects	Normal	Plastic Bag	Sensor Failure	Spoofing	Wrong Connection
2 Floating Objects	53	48	-	-	-	53	-	-	-
7 Floating Objects	5	5	-	-	-	-	-	-	5
Normal	80	58	-	-	-	1	68	-	11
Plastic Bag	85	75	38	-	3	-	24	18	2
Sensor Failure	183	137	-	-	75	53	-	5	50
Spoofing	45	25	-	-	-	37	8	-	-
Wrong Connection	102	72	-	5	23	5	69	-	-

are misclassified to be '2 Floating Objects' (38 instances), 'Sensor Failure' (24 instances), 'Spoofing' (18 instances), 'Normal' (3 instances) and 'Wrong Connection' (2 instances). 75 can be correctly classified with the second probable scenario in consideration.

While the operator is notified with two probable scenarios, it can also be misleading. For this reason our third attempt provides a confidence measure to the operator increasing his situational awareness.

Trial Three and Four

In the third and fourth trials, a single scenario is reported to the operator unless the probability is less than the confidence percentage. Figure 8 shows the results for 75% confidence. In the first case, a single scenario is reported if its probability is greater than or equal to 0.75, otherwise, if the threshold is reached a second scenario is reported as well. The accuracy provided is 91.84%.

This accuracy rises when using an 85% confidence. Figure 8 shows a maximum accuracy of 95.64% using k-NN.

It can be seen from Figs. 7 and 8 that DT accuracy is the same. This is due to the DT output, as a single scenario for each instance is available, therefore it is not possible to output two probable scenarios to the operator.

Finally, the result shows that the fourth operational trial is the most convenient for the operator as a single scenario is provided, unless the threshold is reached. The accuracy provided by the fourth operational scenario also reaches 95.64%, hence reducing the uncertainty of the attack currently at hand, and the ability of the operator to alleviate the attack.

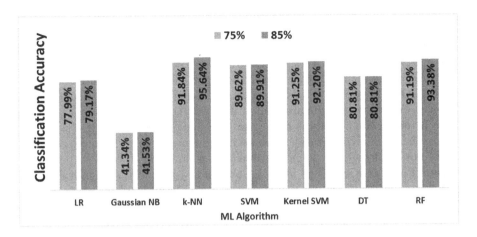

Fig. 8. Scenarios classification accuracy (Alerting with one/two scenario(s) based on 75% and 85% confidence)

5 Discussion and Limitations

In this section, we discuss the main takeaways based on the experiments evaluated in Sect. 4. Additionally, the limitations of our models are listed.

Key Takeaways

- **Using high confidence:** Probabilities are considered to solve the trade-off between the co-related scenarios and reducing the amount of information provided to the operator (i.e. multiple scenarios). This implies reporting the probability of having a scenario occurring. For this piece of work, a confidence interval of 85% is evidenced to provide the best results.
- **Sensors location and architecture:** The position of the sensors and the architecture of the SCADA system affects the collected data and, consequently, affects the model detection accuracy. Moreover, the collection of data greatly affect the pre-processing stages, it is therefore important to gather data consistently.
- **Longer recording periods needed:** In order to increase the accuracy of the machine learning model, the operators should have the recordings of long periods of time for all sensor data. This helps have multiple instances over time and therefore, more instances for training. Moreover, it is recommended to have similar recording duration for the different scenarios. In the case of massively different recording lengths, files need to be serialised in order to avoid bias towards the scenario with the longest recording time.
- **Importance of scenarios:** The more recorded scenarios used for training, the more robust the detection model. With more scenarios, the model can learn variations in scenarios. Moreover, the operator will be provided with higher confidence of reported anomalies.

Limitations

- **Limited Number of Scenarios:** The experiments were conducted using 15 log files which covered 14 scenarios. Any new scenario other than the ones covered in the log files will not likely be reported to the operator.
- **Model Evaluation:** Models are evaluated using six machine learning techniques. Hence, the results are limited to these algorithms.
- **Architecture:** The data is limited to the scale of the CI used in this study. More complex architecture – such as introducing more tanks and sensors – may not yield the same anomaly detection accuracy.
- **Real-Time testing:** The model is built and tested based on the dataset, however, testing the model real-time is essential to measure the performance.

6   Related Work

The area of critical infrastructure protection and Security Information and Event Management has a rich history of books, deployments and lessons learned from both universities and organizations deploying tools and techniques to protect their environments.

Mitchell and Chen [25] presented a survey on recent Cyber-Physical Systems (CPS) intrusion detection systems. They classified CPSs into two categories based on potential detection technique: (1) Knowledge-Based or Misuse Detection and (2) Behaviour-Based. While the survey provides a general overview of potential threats, it focuses essentially on the network traffic rather than on data provenance and data accuracy. This survey, however, provides the stepping stone of the field. In [4] and [3] Amin *et al.* provide an overview a security threat assessment of a networked CI including different layers (i.e. supervisory and control networks). The manuscripts present a grey-box approach where the hacker possesses a certain level of knowledge of the system and is able to perpetrate a deception attack against the system in order to enable liquid spilling from the canal the IDS was tested on. Cheng *et al.* [11] provide a technique to alleviate control-oriented attacks, code-injection attacks or code-reuse attacks on embedded devices. The highlight the lack of existing mechanisms and present 'Orpheus', a program behaviour model, taking advantage of the event-driven nature of embedded devices controlling critical infrastructure. Mathur [24] discusses the limitations of the detecting a incidents in critical infrastructures by analysing processes. The manuscript refers to two methods, the first described is the CUSUM [10]. CUMSUM is a statistical method allowing to detect anomalies in time series, corresponding to a specified process. The technique requires two parameters to operate, the 'bias' and the 'threshold'. The CUMSUM provides the cumulative sum of the deviation for the process measured. By plotting the predicted and observed state, the operator is able to identify the state of the facility and identify changes in behavior. The second methodology is based on State Entanglement (SE) [1]. SE combines the states of multiple components of a system to construct a state space. The state space act as a blacklist, highlighting prohibited states during normal operations.

7   Conclusion and Future Work

This work focused on building an anomaly detection and a SIEM tool for a SCADA water system. The model was evaluated using a real-world dataset covering 14 anomaly scenarios including normal system behavior. The presented scenarios covered a wide range of events, ranging from hardware failure to sabotage. Three experiments were conducted using 6 Machine Learning techniques.

The experiments varied based on the level of information reported to the operator. The First experiment allowed anomaly event to be reported to the operator as a binary output. While events where being detected as either anomalies or normal operation, the operator was unaware of the type of anomaly occurring. The second experiment reported the affected component, providing the operator with information relating to a single or multiple sensor data. Finally, the third experiment - which provided the best results - reported the anomaly with an accuracy level, helping the operator to take subsequent correcting steps.

The overall evaluation showed that k-NN, Decision Tree and Random Forest outperformed Gaussian Naïve Bayes, SVM and kernel SVM. Moreover, k-NN results demonstrated the highest accuracy amongst all algorithms in the three experiments. The experiments achieved the accuracy of **94%** for the binary output and **95.64%** for the scenarios classification. As aforementioned, the scenarios are co-related, therefore, the operator - in the third experiment - is notified with the most probable scenarios/anomaly occurring. Moreover, a confidence level was used to provide the operator with the best information available.

To further enhance the detection accuracy, the following should be considered. Increasing the dataset instances to enhance the training process and building hybrid model to classify subgroups of events.

References

1. Adepu, S., Mathur, A.: Distributed detection of single-stage multipoint cyber attacks in a water treatment plant. In: Proceedings of the 11th ACM on Asia Conference on Computer and Communications Security, pp. 449–460. ACM (2016)
2. Ahmed, I., Roussev, V., Johnson, W., Senthivel, S., Sudhakaran, S.: A SCADA system testbed for cybersecurity and forensic research and pedagogy. In: Proceedings of the 2nd Annual Industrial Control System Security Workshop, pp. 1–9. ACM (2016)
3. Amin, S., Litrico, X., Sastry, S.S., Bayen, A.M.: Cyber security of water scada systems-part ii: attack detection using enhanced hydrodynamic models. IEEE Trans. Control. Syst. Technol. **21**(5), 1679–1693 (2013)
4. Amin, S., Litrico, X., Sastry, S., Bayen, A.M.: Cyber security of water scada systems-part i: analysis and experimentation of stealthy deception attacks. IEEE Trans. Control. Syst. Technol. **21**(5), 1963–1970 (2013)
5. Barber, D.: Bayesian Reasoning and Machine Learning. Cambridge University Press, Cambridge (2012)
6. Bellekens, X., et al.: Cyber-physical-security model for safety-critical IoT infrastructures. In: Wireless World Research Forum Meeting, vol. 35 (2015)

7. Brenner, J.F.: Eyes wide shut: the growing threat of cyber attacks on industrial control systems. Bull. At. Sci. **69**(5), 15–20 (2013). https://doi.org/10.1177/0096340213501372

8. Bujari, A., Furini, M., Mandreoli, F., Martoglia, R., Montangero, M., Ronzani, D.: Standards, security and business models: key challenges for the iot scenario. Mob. Netw. Appl. **23**(1), 147–154 (2018)

9. Calderón Godoy, A.J., González Pérez, I.: Integration of sensor and actuator networks and the scada system to promote the migration of the legacy flexible manufacturing system towards the industry 4.0 concept. J. Sens. Actuator Netw. **7**(2), 23 (2018)

10. Cárdenas, A.A., Amin, S., Lin, Z.S., Huang, Y.L., Huang, C.Y., Sastry, S.: Attacks against process control systems: risk assessment, detection, and response. In: Proceedings of the 6th ACM Symposium on Information, Computer and Communications Security, pp. 355–366. ACM (2011)

11. Cheng, L., Tian, K., Yao, D.D.: Orpheus: Enforcing cyber-physical execution semantics to defend against data-oriented attacks. In: Proceedings of the 33rd Annual Computer Security Applications Conference, pp. 315–326. ACM (2017)

12. Gupta, B., Agrawal, D.P., Yamaguchi, S., Arachchilage, N.A., Veluru, S.: Editorial security, privacy, and forensics in the critical infrastructure: advances and future directions (2017)

13. Hindy, H., et al.: A taxonomy and survey of intrusion detection system design techniques, network threats and datasets. arXiv preprint arXiv:1806.03517 (2018)

14. Hindy, H., Hodo, E., Bayne, E., Seeam, A., Atkinson, R., Bellekens, X.: A taxonomy of malicious traffic for intrusion detection systems. In: Proceedings of the Cyber SA 2018. IEEE, June 2018

15. Huitsing, P., Chandia, R., Papa, M., Shenoi, S.: Attack taxonomies for the modbus protocols. Int. J. Crit. Infrastruct. Prot. **1**, 37–44 (2008)

16. Jensen, E.T.: Computer attacks on critical national infrastructure: a use of force invoking the right of self-defense. Stanf. J. Int. Law **38**, 207 (2002)

17. Jiang, N., Lin, H., Yin, Z., Xi, C.: Research of paired industrial firewalls in defense-in-depth architecture of integrated manufacturing or production system. In: 2017 IEEE International Conference on Information and Automation (ICIA), pp. 523–526. IEEE (2017)

18. Hosmer Jr., D.W., Lemeshow, S., Sturdivant, R.X.: Applied Logistic Regression, vol. 398. Wiley, Hoboken (2013)

19. Langner, R.: Stuxnet: dissecting a cyberwarfare weapon. IEEE Secur. Priv. **9**(3), 49–51 (2011). https://doi.org/10.1109/MSP.2011.67

20. Larose, D.T., Larose, C.D.: Discovering Knowledge in Data: An Introduction to Data Mining. Wiley, Hoboken (2014)

21. Laso, P.M., Brosset, D., Puentes, J.: Dataset of anomalies and malicious acts in a cyber-physical subsystem (2017). https://doi.org/10.1016/j.dib.2017.07.038, http://www.sciencedirect.com/science/article/pii/S2352340917303402, iD: 311593

22. Lee, R.M., Assante, M.J., Conway, T.: Analysis of the cyber attack on the Ukrainian power grid. SANS ICS Report (2016)

23. Lior, R.: Data Mining with Decision Trees: Theory and Applications, vol. 81. World Scientific, Singapore (2014)

24. Mathur, A.: On the limits of detecting process anomalies in critical infrastructure. In: Proceedings of the 4th ACM Workshop on Cyber-Physical System Security, p. 1. ACM (2018)

25. Mitchell, R., Chen, I.R.: A survey of intrusion detection techniques for cyber-physical systems. ACM Comput. Surv. **46**(4), 55:1–55:29 (2014). https://doi.org/10.1145/2542049
26. Steinwart, I., Christmann, A.: Support Vector Machines. Springer, Heidelberg (2008). https://doi.org/10.1007/978-0-387-77242-4
27. Tan, E.E.: Cyber Deterrence in Singapore: Framework & Recommendations, RSIS Working Paper, No. 309. Nanyang Technological University, Singapore (2018)
28. Ten, C.W., Manimaran, G., Liu, C.C.: Cybersecurity for critical infrastructures: attack and defense modeling. IEEE Trans. Syst. Man Cybern.-Part A: Syst. Hum. **40**(4), 853–865 (2010)
29. VanderPlas, J.: Python Data Science Handbook: Essential Tools for Working with Data. O' Reilly Media, Inc., Sebastopol (2016)

Cyber-Attacks Against the Autonomous Ship

Georgios Kavallieratos[1]([⊠]), Sokratis Katsikas[1,2], and Vasileios Gkioulos[1]

[1] Department of Information Security and Communications Technology,
Norwegian University of Science and Technology, Gjøvik, Norway
{georgios.kavallieratos,sokratis.katsikas,vasileios.gkioulos}@ntnu.no
[2] School of Pure and Applied Sciences, Open University of Cyprus,
Latsia, Nicosia, Cyprus
sokratis.katsikas@ouc.ac.cy

Abstract. Autonomous ships transferring valuable cargoes and humans in a more efficient and cost effective manner will soon be state of the art technology. Yet, their ICT system architecture and operations have not been defined in full detail. Moreover, multiple cyber security issues remain open and should be addressed. No study to date has analyzed fully the architecture of the autonomous ship, even less so have potential cyber threats and cyber attacks been identified. In this paper we identify and categorize systems that make up an autonomous ship, we propose a generic system architecture, and we analyze the cyber security of the ship by leveraging the STRIDE threat modeling methodology to identify potential cyber attacks, and to analyze the accordant risk. The results will support ship designers and industry towards improving the autonomous ship system architecture and making ship operations more secure.

Keywords: Autonomous ship · Cyber-security ·
Cyber-physical systems · Risk analysis · STRIDE · Threats

1 Introduction

Information and Communications Technology (ICT) adoption rates on board ships are increasing at an impressive rate over the past few years. Examples of current ship-based cyber systems include:

- navigation, positioning and identification systems;
- communications systems, including voice and data communications;
- integrated bridge systems;
- control systems for electro-mechanical systems on board.

Today's leading manufacturers and ship operators innovate using the latest ICT systems, going beyond traditional engineering to create ships with enhanced

© Springer Nature Switzerland AG 2019
S. K. Katsikas et al. (Eds.): CyberICPS 2018/SECPRE 2018, LNCS 11387, pp. 20–36, 2019.
https://doi.org/10.1007/978-3-030-12786-2_2

monitoring, communication and connection capabilities; such ships are collectively referred to as "Cyber-Enabled Ships (C-ES)". These include ships that can be controlled by remote onshore services, anytime and anywhere [1], and fully autonomous ships. Companies such as Rolls-Royce have already designed crew-less ships which can be controlled from a distance and will be able to sail by the end of 2020 and to travel open seas by 2035 [2]. Most of the cyber systems found on board ships today, and those that will be found in the remotely operated or fully autonomous ships of the future are cyber-physical systems, in which the physical process is controlled by computer-based systems. The interconnections of these systems have not been fully analyzed yet.

The adoption of ICT in any industry has always been accompanied with an enlargement and diversification of the cyber risks that the industry is facing, with existing risks being increased and new risks being introduced. This is mainly due to the fact that whereas traditional operations were designed with no need for cyber security in mind, modern ICT-enabled operations are allowed to be accessed and controlled through the industry's enterprise information system, through interfaces that are rarely adequately secure. As the enterprise system is more often than not connected to the Internet, the end result is that cybersecurity-unaware systems are made potentially accessible to outsiders. Therefore, it is not surprising that almost all known attacks against industrial control systems have been launched by first compromising the enterprise system and subsequently using it as a stepping stone to attack the control system. The shipping industry and the cyber-enabled ship in particular is no exception. As C-ESs become increasingly integrated across freight and passenger transport networks, their security by design becomes an imperative requirement. The EU Directive on the security of network and information systems includes such systems among the most critical societal infrastructures that already rely heavily on digital services, while disruption of their operations can lead to financial and environmental damage, or even endanger human safety.

In this paper we first identify cyber systems that are found on board ships and we define the system architecture of the C-ES. We then use Microsoft's STRIDE methodology [3] to study attacks against such systems. In the sequel, we define specific criteria for the impact and likelihood levels and we determine the risk level that these attacks pose, by leveraging the risk matrix. The contribution of this paper is twofold:

- An ICT system architecture of the C-ES has been defined;
- Attacks against the C-ES have been identified and the accordant risk has been analyzed.

The remainder of this article is structured as follows: Sect. 2 reviews related work. Section 3 presents the proposed C-ES ICT architecture. In Sect. 4 we briefly discuss STRIDE, and the reasons that led us to use it, as well as the results of its application to the C-ES. Finally, Sect. 6 summarizes our conclusions and proposes directions for future work.

2 Related Work

Most of the previous work on autonomous ships is focused on the systems and communication architecture as part of the work within the EU MUNIN project [4]. Namely, the Information and Communications Technology (ICT) architecture of unmanned merchant ships is provided by Rødseth et al. in [5], and the communication architecture is illustrated by Rødseth et al. in [6]. Further, the MUNIN project deliverables analyze the architectures and the operations of the bridge [7], the Shore Control Center [8] and engine rooms [9]. Also, Rødseth in [10] describes a risk assessment method which is safety-oriented and does not examine cyber-security threats and vulnerabilities. Significant work in the field of autonomous vessels has also been done in the AAWA project [2], including the identification of the need for cyber security, and the highlighting of general safety and security issues which have been posed by Jalonen et al. in [2].

Nevertheless, the security of the autonomous ship has been examined and analyzed only scarcely. Specifically, Lloyd's in [1] commented on the cyber-security of the cyber-enabled ship, but only as a consideration. Also, Tam et al. in [11] proposed a method to assess the cyber-risk of C-ES, but the analysis was done for three specific models of ships without extending to all systems and sub-systems, while the potential attacks were only examined from the attacker's perspective. In [12] a generic system architecture is discussed by Katsikas as well as threats, vulnerabilities and risks against this generic architecture. Yet, the system architecture and its components have not been specified. No previous work has proposed a detailed system architecture or has implemented a holistic threat analysis to identify potential attacks that may occur in the systems of such a ship by leveraging specific vulnerabilities.

The methodology to be used is important for the identification of all the attacks, threats and vulnerabilities of a system. Many threat analysis methodologies have been proposed in the literature [13,14]. Among the most prominent ones, Attack Trees requires understanding each subsystem separately and provides an overview about the attack surface, without taking under consideration essential data for the threat scenario. Cheung in [15] concludes that in the Attack Trees the initial attacker's goal must be known, and the method places emphasis in the sophistication of the attack. The Threat Modeling framework based on Attack Path analysis (T-MAP) is another method, which considers the severity weights that derive from attack paths. According to [13], this method works with Commercial Off the Shelf (COTS) systems, hence its is inappropriate for the C-ES case. Risk Reduction Overview (RRO) is a method which depends on the initial risk of the target system [16]. This requires knowing potential vulnerabilities as early as the design phase, which limits its applicability to the C-ES case, whose components' design is not available in sufficient detail. The Petri net methodology is a quite complex one, while the Attack Library method, is based on the attacker's perspective [17]. In contrast, methods with defender perspective examine the targeted systems thoroughly and their scope is to defend them.

Hussain *et al.* in [13] compare different threat modeling methodologies and conclude that most of academia and industry use the STRIDE methodology or its variants. Another comparative analysis of threat models has been carried out in [14]; the authors concluded that the STRIDE method and its variants extract the most rigorous results in contrast with the other six methodologies and frameworks that were considered. It is important to note that most of the threat methodologies require the analysis of the target architecture to be available in full detail; this makes them inappropriate for the C-ES, as such details have not yet become available, and they would be expected to depend on specific implementations. Based on the above findings, STRIDE was selected as the most appropriate method to use to analyze threats against the C-ES. More detail on STRIDE is provided in Sect. 4.1.

3   The ICT Architecture of the Cyber-Enabled Ship

For the definition of the architecture we follow a tree-based structure which consists of the systems and sub-systems of the C-ES according to MUNIN deliverables and the BIMCO report "The Guidelines of Cyber Security Onboard Ships" [18].

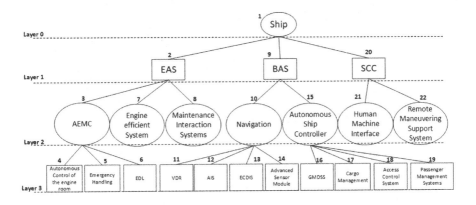

Fig. 1. Systems architecture

Figure 1 presents the schematic of the proposed architecture, structured in three layers. The top layer is the C-ES, while layer one comprises the Engine Automation Systems (EAS), the Bridge Automation Systems (BAS) and the systems in the Shore Control Center (SCC). Layer two comprises the sub-systems of EAS (the Autonomous Engine Monitoring and Control systems-AEMC, the Engine Efficiency System, and the Maintenance Interaction System); the subsystems of BAS (the Navigation systems, and the Autonomous Ship Controller system-ASC); the sub-systems of SCC (the Remote Maneuvering Support System, and the Human Machine Interface-HMI). The third layer comprises the sub-systems of AEMC (the Engine Data Logger-EDL, the Autonomous Control of the Engine Room, and the system for handling emergency situations); the sub-systems of Navigational systems (the VDR, the automatic identification system-AIS, the Electronic Chart Display and Information System-ECDIS, the GPS and the Advanced Sensor Module); and the systems of the Autonomous Ship Controller (the Global Maritime Distress and Safety System-GMDSS, the cargo management systems, the access control systems, and the passenger systems-PSMS). These are discussed in some more detail in the sequel.

1. **Engine Automation Systems-EAS:** Described in full detailed by Schmidt *et al.* in [9], it includes all the systems which are responsible for the generation and management of the ship's power and propulsion systems.

   1.1. **Autonomous Engine Monitoring and Control-AEMC:** Is connected directly with the mechanical parts of the ship.

      1.1.1. **Autonomous Control of the Engine Room:** Is responsible for the correct operation of the engines. It is interconnected with the propulsion system, power generation system, fuel system, rudder systems and evaporation system.

      1.1.2. **Emergency Handling-EmH:** Implements the appropriate countermeasures to avoid potential damage in the infrastructure, and includes the alarm systems.

      1.1.3. **Engine Data Logger-EDL:** Is responsible for recording all the information about the ship's engine operation.

   1.2. **Engine Efficiency System-EES:** Monitors the appropriate ship's operation, consisting of preventive tools for maintenance.

   1.3. **Maintenance Interaction System-MIS:** Provides technical, managerial and administrative maintenance in the engine room.

2. **Bridge Automation System-BAS:** Is fully analyzed in [7] by Burmeister *et al.* and consists of all the sub-systems which exist in a ship's bridge, with the most crucial one being the navigational and the management systems.

   2.1. **Navigation System:** Gives the appropriate directions to the ship for reaching its destination. The NAS interacts directly with many systems.

      2.1.1. **Voyage Data Recorder-VDR:** Gathers and stores all the information about the ship's condition, its position, its movements, and recordings from engine and radio systems. More detail on its operations cabn be found in [19].

      2.1.2. **Automatic Identification System-AIS:** Provides information which, together with other systems, helps authorities and other ships to monitor sea traffic, thereby ensuring the ship's safety.

      2.1.3. **Electronic Chart Display and Information System-ECDIS:** Transmits useful information and contributes to improving the ship's security and safety [20]. It is mandatory for all vessels.

      2.1.4. **Advanced Sensor Systems-ASS:** Produces reliable information about the ship's positioning.

   2.2. **Autonomous Ship Controller:** Is responsible for the data assessment, derived from the sensors and the SCC. It constitutes an additional control for the autonomous systems. A description of the system can be found in [21]

2.2.1. **Global Maritime Distress and Safety System-GMDSS:** Is a set of security procedures, equipment, and communication protocols. Its operation is fully described in [19] and in [20].

2.2.2. **Cargo Management/Cargo Control Room-CCR:** Is responsible for the efficient cargo control and management. BIMCO *et al.* in [18] and Rolls-Royce in [2] describe this system.

2.2.3. **Access Control System:** Is responsible for the ship's access control, either physically or remotely [18].

2.2.4. **Passenger Service System:** Serves the ship's customers/ passengers, with the goal of implementing efficient identity management and access control in the infrastructure [18].

3. **Shore Control Center-SCC:** Is a subsystem that controls and navigates one or more ships from the shore, proposed by MUNIN [8].

3.1. **Human Machine Interface-HMI:** Through this system humans can operate the C-ES under various conditions [2,8].

3.2. **Remote Maneuvering Support System-RMSS:** Is an information system which allows the execution of secure autonomous procedures under the control of the SCC [8].

4 Identifying and Analyzing Attacks Against the Cyber-Enabled Ship

4.1 Methodology

STRIDE stands for Spoofing, Tampering, Repudiation, Information Disclosure, Denial of Service and Elevation of Privilege. The method was developed by Loren Kohnfelder and Praerit Garg in 1999. The STRIDE threats are described by Shostack in [22]. Namely, Spoofing is the capability of the adversary to pretend someone or something else. Tampering is the alteration or disruption of a disk, network or memory of the system. Further, Repudiation is a threat which refers to someone's allegation that didn't do something which influences the system's operation or were not responsible for the results which derived from his actions. Information disclosure is another threat which reveals confidential information to the people who not suppose to see it. The next STRIDE threat is Denial of Service which violates the availability of the system and its task is to absorb all the possible resources which system needs to operate correctly. The last STRIDE threat is the Elevation of Privilege and according to this an adversary could execute unauthorized actions. STRIDE attempts to discover potential threats and vulnerabilities as early as the design phase and analyzes each threat by answering questions according to specific security properties. STRIDE collects and combines the results of active and passive threats.

It is important to note that we implemented STRIDE in the proposed, tree-structured architecture, where each branch is a distinct system or subsystem of the C-ES. This allows us to extract results which remain valid despite internal architectural modifications, as long as each system or subsystem of the architecture remains operationally the same, and regardless of its placement in the ship's architecture. The risk analysis is carried out by considering the likelihood of an attack and its impact. For the risk analysis of the C-ES we employed the risk matrix of Fig. 2 and used the criteria shown in Table 1 and in Table 2 to assess risk. These criteria take into account the attack likelihood and the respective impact, and follow [23].

Likelihood

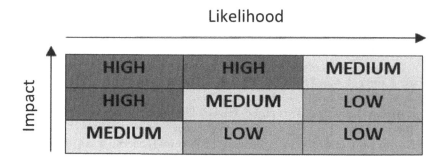

Fig. 2. Risk matrix

Table 1. Threat criteria

High (H)	1. Threats that could result in loss of human life. 2. Threats that could result in wide energy loss. 3. Threats that may cause damage in the infrastructure. 4. Threats that will lead to personal information leakage. 5. Threats that will result in economical damage and client loss. 6. Threats that will result in system malfunction.
Medium (M)	1. Threats that could cause procedure disruption in real time. 2. Threats that could result in miscalculations in the systems, thus influencing the operations. 3. Threats that could result in bad reputation for the company and client's dissatisfaction. 4. Threats that may cause information disclosure. 5. Threats that could influence the system's integrity. 6. Threats that could influence the system's availability. 7. Threats that could result in legal sanctions. 8. Threats that could cause network information leakage.
Low (L)	1. Threats that could result in operation delay or disruption in non-critical procedures. 2. Threats that could result in leakage of non-sensitive data.

Table 2. Likelihood criteria

Very Likely (VL)	1. The adversary is highly motivated and capable, and there are no deployed countermeasures. 2. Existing popular exploits which can be executed at any time. 3. High system's exposure to the Internet.
Moderate (M)	1. The adversary is highly motivated and capable, while the systems countermeasures are not enough to prevent the attack. 2. The system's vulnerability is widely known, but the attacker has to gain physical access to the system. 3. Systems are not directly exposed to the Internet.
Rare (R)	1. The attacker is not highly motivated or does not have the necessary knowledge to perform an attack, or the deployed countermeasures are sufficient. 2. An attacker must have administrative rights to perform the attack. 3. The system is not connected with external networks or systems.

4.2 Applying STRIDE to the Cyber-Enabled Ship

A full analysis of attacks against the systems and subsystems of the Cyber-Enabled Ship as shown in Fig. 1 using STRIDE has been carried out in [24]. In the interest of adhering to space limitations, in this section we present a selected subset of the results of [24]. The selection criteria were the diversity and representativeness of the results. In the tables that follow "I" stands for "Impact", "L" stands for "Likelihood" and "R" stands for "Risk".

Table 3. Engine Automation Systems-EAS

T	Engine Automation System-EAS	I	L	R
S	An adversary providing false information that the lubrication systems do work efficiently, when they do not, could result in engine damage. The system's exposure to the Internet is medium.	H	M	H
T	Tampering with a command to the engine control could lead to physical damage to the ship or to human injury.	H	R	M
R	Most of the system's operations are crucial for the ship; thus, the repudiation of actions is not acceptable.	M	R	L
I	Information disclosure will not adversely affect operations or the environment.	L	R	L
D	The availability of this system is very important, since the interruption of its operations will restrain the ship and most of its subsystems.	H	M	H
E	An attacker that gains administrative rights, may execute commands that can be catastrophic to the infrastructure.	H	R	M

Table 4. Bridge Automation Systems-BAS

T	Bridge Automation Systems-BAS	I	L	R
S	Identity spoofing caused by malware can be used to cause damage to the infrastructure and/or to humans. The system's exposure to the Internet is high.	H	M	H
T	Data tampering could cause disruption of crucial operations. This can lead to damage to the cargo, the ship or the infrastructure	H	R	M
R	The repudiation of actions is not allowed in this system, as it is a crucial component and these actions could adversely affect human safety.	H	R	M
I	A breach of confidentiality may pose serious risks to the security of the cargo and to the infrastructure in general.	M	M	M
D	In systems which are responsible for ensuring the security and safety of operations, a data delay or loss is unacceptable. Loss of availability in such a system could expose the ship to a high risk.	H	M	H
E	An attacker with administrator access in the system has full ship control.	H	R	M

Table 5. Shore Control Center-SCC

T	Shore Control Center-SCC	I	L	R
S	The SCC could be compromised by an adversary with access to another users credentials. This could lead to a catastrophic scenario for the ships cargo, or the ship itself, and could put human lives at risk. The system's exposure to the Internet is high.	H	M	H
T	Data tampering could lead to a system crash. Changing the navigation information, for example, can cause a change of destination.	H	R	M
R	The consequences of repudiation are crucial and not acceptable. Every action must be attributable to a known person.	M	R	L
I	A breach of confidentiality could lead to loss of cargo and could induce economic damage to the shipping company.	L	R	L
D	Loss of availability could cause loss of the capability to monitor the ship, and to acquire data which contribute to the efficient sailing. This sub-system works in real time and this makes its availability crucial.	H	M	H
E	This threat could cause violation of the systems integrity, availability and confidentiality since an adversary with elevated privileges could control the entire ship.	H	R	M

Table 6. Autonomous Engine Monitoring and Control-AEMC

T	Autonomous Engine Monitoring and Control-AEMC	I	L	R
S	An adversary with elevated privileges could execute unauthorized actions which will expose the engines to high risk. The system's exposure to the Internet is medium.	H	R	M
T	Data integrity violations can cause malfunctions, since critical operations are executed by this sub-system, e.g. rudder control.	H	M	H
R	The repudiation of actions is critical, since process disruption can lead to the shipping company's economic loss or even to jeopardize human safety.	H	R	M
I	The leak of information will not cause an operational malfunction to the system.	L	M	L
D	Loss of availability could cause significant consequences to the infrastructure, since the AEMC is the main control system of the engines, the vessel's speed and the power production.	H	M	H
E	The acquisition of administrative rights will cause the execution of unauthorized actions which could damage the infrastructure.	H	R	M

Table 7. Engine Efficiency System

T	Engine Efficiency System-EES	I	L	R
S	An adversary could alter fuel consumption data. This may lead to engine malfunction and could cause delay to the ship's operations. The system's exposure to the Internet is medium.	H	M	H
T	The violation of integrity will put at risk the entire infrastructure, by impeding maintenance in case of errors.	H	R	M
R	The repudiation of an action is unacceptable; every action must be fully attributable.	M	R	L
I	Disclosure of system information will not cause significant impact to the ship or to the shipping company.	L	R	L
D	Disruption of system operation could lead to a malfunction of engine systems without, however, extended damage.	H	M	H
E	An attacker with administrative rights will be able to stop the operation of many systems, and to alter data which adversely affect the capability to monitor the ship's operation from the shore.	H	R	M

Table 8. Maintenance Interaction Systems

T	Maintenance Interaction Systems-MIS	I	L	R
S	An adversary with elevated privileges could interrupt operations by preventing a maintenance procedure. The system's exposure to the Internet is medium.	H	R	M
T	By tampering the Key Performance Indicator values, an attacker could effect a false notification to the SCC of need for maintenance of the system.	H	M	H
R	Repudiation of actions in this sub-system is unacceptable, as responsibilities must be fully attributable to specific persons.	M	R	L
I	The system's operation does not entail sensitive data, so a possible information disclosure does not have significant impact to the system's operation or to the ship.	L	R	L
D	The availability of this system is crucial. If an attacker manages to render this system unavailable, s/he could inflict a malfunction in the infrastructure and/or economic loss.	H	M	H
E	Gaining administrative rights in this system could cause economic damage and bad reputation for the shipping company.	H	R	M

Table 9. Navigation Systems

T	Navigation Systems-NavS	I	L	R
S	An adversary using another user's credentials could inflict a malfunction, and will be able to change the ship's course. This could cause economic damage for the shipping company and damages to infrastructure. This sub-system's exposure to the Internet is high.	H	M	H
T	The violation of system's integrity could cause cargo loss or damage to the components of the ship or even to the entire infrastructure.	H	M	H
R	The repudiation of actions in this sub-system is unlikely, since the persons who manage and operate it are known.	H	R	M
I	The leak of navigational information could lead to cargo loss and damage to the infrastructure. Legal consequences may arise for the shipping company too.	H	M	H
D	Loss of availability could cause economic damage to the company, since the vessel will not be able to sail.	H	M	H
E	If an adversary gains elevated privileges in this sub-system, s/he will be able to change the ship's destination.	H	R	M

Table 10. Autonomous Ship Controller-ASC

T	Autonomous Ship Controller-ASC	I	L	R
S	Malware infection could cause damage to the cargo management systems or to the GMDSS. This system's exposure to the Internet is high.	H	M	H
T	The alteration of data and files in this sub-system is unacceptable, since it could result in system destruction. Also an attacker could change the ship's course.	H	R	M
R	This system handles crucial sub-systems; this is why all the actions and procedures are fully attributable to each person separately and repudiation is unacceptable.	M	R	L
I	The data handled by this sub-system are related to the ship information and its environment, and most of them are sensitive.	M	R	L
D	The availability of this system is very important since without it the ship may not be able to sail.	H	M	H
E	An adversary with administrative rights will be capable to change system parameters and influence operations. This could harm the infrastructure and result in litigation against the shipping company.	H	R	M

Table 11. Human Machine Interface-HMI

T	Human Machine Interface-HMI	I	L	R
S	An attacker could obtain access to the system and critical information. This will influence the entire infrastructure and cause bad reputation for the company or even litigation. This sub-system's exposure to the Internet is high.	H	M	H
T	Data tampering in this system will put the ship in danger since through this system, unauthorized humans in the shore are able to control and monitor the ship.	H	M	H
R	Repudiation of actions in this system is not possible, because its operation is fully defined and its internal procedures stem from other sub-systems.	M	R	L
I	The HMI contains information which are crucial for the ship's sailing. A disclosure of this information could lead to damage, since these relate to the vessel's navigation and management.	H	M	H
D	Availability is critical for secure sailing. If this system becomes unavailable, the vessel will be control-less and invisible to the SCC.	H	M	H
E	An attacker with administrative rights to the system will be able to access sensitive data about the vessel's condition, its customers, and passengers. This could raise legal issues for the shipping company.	H	M	H

Table 12. Remote Maneuvering Support System-RMSS

T	Remote Maneuvering Support System-RMSS	I	L	R
S	An adversary with access privileges could alter the ship's control and manipulate its operation. This could cause malfunction to the ship's systems and delay to its operation. This sub-system's exposure to the Internet is medium.	M	M	M
T	Data tampering can cause damage to the ship's engines, due to the close connection with the EAS.	M	M	M
R	All the actions and procedures in RMSS are predefined and their repudiation is not acceptable.	M	R	L
I	A breach of data confidentiality could reveal information about the vessel's position, but would not cause the malfunction of other systems.	H	M	H
D	An attack which targets the system's availability will influence the infrastructure to high extent and could result in delays in the process.	M	M	M
E	An access to the system with high privileges could cause crucial problems to the infrastructure, as the RMSS is connected directly with the engines and an attacker could manipulate their operation.	H	R	M

Table 13. Emergency Handling

T	Emergency Handling-EmH	I	L	R
S	If an attacker spoofs the identity of the fire alarm system, s/he will be able to activate or deactivate the firefighting system and destroy some ship components. This sub-system's exposure to the Internet is low.	M	M	M
T	The violation of data integrity in this system could start the wrong alarm in the ship. This could lead to ship's flooding and harm the infrastructure.	M	M	M
R	The repudiation of action in this system is unacceptable. All the roles are predefined, and no one should be able to claim that s/he did not start the alarm in case of emergency.	M	R	L
I	A breach of the system confidentiality could not harm the infrastructure to a high extent.	M	R	L
D	Loss of availability could pose a risk to the ship and its cargo, because in a case of emergency SCC will not be notified.	H	M	H
E	If the attacker gains administrative rights in this system, s/he will able to deactivate system alarms.	H	R	M

Table 14. Automatic Identification System-AIS

T	Automatic Identification System-AIS	I	L	R
S	An adversary using another AIS device is able to spoof their identity and receive system information. This sub-system's exposure to the Internet is low.	M	V	M
T	Altering the system's data is an important problem for the ship since AIS has information which may be confidential.	H	M	H
R	AIS is an automatic system and its internal procedures are well defined. Repudiation of its actions is not acceptable and could result in economic damage to the ship owner.	H	V	H
I	As already noted, this system's information is confidential, and its disclosure could cause problems to the infrastructure. Information about cargo and destination are included in this sub-system, so a potential leak may influence the ship's operation.	H	M	H
D	The loss of availability could affect the ship's operations directly, because AIS handles ship traffic information and other static and dynamic information on the vessel.	H	R	M
E	If an adversary gains administrative rights in the system, s/he will be able to execute unwanted action, such as changing ship navigation information.	H	M	H

Table 15. Electronic Chart Display and Information System-ECDIS

T	Electronic Chart Display and Information System-ECDIS	I	L	R
S	If an unauthorized user gains the credentials of a legitimate user, s/he could inflict damage to the ships infrastructure. This system's exposure to the Internet is medium.	H	M	H
T	Tampering with ECDIS data could cause problems to the ship's operation, since an attacker could intercept the ship's course by changing the maps.	M	M	M
R	The system's actions are well defined, and their repudiation is not acceptable.	M	M	M
I	ECDIS has many interconnections with other systems and subsystems; as such, it handles various pieces of information which may be personal or sensitive. The disclosure of these information could raise legal issues for the shipping company.	H	M	H
D	The loss of ECDIS's availability is unacceptable, since the ship could not sail without it.	H	M	H
E	Gaining administrative rights by unauthorized persons for this system could cause crucial issues for the vessel. An attacker could execute unwanted actions like altering maps. This may lead to economic loss and bad reputation.	M	R	L

Table 16. Global Maritime Distress and Safety System-GMDSS

T	Global Maritime Distress and Safety System-GMDSS	I	L	R
S	An attacker could spoof the identity of another ship through GMDSS and transmit false data between the two ships. This will influence the cargo security, raise economic issues and even adversely affect the safety of people on board. This system's exposure to the Internet is high.	H	M	H
T	The violation of data integrity is important, since information about weather conditions and the ship's position are transmitted through this system. The alteration of these could cause economic damage and human injury.	H	M	H
R	Most of the system's actions are crucial for the ship's security and safety. Therefore, repudiation of these actions is unacceptable.	M	M	M
I	GMDSS interacts directly with the SCC and exchanges sensitive information about the ship and its operations. A breach of confidentiality in this system could harm the entire infrastructure.	H	M	H
D	A Disruption of operation of the GMDSS could pose a high risk to the vessel's operation, since this system is the main communication channel in case of emergency.	H	R	M
E	An adversary that has gained access with high privileges could activate or deactivate the vessel's alarms and emergency communication.	H	R	M

5   Summary of Results and Discussion

Figure 3 summarizes the results and main contributions of our study. Specifically, in accordance to the proposed system taxonomy, the connections between parent nodes and their children in Fig. 1 are illustrated by arrows, where each arrow is directed from the children systems towards the parent systems. Furthermore, the table depicts all the calculated risk levels. The table also enumerates the number of high, medium and low level threats per system (vertical count), and records the number of times where each threat has appeared across the systems (horizontal count).

The C-ES systems that have been identified to be the most vulnerable are the HMI, NavS, AIS, ECDIS and GMDSS. It is important to highlight that both AIS and ECDIS are sub-systems of NavS, which also reached high risk levels. By leveraging the information in Fig. 3, we can conclude that parent nodes with highly vulnerable children inherit the vulnerabilities of their subsystems. Further, we should note that the AIS, ECDIS and GMDSS, which have reached the highest risk level in four out of six STRIDE threats, are parts of the infrastructure that has already been adopted by the shipping industry as part of the traditional ship, within the context of the C-ES. Furthermore, these systems are crucial for the efficient and effective operation of the C-ES, since they are strictly connected with the BAS systems. Further, we should focus on the HMI system, since it has reached high risk levels, its exposure to the internet is high,

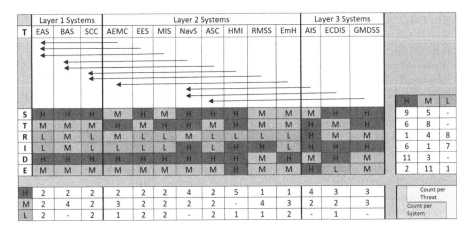

Fig. 3. Summary

and it is being used by the SCC. Hence, its vulnerabilities should be addressed promptly to avoid critical system malfunctions.

Analyzing the information in Fig. 3 from the perspective of threats, it becomes apparent that Denial of Service and Spoofing are the most critical threats for the C-ES systems. Specifically, Denial of Service and Spoofing have been found to be high level threats eleven and nine times respectively. STRIDE threats such as Tampering and Elevation of Privileges have been recognized as medium level threats, since they refer to more sophisticated and difficult to execute attacks, while in order to exploit these vulnerabilities the adversary should be highly motivated. Finally, Repudiation and Information Disclosure are low criticality threats for the C-ES systems.

6   Conclusions and Future Work

In this work we systematically classified the systems and sub-systems of Cyber-Enabled Ships, providing a taxonomy of the components that constitute the C-ES's ICT architecture; this was used as input to the STRIDE threat modeling methodology to identify attacks against the C-ES and to assess the accordant risk. The results show that the C-ES faces some high risks, related particularly to the AIS, the ECDIS and the GMDSS. At the sub-system level, high risks are posed by attacks against the HMI and the Navigation system, whereas their own sub-systems have been found to be vulnerable in high risk attacks as well. These risks propagate upwards in the architecture, resulting in high risks for the BAS and the SCC, whereas the risk associated with the EAS is lower. For future work, we intend to extend these results by utilizing other threat modeling and analysis methods, and also to integrate the notion of safety risk in the analysis. We also intend to define appropriate countermeasures to reduce the identified risks.

References

1. Lloyd's Register. Cyber-enabled ships, p. 20 (2016)
2. Rolls-Royce. Remote and autonomous ship-the next steps, p. 88 (2016)
3. Microsoft. The stride threat model (2009)
4. MUNIN. Maritime unmanned navigation through intelligence in networks (2016)
5. Rødseth, Ø.J., Tjora, A.: A system architecture for an unmanned ship, May 2014
6. Rødseth, Ø.J., Kvamstad, B., Porathe, T., Burmeister, H.C.. Communication architecture for an unmanned merchant ship. In 2013 MTS/IEEE OCEANS - Bergen, pp. 1–9, June 2013
7. Burmeister, H.C., Bruhn, W., Walther, L., Moræus, J.A., Sage-Fuller, B.: Munin d8.6: final report: autonomous bridge. Technical report (2015)
8. MacKinnon, S.N., Man, Y., Baldauf, M.: Munin d8.8 final report shore control centre. Technical report (2015)
9. Schmidt, M., Fentzahn, E., Atlason, G.F., Rødseth, H.: Munin 8.7 final report autonomous engine room. Technical report (2015)
10. Rødseth, Ø.J., Burmeister, H.-C.: Risk assessment for an unmanned merchant ship. TransNav **9**(3), 357–364 (2015)
11. Tam, K., Jones, K.: Cyber-risk assessment for autonomous ships, p. 9 (2018)
12. Katsikas, S.K.: Cyber security of the autonomous ship. In Proceedings of the 3rd ACM Workshop on Cyber-Physical System Security, CPSS 2017, pp. 55–56. ACM, New York (2017)
13. Hussain, S., Kamal, A., Ahmad, S., Rasool, G., Iqbal, S.: Threat modelling methodologies: a survey. Sci. Int. (Lahore) **26**(4), 1607–1609 (2014)
14. Sidi, F., et al.: A comparative analysis study on information security threat models: a propose for threat factor profiling. J. Eng. Appl. Sci. **12**, 548–554 (2017)
15. Cheung, C.Y.: Threat modeling techniques (2016)
16. Havinga, H., Sessink, O.: Risk Reduction Overview Manual, version 1.0 edition (2014)
17. Krishnan, S.: A hybrid approach to threat modelling, p. 24 (2017)
18. ICS INTERCARGO INTERTANKO OCIMF BIMCO, CLIA and IUMI. The guidelines on cyber security onboard ships, p. 51 (2017)
19. Bruhn, W., et al.: Munin D5.2: process map for autonomous navigation. Technical report (2013)
20. Kokotos, D., Linardatos, D., Nikitakos, N.B., Tzannatos, E.S.: Information and communication technologies in shipping industry (In Greek). Stamoulis (2011)
21. Nordahl, H., Rødseth, Ø.J.: NFAS-definitions for autonomous merchant ships, p. 10 (2017)
22. Shostack, A.: Threat Modeling: Designing for Security, 1st edn. Wiley, Hoboken (2014)
23. Jelacic, B., Rosic, D., Lendak, I., Stanojevic, M., Stoja, S.: STRIDE to a secure smart grid in a hybrid cloud. In: Katsikas, S.K., et al. (eds.) CyberICPS/SECPRE -2017. LNCS, vol. 10683, pp. 77–90. Springer, Cham (2018). https://doi.org/10. 1007/978-3-319-72817-9_6
24. Kavallieratos, G.: Cyber-attacks against the cyber-enabled ship. M.Sc. thesis. University of Piraeus, Greece (2018)

EPIC: An Electric Power Testbed for Research and Training in Cyber Physical Systems Security

Sridhar Adepu$^{(\boxtimes)}$, Nandha Kumar Kandasamy, and Aditya Mathur

iTrust, Center for Research in Cyber Security, Singapore University of Technology
and Design, 8 Somapah Road, Singapore 487372, Singapore
adepu_sridhar@mymail.sutd.edu.sg,
{kumar_kandasamy,aditya_mathur}@sutd.edu.sg

Abstract. Testbeds that realistically mimic the operation of critical infrastructure are of significant value to researchers. One such testbed, named Electrical Power and Intelligent Control (EPIC), is described in this paper together with examples of its use for research in the design of secure smart-grids. EPIC includes generation, transmission, smart home, and micro-grid. EPIC enables researchers to conduct research in an active and realistic environment. It can also be used to understand the cascading effects of failures in one Industrial Control System (ICS) on another, and to assess the effectiveness of novel attack detection algorithms. Four feasible attack scenarios on EPIC are described. Two of these scenarios, demonstrated on EPIC, namely a power supply interruption attack and a physical damage attack, and possible mitigation, are also described.

Keywords: Critical infrastructure · Cyber Physical Systems ·
Smart-grid testbed · Smart-grid security · Cyber attacks

1 Introduction

A Cyber Physical System (CPS) [26] consists of a physical process controlled by a computation and communications infrastructure. Typically, a CPS contains Programmable Logic Controllers (PLCs) for computing control actions. The control actions are based on the current state of the system obtained through a network of sensors. A Supervisory Control and Data Acquisition (SCADA) workstation enables the control and monitoring of the physical process. This integration of PLCs, SCADA workstation, and other computing and communications elements is often referred to as an Industrial Control System (ICS).

Attacks against ICS have been reported on a regular basis [14]. Given our dependence on water, power, and other critical infrastructure, it is important that such infrastructure be secured against external and internal malicious actors. Researchers are investigating current and future challenges in smart grid security [16,31], and focusing on the importance of cyber security in smart grid

© Springer Nature Switzerland AG 2019
S. K. Katsikas et al. (Eds.): CyberICPS 2018/SECPRE 2018, LNCS 11387, pp. 37–52, 2019.
https://doi.org/10.1007/978-3-030-12786-2_3

systems. Grid modernization to realise smart grid scenarios could only be effective [36] when the overall system's safety from the perspective of cyber security, be certifiable. Researchers are utilizing real time digital simulators [22] to conduct similar studies. However, in such cases, an additional step (eventually evaluating it in a real system) would be required for implementation/translation of developed technologies. From, the survey in [11], it was observed that having the defense mechanisms evaluated in a physical testbed facilitates smoother translation of developed technologies. This motivates us to study the security in a physical smart-grid environment and contribute to the existing work.

Contributions: (a) Description of an operational Electric Power and Intelligent Control (EPIC)[1] testbed. (b) Use of EPIC in the design of novel cyber attacks on a smart-grid and assessment of the effectiveness of methods for defense against such attacks.

Organization: The remainder of this work is organized as follows: Sect. 2 presents the architecture of EPIC including physical process and communication network. Attack models and feasible attack scenarios are presented in Sect. 3 including experimental validation and the impact of selected attacks. A brief discussion on cascading effects is in Sect. 4. Similar testbeds and related work is in Sect. 5. We conclude in Sect. 6.

2 Architecture of EPIC

EPIC (Fig. 1) is an electric power testbed that mimics a real world power system in small scale smart-grid. Comprising of four stages, namely Generation, Transmission, Micro-grid, and Smart Home, EPIC is capable of generating up to 72 kVA power. It is designed to enable cyber security researchers to conduct experiments and assess the effectiveness of novel cyber defense mechanisms.

Fig. 1. EPIC control room: 360° view.

2.1 Views of EPIC

The following four views of EPIC are described next: physical process view, network architecture view, communication layout, and electrical layout.

---

[1] https://itrust.sutd.edu.sg/testbeds/electric-power-intelligent-control-epic/.

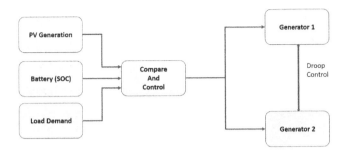

Fig. 2. EPIC physical process connectivity

Physical Process: EPIC physical process connectivity is shown in Fig. 2. It has two motor-driven generators (Generator1 and Generator2), Photovoltaic (PV) panels, Battery system–with state-of-charge (SOC) based control– and Load demand. Power required for the load demand is generated from two types of sources: motor-driven generators, and PV panels. The motor-driven generators replicate typical diesel engine-driven generators in which the mechanical power/energy is derived from the diesel engine and converted into electrical power/energy by the generator. However, having a diesel engine inside EPIC is not feasible due to laboratory constraints. Hence, a variable speed motor is used to drive the generators.

Solar power is used to meet part of the demand from critical and non-critical loads. This allows us to simulate different types of load scenarios such as peak demand, normal demand, etc. The load demand can be decoupled into real and reactive power. In any electrical bus, the real and reactive power generated needs to be balanced with the load demand for maintaining stability. In the case of EPIC, the real and reactive power balance is maintained by controlling the power from the generators and the charging process of the battery system based on the load demand (as shown by the compare and control block in Fig. 2). Droop control is used for controlling the operation of generators connected in parallel. It ensures that load shared by each generator replicates its characteristics, i.e., the speed or voltage changes with respect to the load demand, in the overall system.

EPIC Architecture: EPIC (Fig. 3) has four stages, namely Micro-grid, Smart Home, Transmission, and Generation. These atages are connected to a master PLC using a communication bus. The master PLC connects to SCADA workstation using a gateway. Each of the four stages in EPIC has its own switches, PLCs, a power supply unit, and protection and communication systems in a fiber optic ring network. The individual ring networks are shown in Fig. 4. For example, in ring HSR1, MIED1, MIED2, MSW1 and MSW2 are connected using fiber optic cables in a ring format.

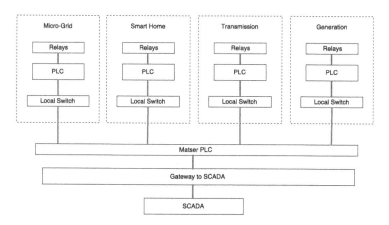

Fig. 3. EPIC architecture

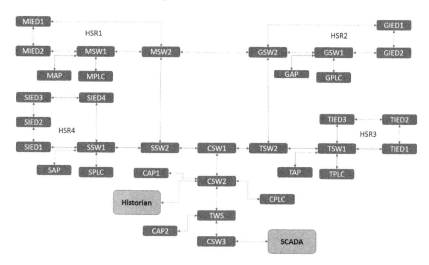

Fig. 4. The EPIC communication layout; Programmable Logic Controllers (PLCs), Intelligent Electronic Devices (IEDs), Access points (APs), Switches (SWs). PLC in generation is represented as GPLC, similarly Transmission (TPLC), smart home (SPLC), Micro-grid (MPLC). All other components in the communication layout also prefixed with G, T, S and M, respectively, for generation, transmission, smart home and micro grid.

The master PLC is responsible for the control of the overall operation. The SCADA workstation is used to monitor the entire system and provides supervisory control. PLCs manufactured by WAGO [1] corporation are used for controlling the opening/closing of breakers and also for implementing the synchronization logic for the generators. Breaker interlocks are implemented between transmission, smart home, and micro-grid to prevent a clash in the system voltages and frequency. Breaker interlocks are physical contacts that implement a certain group of logical protection functions. For instance, an auxiliary contact from the breaker used for one generator could be used for preventing the closing of the breaker in the second generator when synchronization is not complete.

Communications Layout: The communication layout of the EPIC is shown in Fig. 4. High-availability Seamless Redundancy (HSR) and Media Redundancy Protocol (MRP) switches are used in the ring network. HSR is primarily designed for use in redundantly coupled ring topologies. It uses two network ports and incorporates a DAN H (Double Attached Node for HSR) that connects the two interfaces to form a ring. HSR achieves redundancy by sending duplicate frames from both the ports of an HSR connection. In the event of a failure of one frame, data will be transmitted via the other network path which is still intact. In case of similar failure in MRP, the network employs the Ring-Open status mode of communication. For instance, in case of failure of a link connecting two clients, both ring ports of the manager will be forwarding the packets; the clients adjacent to the failure have a blocked and a forwarding ring port; the other clients have both ring ports forwarding. Hence redundancy would be achieved.

EPIC uses the IEC 61850 [28, 29] standard as a communication protocol for the electrical substation and automation system. This protocol runs over TCP/IP and is capable of obtaining a response from different parts of the system within four milliseconds. IEC 61850 includes standard features such as standardization of data names, fast transfer of events and data storage, etc.

Generic Object Oriented Substation Event (GOOSE) [15] and Manufacturing Message Specification (MMS) [40] are used in the ring network for data transfer between Intelligent Electronic Devices (IEDs) and the SCADA workstation. The fieldbus communication among physical processes to PLCs, master PLC, and SCADA is realized through selectable wired and wireless channels. Here, the operator has to choose the option of using either wired mode or wireless mode of communication. This feature enable researchers to investigate the cyber security of power grid systems in both wired and a wireless channels. For example, jamming related attacks could be studied for the wireless mode of operation.

In the communication layout (as shown in Fig. 4), apart from the SCADA and Historian, we have PLCs, IEDs, Access points (APs), Switches (SWs). PLC in generation is represented as GPLC, similarly Transmission PLC as TPLC, smart home PLC as SPLC, Micro-grid PLC as MPLC. All other components (some of the components details are shown in Table 1) in the communication layout also prefixed with G, T, S and M respectively for the generation, transmission, smart home and micro grid.

Electrical Layout: The electrical layout of EPIC is shown in Fig. 5. Main power supply for driving the prime-mover motors, referred to as M1 and M2, are obtained from the university's grid through the main circuit breaker (main CB). Having a prime-mover based generator, instead of grid-emulator [11], opens up the possibility of studying the security issues related to Automatic Governor Controllers (AGCs). AGC could be realized through variable speed drives VSD1 and VSD2. The generators referred to as G1 and G2, and the power supply

Table 1. Components in the communication layout

Component	Model	Location
SCADA system	SCADA System from PCvue solutions is used for the application. PCvue 11 is used in EPIC	SCADA System computer running on Windows 7
PLCs	PLC series 'PFC200 CS 2ETH RS' from WAGO is used in EPIC to controll various operations	Control and network panel and works based on the firmware and control logic program. Communicates with Modbus TCP/IP communication in few cases
IEDs	SIPROTEC relays from Siemens is used for protection and control in EPIC	Located in the control center and communicates with rest of the system using IEC-61850 standards. Firmware and the control logic maintains the overall process
VSD motors with dedicated firmware and control logic	SEW Eurodrive-8227136	Located at the generator room near the generators
PV and battery inverters	SMA Sunny Tripower for PV (on roof top), SMA Sunny Island for battery system (battery room). A dedicated SMA cluster controller is also used in EPIC	Control option is only enable with a 'GRID GUARD CODE', if it is enabled MODBUS TCP/IP can be used for read/write operation. Firmware update can be carried out from SCADA PC (SMA's Web portal)
Network switches	HIRSCHMANN	Network Control panel
Access points	HIRSCHMANN OpenBAT-R is used in EPIC for Wifi access points	Network Control panel

from PV and battery system is tied together in a bus, which enables options for having grid-connected as well as an islanded mode of operations. The grid-connected mode is the mode where the sources and load demand are operated in the presence of the main grid, whereas in the islanded mode only the local generators supply power to meet the demand and grid connection is disabled.

The security issues related to a transmission system could be studied using the Transformer (T1) based Tie-line. Tie-line is usually a power supply line connected in parallel to the existing distribution system and can supply additional power in the event of excess load demand or insufficient power generation.

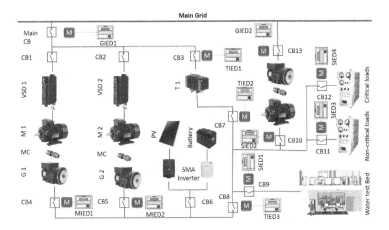

Fig. 5. Electrical layout in EPIC.

Since the transformer has the on-line tap changing functions, the security issues associated with such operations, often given less importance than deserved in the literature, could be studied. On-line tap changing function is employed in distribution transformers to avoid voltage deviations beyond the allowed limits. In many distribution systems, the allowed voltage fluctuations are to be maintained within ±5%. Whenever the voltage fluctuates beyond the allowed limits due to load fluctuations, the tap settings are changed to maintain the voltage within the limits. Hence, if an adversary gets control of the PLC in-charge of the tap-changing functions, serious voltage related issues may arise.

Components Description: (1) Two conventional generators (10 KVA each) are run by 15 kW VSD driven motors. (2) A 34 kW PV system, together with an 18 kW battery system. (3) A 15 kVA 3-phase voltage regulator. (4) Two load banks capable of emulating 45 kVA load bank. (5) 10 kW motor-generator. (6) Molded Case Circuit Breakers. (7) A SCADA system and a historian, PCvue [35] is used for programming SCADA. (8) PLC series *'PFC200 CS 2ETH RS'* from WAGO [1] is used in EPIC to control the process, and Codesys[2] [12] for programming the PLCs.

3   Experiments with EPIC

The following attack scenarios were designed using the attacker profiles in [37]: power supply interruption attacks (nation-state profile), nuisance tripping attacks (cyber-criminal), physical damage attacks (insider profile), and attacks related to economic advantage (nation-state). The four attack scenarios, and two selected scenarios implemented in EPIC, are described next.

---

[2] CoDeSys is an integrated development environment for programming controllers such as WAGO PLCs.

3.1   Feasible Attack Scenarios

Based on the vulnerability analysis of the power grid, different attacks can be designed and launched to capture the grid behavior in terms of affected components, properties, performance [5] and the cascading failures of the system. It is feasible to launch a variety of attacks on EPIC and study their impact. Four such attack types, discussed in the literature, are described below.

1. *Power supply interruption:* These are false data injection attacks on SCADA and PLC system that can lead to power supply interruption or tripping the overall system. An attack on the load demand control, either on the load banks or on other connected test-beds, can result in underutilization of the system components. False data injection attacks on local EMS may increase the active power from the renewable energy source and battery system.
2. *Nuisance tripping:* Malware attack on the firmware of PLCs can result in nuisance tripping by triggering the protection functions in IEDs. Such an attack could result in extended power supply interruption (intermittent). Nuisance tripping attacks can also be launched on secondary control from utilities or local EMS by disabling active power curtailment of renewable energy sources [25].
3. *Physical damage:* Though attacks that can cause physical damage [44] are not directly launched on EPIC, the process can be emulated using the motor-generator load combination and load banks for power system components such as battery systems. The attack could be false data injection such as erroneous voltage and temperature measurement in battery systems or attack on the firmware of power conversion system.
4. *Economic advantage:* These are false data injection attacks which can create an economic gain [21] to the attacker such as recording reduced or increased amount of power injected from the renewable energy sources. False data injection attacks on the control systems of various components, to cause accelerated aging or over utilization, can also be launched on the local EMS, PLCs, and the SCADA workstation.

From the four possible attack scenarios mentioned above, two attacks were selected and are explained in detail in the remainder of this section.

3.2   Power Supply Interruption Attack

During the normal operation of EPIC, circuit breakers CB1, CB4, CB8, and CB12 must be closed to supply power to the critical loads (Fig. 5). The SPLC (smart home PLC) controls the opening and closing of CB12. Whenever power supply is required for the critical load, a close command is issued from the SCADA to the SPLC. Subsequently, the SPLC (Control CodeX as in Fig. 6) issues a command to the IEDs to close CB12. The affected IED will eventually control the closing operation of the breaker thus enabling power to the critical loads.

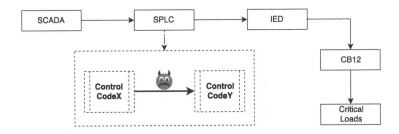

Fig. 6. Power supply interruption attack

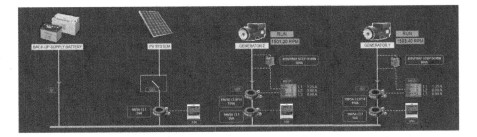

Fig. 7. Protection with machine learning predictors in IED layer for attack targeting complete destruction of SBS.

Attack Design: We assume that the attacker's intention is to interrupt power to the critical loads. The attacker can achieve this intent by opening the circuit breaker CB12, giving a false indication, i.e. "the breaker is closed," to the operator through the SCDA workstation, and disabling further closing of the circuit breaker.

Attack Vector: The attacker uses the vulnerabilities [13,33] to enter the SCADA workstation. Vulnerabilities in CoDeSys (see footnote 2) are used to modify the control code inside a PLC.

EternalBlue [10,24]: This exploit focuses on Microsoft Windows and was used in the WannaCry ransomware attack in 2017. EternalBlue [33] is vulnerability CVE-2017-0144 [13] in the server message block (SMB) protocol.

CoDeSys Unauthenticated Command-Line Access [32]: The CODESYS allows remote attackers to execute commands via the command-line interface and transfer files. This vulnerability allows an attacker to obtain administrative access to the PLC logic thus enabling the modification of the control logic.

Experiments and Results: Two experiments were conducted. In each case, EPIC was run in normal mode and then the attack was launched. In the first experiment power was supplied to the critical loads as desired. In the second experiment, the EternalBlue exploit was used to enter the SCADA workstation and used the vulnerabilities in CoDeSys to upload the malicious control code to the SPLC. The original control code is shown as *Control CodeX* in Fig. 6 and the malicious control code as *Control CodeY*. As a result, the circuit breaker opened immediately, the command to close the breaker was disabled, and the SCADA workstation reported the circuit breaker as closed. Hence, the operator observing the screen at the SCADA workstation was unable to control the circuit breaker (CB12). As intended, this attack resulted in power supply interruption to the critical loads.

Mitigation: To overcome the EternalBlue vulnerability, the windows-based machine needs to be updated to the latest version of the operating system. However, CoDeSys vulnerability does not have any possible mitigation measures at the time of writing this paper.

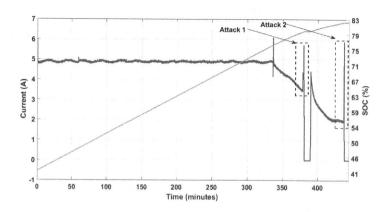

Fig. 8. Impact of Attack 1 and Attack 2 on the charging current of the battery system.

3.3 Physical Damage Attack

Figure 7 shows the portion of EPIC used for in this study, namely the "BACKUP-SUPPLY BATTERY" used only for supplying control power during a complete black-out. The "BACKUP-SUPPLY BATTERY" is charged using Generator 1 and Generator 2. The measurements from MIED1 and MIED2 represent the charging current of the battery. During normal operation, the battery is charged with a constant current (approximately 5A) until 75% SOC and a continuously decreasing current beyond 75% SOC.

Attack Design: The intention of the attacker is to increase the charging current in the region beyond 75% SOC and lead to increased temperature and eventually physical damage to the battery.

Attack Execution: It is assumed that the attacker is capable of modifying the measurements carried out by the Battery Management System (BMS) of the inverters, and can cause overcharging resulting in physical damage to the batteries. The attack scenario of overcharging the battery is implemented by adding load in the downstream to avoid any possible physical damage to the battery system. Doing so will result in increased charging current as seen by MIED1 and MIED2.

Experiment and Results: I Fig. 8, shows the impact of Attack 1 and Attack 2 on the battery charging current. Inherently, the IDMT scheme in IEDs is not designed to protect the increase in current during the CV region as technically no over current is seen by the system. However, continuously supplying higher current in the CV region will result in increased temperature and hence physical damage to the battery system.

Mitigation: A new model is proposed by combining the Inverse Definite Minimum Time (IDMT) concept in over-current protection with machine-learning based predictors and the actual charging current of the battery system. The tripping time, i.e. enabling protection against physical damage is given as follows.

$$T_{trip} = \frac{k * m}{\int_{n-k}^{n} \left(\frac{|I_n^m| - |I_n^p|}{I_n^p}\right)^2}, \tag{1}$$

where $\forall\ I_n^m > 0$ & $|I_n^m| - |I_n^p| > 0$, k is the time taken for charging/discharging at rated current, I_n^m is the current measured at n^{th} time stamp, I_n^p is the output from machine learning algorithm which is not described in this paper (the algorithm similar to the one described in [23] can be used for prediction), and m is the on-field trip setting multiplier.

The equation for the tripping time is derived from the standard IDMT protection [34] by including I_n^p along with I_n^m rather than using I_n^m alone. Hence, the scheme, instead of relying only on the measured value, uses the deviation from usual value predicted by the machine learning predictors. The square term in the equation is used for getting an extremely inverse characteristics, i.e., speed of tripping increases at a much faster pace compared to the error, as described in standard IDMT and summation of past k values to identify the cumulative variation rather than instantaneous transients. Such transients are usually eliminated by including the time component [34]. In practice, m is selected by the operator based on heuristics, a usual procedure for IDMT protection. In the experiment, m is chosen as 1, and the authors did not change m as no nuisance tripping was observed. As the IEDs do not have in-built modules for implementing the protection scheme, the above protection scheme is implemented using PLCs (MPLC) for the system in Fig. 7 and the results are in Fig. 8.

Figure 8 shows the charging current of the battery system. It can be observed that the transient at the 325th minute is not identified as an attack as the cumulative error was within the limit. The system restored quickly back to the normal state from the transient state. The attack scenarios near 360th minute (Attack 1) and 440th minute (Attack 2) were successfully identified and the system protected. It can be observed from Fig. 8 that the battery system is protected by tripping the entire system based on the measurement from IEDs through circuit breaker 'Q2' in the distribution control/switchboard. Tripping is indicated with zero current in Fig. 8.

The transients post attack scenario (after Attack 1 around 400th minute) is not mis-identified as an attack. The speed at which the system should trip could be controlled by changing the value of m which is an on-field variable similar to trip selector setting in the IDMT protection scheme. Choice of m is crucial as higher value for m results in under protection (higher possibility of damage) and lower value for m results in over protection (nuisance tripping). A heuristic approach would be suitable for selecting m. It was observed that the overall time taken for the protection scheme to identify the attack and protect the system was in the order of seconds.

4   Cascading Effects

Many CPSs depend on one another and are connected via some physical or cyber infrastructure. For example, a public transit system uses electricity and hence is connected to the power grid via several intermediate elements each of which could also be considered a CPS. Such interconnections through one or more infrastructure CPS lead to the following challenge. *What methods and tools are needed to understand the cascading effects of cyber attacks in one CPS on other connected CPS?* It is important to consider this challenge in the context of interconnected CPSs. For example, the impact of cyber attacks on a smart meter in a smart grid could propagate to other subsystems in the grid before progressing outside of the grid to other connected systems.

EPIC supplies power to two testbeds, namely a Secure Water Treatment (SWaT) and a Water Distribution (WADI) SWaT [30] is a scaled down water treatment plant that is capable of producing five gallons/minute of filtered water. SWaT has a six-stage filtration process that mimics a large modern water treatment plant. WADI [8] is an operational testbed supplying 10 US gallons/min of filtered water. It represents a scaled-down version of a large water distribution network in a city. This connection between three plants allows one to study the interdependencies between CPS and how cyber attacks on one can affect the other. Such work is helpful in advancing the design of secure interconnected public infrastructures. CPSs often depend on each other implying that a disturbance due to cyber attack in one is likely to have a significant impact on the operation of another. Significant attention is currently being devoted to ensuring that such systems are resilient to cyber attacks. The notion of cyber security was nearly non-existent when many of these systems were designed and built. Hence, while such systems may be functionally sound, they are prone to successful cyber attacks as has been demonstrated in the past [43]. Thus, subsystems for intrusion prevention and detection, network attack detection, and the like are being installed in the existing CPSs to prevent and detect cyber attacks.

5   Related Work

Research related to work in this paper is divided into two parts: work related testbeds and that related to attack scenarios.

Similar Testbeds: There exist a number of electric power testbeds. Some of these allow simulation of large systems and do not actually produce electric power. Simulation based testbeds allow large scale attack analysis. Operational testbeds offer more realistic environments and scenarios than those based exclusively on simulation. [9] presents efforts to model the smart power grid in real time by developing a *"smart grid testbed"*. A smart grid testbed for electric power distribution system is presented in [42]. This system is designed to emulate distribution grid by focusing on analyzing power system components, renewable energy integration, power quality issues, and consumer load behavior in the smart distribution grid. Pulau Ubin pilot Micro-grid Test-Bed [17] is located in Singapore at the jetty area of Pulau Ubin– an island north-east of Singapore. This test-bed aims to assess the reliability of electricity supply within a micro-grid infrastructure using intermittent renewable energy sources such as solar photovoltaic (PV) technology. This micro-grid mainly focuses on clean energy, reliable electricity supply, cost competitive electricity and scalability issues at present. A software based smart grid testbed for evaluating substation cyber security was reported in [20]. Due to the importance of smart-grid security, researchers have focused on the development of smart grid testbeds. [11] provides a four step taxonomy based on smart grid domains, research goals, test platforms, and communication infrastructure. The Cyber-Physical Experimentation Environment for RADICS (CEER) at The University of Illinois at Urbana-Champaign employs a production quality software to flexibly (and remotely) define experiments, configure testbed resources, and run an experiment. EPIC can serve as a useful hybrid of the above systems (the hybrid of physical process and cyber-layer forming an ICS), by implementing both cyber and physical processes for security research. The physical process can be defined and configured using the PLCs and SCADA system, as well as any specific Energy Management System. Based on the physical process, the desired attack scenarios and defense mechanisms can be implemented and tested using an array of network components available in EPIC.

Attacks and Attack Scenarios: Grid modernization to realize smart grid scenarios could only be effective [36] if the overall system's safety from cyber security perspective is satisfied. Though, many research efforts utilizing real time digital simulators [22] are underway, having the defense mechanisms evaluated in a physical testbed offers advantages in terms of implementation/translation of developed technologies as indicated in [11]. A resilient architecture for the smart grid is presented in [27]. Researchers have reported case studies on power substation networks [18]. Privacy preserving methods in the advanced metering infrastructure based on the influence of dataset characteristics is presented in [41]. Integrity attacks on real time pricing in smart grids [19] were investigated against their impact and countermeasures. Security of economic dispatch in power system operations has been investigated [38]. In [39], authors present an overview of the network services provided by devices found in EPIC and discuss how this information can be used to implement practical threat scenarios.

In the future, we are planning to use EPIC testbed similar to our water testbed and conduct experiments [2–4,6,7] which we already conducted on SWaT.

6   Conclusion and Future Work

This paper presents a smart grid testbed named EPIC for research in the design of secure smart-grids. Also presente are possible attack scenarios, consequences of such attacks, and potential mitigations. The combination of testbeds and dependency among the testbeds enables the design of realistic scenarios. The connection of EPIC to two other testbeds for water treatment and water distribution enables the study of impact of multiple simultaneous attacks on two or more CPSs. Design of additional attacks, and mitigations, are planned for the future.

References

1. Wago Programmable Logic Controllers (2009). http://www.wago.us
2. Adepu, S., Mathur, A.: An investigation into the response of a water treatment system to cyber attacks. In: Proceedings of the 17th IEEE High Assurance Systems Engineering Symposium, Orlando, January 2016
3. Adepu, S., Mathur, A.: Distributed attack detection in a water treatment plant: method and case study. In: IEEE Transactions on Dependable and Secure Computing (2018, to appear)
4. Adepu, S., Mathur, A.: Distributed detection of single-stage multipoint cyber attacks in a water treatment plant. In: Proceedings of the 11th ACM Asia Conference on Computer and Communications Security, pp. 449–460. ACM, New York, May 2016
5. Adepu, S., Mathur, A.: Generalized attacker and attack models for cyber-physical systems. In: Proceedings of the 40th Annual International Computers, Software and Applications Conference, Atlanta, USA, pp. 283–292. IEEE, June 2016
6. Adepu, S., Shrivastava, S., Mathur, A.: Argus: an orthogonal defense framework to protect public infrastructure against cyber-physical attacks. IEEE Internet Comput. **20**(5), 38–45 (2016)
7. Adepu, S., Mathur, A.: Assessing the effectiveness of attack detection at a hackfest on industrial control systems. arXiv preprint arXiv:1809.04786 (2018)
8. Ahmed, C.M., Palleti, V.R., Mathur, A.: WADI: a water distribution testbed for research in the design of secure cyber physical systems. In: The 3rd International Workshop on Cyber-Physical Systems for Smart Water Networks, April 2017
9. Biswas, S.S., Kim, J.H., Srivastava, A.K.: Development of a smart grid test bed and applications in PMU and PDC testing. In: 2012 North American Power Symposium (NAPS), pp. 1–6 (2012)

10. Caulfield, T., Ioannidis, C., Pym, D.: The U.S. vulnerabilities equities process: an economic perspective. In: Rass, S., An, B., Kiekintveld, C., Fang, F., Schauer, S. (eds.) GameSec 2017. LNCS, vol. 10575, pp. 131–150. Springer, Cham (2017). https://doi.org/10.1007/978-3-319-68711-7_8
11. Cintuglu, M.H., Mohammed, O.A., Akkaya, K., Uluagac, A.S.: A survey on smart grid cyber-physical system testbeds. IEEE Commun. Surv. Tutor. **19**(1), 446–464 (2017)
12. CODESYS: Codesys-industrial IEC 61131–3 PLC programming (2018). https://www.codesys.com/
13. CVE-2017-0144: Windows SMB remote code execution vulnerability (2017). https://www.cve.mitre.org/cgi-bin/cvename.cgi?name=CVE-2017-0144
14. ICS-CERT Advisories (2018). https://ics-cert.us-cert.gov/advisories
15. Du, L., Liu, Q.Y.: The design of communication system on the real-time relay protection based on goose. In: 2012 Asia-Pacific Power and Energy Engineering Conference, pp. 1–5 (2012)
16. Dumitrache, I., Dogaru, D.I.: Smart grid overview: infrastructure, cyber-physical security and challenges. In: 2015 20th International Conference on Control Systems and Computer Science, pp. 693–699 (2015)
17. EMA: Pulau ubin micro-grid test bed (2013). https://www.ema.gov.sg/Pulau_Ubin_Micro-grid_Test_Bed.aspx
18. Formby, D., Walid, A., Beyah, R.: A case study in power substation network dynamics. Proc. ACM Meas. Anal. Comput. Syst. **1**, 19 (2017)
19. Giraldo, J., Cárdenas, A., Quijano, N.: Integrity attacks on real-time pricing in smart grids: impact and countermeasures. IEEE Trans. Smart Grid **8**, 2249–2257 (2017)
20. Gunathilaka, P., Mashima, D., Chen, B.: SoftGrid: a software-based smart grid testbed for evaluating substation cybersecurity solutions. In: Proceedings of the 2nd ACM Workshop on Cyber-Physical Systems Security and Privacy. CPS-SPC 2016 (2016)
21. He, Y., Mendis, G.J., Wei, J.: Real-time detection of false data injection attacks in smart grid: a deep learning-based intelligent mechanism. IEEE Trans. Smart Grid **8**(5), 2505–2516 (2017)
22. Hernandez, M., Ramos, G., Lwin, M., Siratarnsophon, P., Santoso, S.: Embedded real-time simulation platform for power distribution systems. IEEE Access **6**, 6243–6256 (2017)
23. Kandasamy, N.K., Badrinarayanan, R., Kanamarlapudi, V.R.K., Tseng, K.J., Soong, B.H.: Performance analysis of machine-learning approaches for modeling the charging/discharging profiles of stationary battery systems with non-uniform cell aging. Batteries **3**(2), 18 (2017)
24. Kharraz, A.: Techniques and solutions for addressing ransomware attacks (2017)
25. Langner, R.: Stuxnet: dissecting a cyberwarfare weapon. IEEE Secur. Priv. **9**(3), 49–51 (2011)
26. Lee, E.A.: Cyber-physical systems: design challenges. Technical Report UCB/EECS-2008-8, EECS Department, University of California, Berkeley, January 2008. http://www.eecs.berkeley.edu/Pubs/TechRpts/2008/EECS-2008-8.html
27. Lopez, J., Rubio, J.E., Alcaraz, C.: A resilient architecture for the smart grid. IEEE Trans. Industr. Inf. **14**, 3745–3753 (2018)
28. Mackiewicz, R.: Overview of IEC 61850 and benefits. In: Power Systems Conference and Exposition, 2006. PSCE 2006. 2006 IEEE PES, pp. 623–630. IEEE (2006)

29. Mascarella, D., Chlela, M., Joos, G., Venne, P.: Real-time testing of power control implemented with IEC 61850 GOOSE messaging in wind farms featuring energy storage. In: 2015 IEEE Energy Conversion Congress and Exposition (ECCE), pp. 6710–6715 (2015)

30. Mathur, A.P., Tippenhauer, N.O.: SWaT: a water treatment testbed for research and training on ICS security. In: International Workshop on Cyber-Physical Systems for Smart Water Networks (CySWater), USA, pp. 31–36. IEEE, April 2016

31. McDaniel, P., McLaughlin, S.: Security and privacy challenges in the smart grid. IEEE Secur. Priv. **7**, 75–77 (2009)

32. MITRE: CVE-2012-6068 (2012). https://cve.mitre.org/cgi-bin/cvename.cgi?name=CVE-2012-6068

33. Nakashima, E., Timberg, C.: NSA officials worried about the day its potent hacking tool would get loose. Then it did. Washington Post (2017). https://www.washingtonpost.com/business/technology/nsa-officials-worried-about-the-day-its-potent-hacking-tool-would-get-loosethen-it-did/2017/05/16/50670b16-3978-11e7-a058-ddbb23c75d82_story.html

34. Paithankar, Y.G., Bhide, S.: Fundamentals of Power System Protection. PHI Learning Pvt. Ltd., New Delhi (2011)

35. PcVue: PcVue: versatile HMI-SCADA software (2018). https://www.pcvuesolutions.com/index.php/products-a-technology/pcvue-hmiscada-48583

36. Qi, J., Hahn, A., Lu, X., Wang, J., Liu, C.C.: Cybersecurity for distributed energy resources and smart inverters. IET Cyber-Phys. Syst.: Theory Appl. **1**(1), 28–39 (2016)

37. Rocchetto, M., Tippenhauer, N.O.: On attacker models and profiles for cyber-physical systems. In: Askoxylakis, I., Ioannidis, S., Katsikas, S., Meadows, C. (eds.) ESORICS 2016. LNCS, vol. 9879, pp. 427–449. Springer, Cham (2016). https://doi.org/10.1007/978-3-319-45741-3_22

38. Shelar, D., Sun, P., Amin, S., Zonouz, S.: Compromising security of economic dispatch in power system operations. In: 2017 47th Annual IEEE/IFIP International Conference on Dependable Systems and Networks (DSN) (2017)

39. Siddiqi, A., Tippenhauer, N.O., Mashima, D., Chen, B.: On practical threat scenario testing in an electric power ICS testbed. In: Proceedings of the 4th ACM Workshop on Cyber-Physical System Security, pp. 15–21 (2018)

40. Sørensen, J.T., Jaatun, M.G.: An analysis of the manufacturing messaging specification protocol. In: Sandnes, F.E., Zhang, Y., Rong, C., Yang, L.T., Ma, J. (eds.) UIC 2008. LNCS, vol. 5061, pp. 602–615. Springer, Heidelberg (2008). https://doi.org/10.1007/978-3-540-69293-5_47

41. Tudor, V., Almgren, M., Papatriantafilou, M.: The influence of dataset characteristics on privacy preserving methods in the advanced metering infrastructure. Comput. Secur. **76**, 178–196 (2018)

42. Tunaboylu, N.S., Shehu, G., Argin, M., Yalcinoz, T.: Development of smart grid test-bed for electric power distribution system. In: 2016 IEEE Conference on Technologies for Sustainability (SusTech), pp. 184–187 (2016)

43. Weinberger, S.: Computer security: is this the start of cyberwarfare? Nature **174**, 142–145 (2011)

44. Zeller, M.: Myth or reality? Does the aurora vulnerability pose a risk to my generator? In: 2011 64th Annual Conference for Protective Relay Engineers, pp. 130–136 (2011)

A Hardware Based Solution for Freshness of Secure Onboard Communication in Vehicles

Sigrid Gürgens$^{(\boxtimes)}$ (ID) and Daniel Zelle (ID)

Fraunhofer Institute for Secure Information Technology, Darmstadt, Germany
{sigrid.guergens,daniel.zelle}@sit.fraunhofer.de
http://www.sit.fraunhofer.de

Abstract. Information Technology has become eminent in the development of modern cars. More than 50 Electronic Control Units (ECUs) realize vehicular functions in hardware and software, ranging from engine control and infotainment to future autonomous driving systems. Not only the connections to the outside world pose new threats, also the in-vehicle communication between ECUs, realized with bus systems like CAN, needs to be protected against manipulation and replay of messages. Multiple countermeasures were presented in the past making use of Message Authentication Codes and specific values to provide message freshness, most prominently AUTOSAR's Secure Onboard Communication (SecOC). However, the currently considered solutions exhibit deficiencies which are hard if not impossible to overcome within the scope of the respective approaches. In this paper we present a new, hardware-based approach that avoids these deficiencies and formally prove its freshness properties.

Keywords: Security · Automotive engineering · Formal analysis · Replay protection · Freshness

1 Introduction

In modern cars more than 50 interconnected Electronic Control Units (ECUs) realize vehicular functions in hardware and software ranging from engine control and connected infotainment systems to future autonomous driving systems. The usage of IT however introduces new threats, one of the possible attack vectors being the in-vehicle communication between ECUs realized by bus systems like CAN (Controller Area Network Bus [7]). The vehicle owner can for example install a tuning box to suppress or inject messages that control engine operations in order to achieve more horse power. This in turn may damage the engine and violate the warranty. Moreover third party devices connected to the On-board diagnostics (OBD) port can inject messages to the regular in-vehicle network. In [8] Koscher et al. have shown various attack techniques like *Packet Sniffing and Targeted Probing*, *Fuzzing*, and *Reverse-Engineering*.

© Springer Nature Switzerland AG 2019
S. K. Katsikas et al. (Eds.): CyberICPS 2018/SECPRE 2018, LNCS 11387, pp. 53–68, 2019.
https://doi.org/10.1007/978-3-030-12786-2_4

Multiple countermeasures were presented in the past to protect in-vehicle networks (see Sect. 2). Early work can be traced back to EVITA [14] that introduced Message Authentication Code (MAC) truncation in order to cope with the small bandwidth of CAN buses. This approach has been adapted by AUTOSAR in Secure Onboard Communication (SecOC) [1]. Including a freshness value in a message's MAC can in principle prohibit fuzzing or replay attacks. Two different approaches are currently being considered. However, both suffer from security gaps they cannot cope with (see Sect. 2.1 for a detailed discussion).

In this paper we suggest another method to generate freshness in bus systems that avoids disadvantages of current approaches. The principle idea is to use the messages that are sent on a specific bus as a pulse generator for the counter of this bus, resulting in only one counter per bus. The fundamental difference to other approaches is that there is no way for an attacker to circumvent the change of counter values. In order to cope with loss of counter values for example caused by technical problems or an attack, our approach includes counter synchronization. Our method requires messages to be read by all ECUs connected to a bus including the sender and demands each ECU to be active during the complete trip. Software implementations would be hard to realize since transceivers normally filter broken messages. Therefore we propose a hardware based solution: The transceiver is enhanced by the functionality to maintain a counter and to manage MAC generation and verification while the main ECU processors can be inactive at times.

The next section discusses related work and in particular limitations of current approaches. Section 3 presents the assumed setting. Section 4 then describes the details of the proposed solution, and Sect. 5 introduces a summary of its formal verification. Finally Sect. 6 discusses our approach as opposed to current ones and presents our conclusions.

2   Related Work

Security of bus communication in current vehicle networks has already been discussed in literature and standardization. In this section we give an overview of related work with a focus on replay protection in CAN bus systems.

Proposed solutions for authenticated bus communication by Chavez et al. [2] and Nilsson et al. [11] do not include protection against replay attacks. In [2] CAN messages are encrypted using RC4. [11] proposes to calculate a MAC covering four messages which implies a delay between data reception and validation.

Often only truncated MAC values are actually sent with the message. Early work on MAC truncation can be traces back to [14]. More recently Szilagyi and Koopman [16] proposed to send truncated MACs (8-bit) with each message. Each pair of communication partners shares a symmetric key. Since truncation of MACs decreases the security the authors suggest to verify MACs over multiple messages. Freshness of the message is not part of their solution, they simply suggest to introduce replay protection by adding a time stamp and a secure time synchronization protocol without elaborating any details.

Nürnberger and Rossow [12] developed an HMAC based authentication procedure that sends a MAC in a separate message after the original CAN message. The MAC is then validated with a delay of about 4 ms. Replay protection is implemented by assigning a counter to every message ID. The authors recommend this procedure only for few CAN messages since it increases the bus load. Similar to this approach is the LeiA protocol [13] with a different synchronisation mechanism addressing the case of corrupted counters.

The LiBrA-CAN protocol [5] uses a central component for the authentication algorithm and different MAC keys depending on the intended receivers. Instead of one MAC, LiBrA mixes multiple MACs with different keys for the authentication process. For replay protection they use counters as well.

AUTOSAR (AUTomotive Open System ARchitecture) specifies the use of secure communication in vehicle networks with MAC. The specification of the Secure Onboard Communication (SecOC) [1] module suggests to add a truncated time stamp or message counter and a truncated authenticator to every message. The specific counter mechanism is based on splitting the counter into three different parts: the so-called "trip counter" that only changes essentially with every new trip, a "reset counter" that is reset periodically, and the actual "message counter". Only the trip counter is stored in non-volatile memory, thus mitigating loss of counter values in case of sudden ECU shutdown. The truncated freshness value has a length between 0 and 8 bit. The truncated authenticator covers the freshness value and the message, the least 24 to 28 bits are actually sent.

Some works are also considering the implementation of a secure CAN Bus transceiver. These approaches introduce calculation of MACs, denial of service counter measures or intrusion prevention mechanisms. Elend and Adamson [3] suggest hardware extensions for CAN transceivers that prevent spoofing, tampering and denial of service attacks by "invalidating messages on the bus based on ID, filtering messages in transmit path based on ID, invalidating tampered messages on bus and rate control with a leaky bucket in transmit path". [15] implemented a CAN transceiver including physical unclonable function implementation, key generation and storage, encryption and decryption allowing authenticated communication over CAN. However the approach does not consider replay protection. Ueda et al. presented a CAN transceiver with integrated HMAC in [17]. To ensure replay protection a monotonic counter value of 4 bits is part of every message.

A first comparison of using time stamp vs. counter to establish freshness was given in [18]. The comparison only focuses on message transmission, but does not regard synchronization and persistent storage of freshness values.

Very few of these approaches address message freshness in detail. Those that do so result in additional bus load caused by the need to include (truncated) freshness values in the messages. Limitations of the respective freshness solutions (see Sect. 2.1) are not discussed. In contrast, our hardware based solution that we will describe in detail in Sect. 4 does not increase the bus load and allows the storage of counter values in non-volatile memory (each ECU has only to handle as many counters as buses it is connected to). Further, it avoids most of the security gaps other solutions suffer from which will be formally proven in Sect. 5. It must be noted, though, that it cannot be implemented in currently available ECUs.

2.1 Limitations of Current Approaches

While a MAC provides authenticity of a message, only in combination with a freshness value replay attacks can be mitigated. Two different approaches are currently considered (discussed e.g. in [18]), both exhibit some drawbacks.

Time Stamps. Each ECU is equipped with a clock providing time stamps which are included in messages' MACs. Since Real Time Clocks are considered too costly, most ECUs included in a vehicle dispose of software based clocks. These however diverge and thus require regular synchronization. Further, viewed from the moment of message reception, if sender and recipient clocks are synchronized, the time stamp used for the message's MAC is always generated in the past. Thus an acceptance interval is required that, deduced from the recipient's time stamp, determines the range within which a message's time stamp is accepted. This in combination with clock synchronization can lead to serious problems. Depending on the choice of acceptance intervals, an attacker can keep ECUs' clocks in a specific time interval by continuously replaying the same synchronization message within the allowed interval. Furthermore, an attacker may relay the synchronization messages within the acceptance interval which may cause the local clocks of the recipient ECUs to slow down.

Counter. The second approach is to assign to each message type a counter which is incremented by the sender ECU and accepted and adopted by the recipient if it is equal to or bigger than its local one. Counters must increase monotonically across trips in order to prohibit message replay, hence the necessity for ECUs to store all counter values in non-volatile memory. This is costly and cannot be assumed to be possible for all ECUs in case of suddenly being switched off, given the number of message types and thus counters that need to be stored. A solution taking this into account is presented in AUTOSAR SecOC [1] where the complete counter is split into different parts (as explained in Sect. 2). However, by its very nature, the current counter based approaches allow relaying of messages as there is no link between a counter and the actual point in time it is used. Hence they are susceptible to replay attacks.

A further disadvantage for both the time stamp and the sequence number based approach is that at least a truncated freshness value needs to be transmitted, thus increasing the playload.

3 The Setting

In this section we describe the assumed setting consisting of a vehicular reference architecture, the basics of CAN Bus communication, and an attacker model.

3.1   The Reference Architecture

Vehicle networks can differ a lot regarding model and manufacturer. An overview of different network structures is given in [10]. Most connections in modern cars are realized using Controller Area Network (CAN) Bus [7]. Each bus interconnects multiple ECUs and an ECU can be connected to multiple buses. Some manufacturers integrate a gateway in the vehicle networks that can forward messages between different buses. Moreover each car has specific access points connecting the outside world with the internal bus systems. The On-Board-Diagnose (OBD) port is one of these access points allowing repair shops to access the car network; but there are also third party devices connecting this port with the internet for different use cases.

3.2   The Characteristics of CAN Communication

The CAN bus, specified in [7], is designed to reduce weight and cost of cables as well as to provide a safe connection between ECUs. Each entity connected to a CAN bus is able to send messages and can listen to every message sent on the bus. Only recently the necessity arose to protect its messages against malicious entities. The maximum transfer rate of the highspeed-CAN is 1 Mbit/s. A standard CAN message consists of 7 segments: the "Start of message" bit, a message identifier, a control field, a data field, a check sum, a confirmation field, and an "end of message" sequence. The 11 bit message identifier additionally represents the message's priority which is used to handle collisions. The CAN Bus uses Carrier Sense Multiple Access/Collision Resolution (CSMA/CR) to prevent collisions: All ECUs start simultaneously sending a CAN message and monitor its identifier while sending. In case a dominate 0 overwrites a 1 the ECU with the lower priority stops its transmission, hereby avoiding collisions. Once a message has been transmitted, i.e. its "end of message" sequence has been written, every ECU checks the correctness of its CRC (cyclic redundancy check). If correct, it adds the message to a temporary memory. A higher-level ECU part reads all such messages in certain time intervals (in the order they had been stored) and checks them regarding their message ID. Messages with message IDs irrelevant for the recipient are discarded.

3.3   Attack Model

There are multiple possibilities to manipulate CAN bus communication. For this paper we define an attacker based on attacks presented in [8] that has access to multiple CAN buses. Thus an attacker may attach a device to the bus system of a car, including ECUs of other cars she has access to, but also tuning devices, AdBlue emulators, unauthorized OBD dongles, etc. The attacker can send arbitrary messages on any bus it has access to. Moreover she can overhear and record all communication on a bus and replay all recorded messages on any bus she is connected to. Finally an attacker is able to flip bits of messages. This enables her to invalidate messages for other ECUs after having recorded them herself. In our scenario an attacker does not have access to any cryptographic keys. This also includes that the attacker cannot manipulate ECUs by e.g. corrupting firmware.

4   Hardware Based Bus Count Solution

In this section we describe our approach to defend a CAN bus against attackers with the abilities presented in the previous section. As already explained in Sect. 1, the principle idea is to equip each bus of the system with its own counter. An ECU connected to a bus decrements the bus counter each time it sees a message being sent on the bus. The procedures are described in more detail as follows (see Fig. 1 for a schematic representation of the message send process):

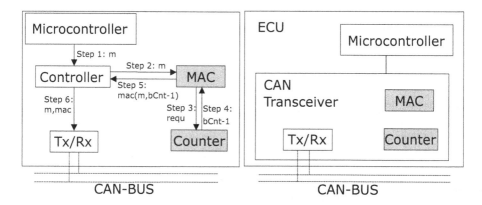

Fig. 1. Schematic representation of send   **Fig. 2.** ECU components

1. For sending a message m on a bus, the sender ECU generates the message's MAC including its local bus counter value (subsequently denoted by busCnt) decremented by 1 and the message ID. Note that it does not change the value of its local busCnt.
2. Once the MAC has been generated, the ECU starts writing the message's bits to the bus unless it has meanwhile started reading another message m' from the bus. In the latter case it discards m's MAC and sending of m. Note that if sending, the ECU still does not decrement its local busCnt.
3. All ECUs including the message sender read all messages on the bus. When reading the "start of message" bit initializing a CAN frame, all ECUs decrement their local busCnt value by 1.
4. After having read the message, the transceiver verifies it, using its current local busCnt value (just decremented when reading the message) for MAC verification. Successful MAC verification implies that the busCnt included in the MAC is equal to the ECU's local busCnt value.

5. Since ECUs may lose the correct counter value (e.g. because of having been switched off or disconnected from the bus), all ECUs simultaneously send a synchronization message containing their respective current local busCnt. More precisely, each time an entity starts sending a synchronization message, all ECUs join in sending. In order to determine the ECU that finalizes the synchronization message we apply the same mechanism as is used with respect to CAN Bus collision resolution: The ECUs with the lowest busCnt value are the ones that send their full message, ECUs with bigger busCnt values stop writing to the bus and adjust their local busCnt accordingly. The sending and receipt of these messages is carried out by two different components of the transceiver and analogously to sending and receiving other messages, hence all ECUs simultaneously decrement their busCnt value by 1. This ensures that after synchronization all ECUs own the correct busCnt.

We assume an appropriate MAC mechanism to be in place (e.g. CMAC with AES-128 as specified by Autosar SecOC). While SecOC's truncated MAC has a length of 24 bit, the fact that we do not transmit freshness values explicitly allows to use a truncated MAC of 32 bit.

The transmission of messages can fail due to technical problems or attacks. Further our approach requires messages to be read by all ECUs connected to a bus including the sender. Moreover it is necessary to calculate a MAC including the current counter directly before sending the message. Thus a pure software solution is not suitable and we propose a hardware based implementation of the mechanism. The resulting new transceiver allows ECUs additionally to sending and receiving of messages, respectively, to concurrently manage counters and to generate and verify MACs (see Fig. 2).

Our approach has multiple advantages. Our solution does not need any additional component such as a real time clock. The number of messages as an inherent part of the system is used to replace a clock. Moreover our solution allows to reduce the bus load since it does not have the need to send the busCnt with any of the messages. There is the further advantage of reducing the number of counters needed per bus. Approaches so far always use a separate counter for each message id, in contrast our approach can manage with just one counter per bus. This reduces the amount of storage necessary in each ECU.

Our solution has the further advantage that it is independent of functional disruptions regarding a central synchronization entity. All we need to assume in order for it to work is that there is always at least one ECU that owns the correct counter, i.e. the one corresponding to the number of messages that have been written onto the bus. Situations that violate this assumption, e.g. simultaneous loss of the correct counter value by all ECUs caused by a sudden power-off, can be prevented by an appropriate software and hardware realization of the proposed solution. A detailed discussion is out of the scope of this paper.

There are a couple of technical details that influence the security of our solution. One of them is the counter size. It needs to be small enough so as not to waste storage, but big enough to prevent an overflow during the vehicle lifetime that could be abused by an attacker for message replay. With the proposed hardware it will be easy to generate up to 1000 messages per second on a CAN Bus and we can assume an attacker that tries to provoke an overflow to have similar capabilities. Thus the number of messages per year cannot exceed 3.1536×10^{10}. Since a 32 bit counter would overflow after approximately 50 days we suggest to use a 64 bit counter that would be able to last a car's life time estimated by [9] to be about 25 years multiple times. Alternatively a replay protection with shorter counters could be implemented by changing keys before the counter overflows.

Another technical aspect that needs to be taken care of is the frequency of synchronization messages. As our proof (see Sect. 5.3) will show, replay is in general possible in the time interval between an ECU losing its counter value and receiving the next synchronization message. Thus the frequency of synchronization messages must be as high as possible but must on the other hand not disrupt the actual functionality of the bus. However, the optimization between overhead on the bus on the one hand and reaction time of an ideal ECU on the other hand is out of the scope of this paper.

Finally, while key management is not in the scope of this paper, our proof will show that using only one MAC key for all buses is not sufficient in order to distinguish senders of different buses. Since the busCnt values of different buses may differ, i.e. one bus may have a lower value than another bus, an attacker can in principle monitor the messages on the one and replay them on the other one, even across cars.

5   Formalization and Proof

In this section we introduce a formal model of a system implementing our approach and the formal proof regarding the freshness properties provided by it.

5.1   The Security Modeling Framework SeMF

We use our Security Modeling Framework SeMF [6] to formally verify the busCnt system introduced in the previous section. In SeMF, the specification of a cooperating system is composed of (i) a set $\mathbb{P}$ of agents (e.g. a set of ECUs), (ii) a set Σ of actions (e.g. send and receive actions on a bus), (iii) the system's behavior $B \subseteq \Sigma^*$ (Σ^* denoting the set of all words composed of elements in Σ), (iv) the local views $\lambda_P : \Sigma^* \to \Sigma_P^*$, and (v) initial knowledge $W_P \subseteq \Sigma^*$ of all agents $P \in \mathbb{P}$. The behavior B of a discrete system can be formally described by the set of its sequences of actions. An agent P's initial knowledge W_P about the system consists of all traces the agent initially considers possible. An agent may assume for example that a message that was received must have been sent before. The agents' initial knowledge is used to formalize the system properties that are certain to hold. It is specified once and does not change when the system evolves. Finally, an agent's local view essentially captures what an agent can see from the system. ECUs connected to a CAN bus for example see all messages written to the bus but do not see the respective senders.

In what follows, $alph(\omega)$ denotes the alphabet of a word $\omega \in \Sigma^*$, $pre(\omega)$ its set of prefixes and $pre(\Gamma)$ the set of prefixes of all words in $\Gamma \subseteq \Sigma^*$, $suf_1(\omega)$ its last action, $card(a, \omega)$ the frequency of an action a in ω, and for $L \subseteq \Sigma^*$, $\omega^{-1}(L)$ is its left quotient and denotes the set of all its continuations of ω in L.

The security property provided by a MAC mechanism can be formally specified by the following definition introduced in [6], the weaker property below describes links between specific actions:

Definition 1 (Authenticity). *A set of actions $\Gamma \subseteq \Sigma$ is authentic for $P \in \mathbb{P}$ after a sequence of actions $\omega \in B$ with respect to W_P if $alph(x) \cap \Gamma \neq \emptyset$ for all $x \in \lambda_P^{-1}(\lambda_P(\omega)) \cap W_P$.*

Definition 2 (Precedence). *For $L \subseteq \Sigma^*, \Gamma \subseteq \Sigma, b \in \Sigma$ the property $prec_L(\Gamma, b)$ holds if for all $\omega \in pre(L)$ with $b \in alph(\omega)$ follows $\Gamma \cap alph(\omega) \neq \emptyset$. We simply write $prec(\Gamma, b)$ if from the context the language referred to is clear.*

In order to capture message freshness we use phase classes (based on the concept of a *phase* introduced in [4]) that allow to model that a particular action occurred within a particular period in time. It is characterized by being closed with respect to concatenation.

Definition 3 (Phase class). *Let $\Upsilon \subseteq \Sigma^*$. A language $\Phi(\Upsilon) \subseteq \Sigma^*$ is a phase class for Υ if $\Phi(\Upsilon) \cap \Sigma \neq \emptyset$ and for all $\omega, u \in \Upsilon$ with $\omega = uv$ and $v \in \Phi(\Upsilon) \setminus (max(\Phi(\Upsilon)) \cup \{\varepsilon\})$ holds $\omega^{-1}(\Upsilon) \cap \Sigma \subseteq v^{-1}(\Phi(\Upsilon)) \cap \Sigma$.*

Phase classes defined by their starting and terminating actions are particularly usefull:

Definition 4 ((S,T)-phase class). *Let $\Upsilon \subseteq \Sigma^*, S, T \subseteq \Sigma, S \cap T = \emptyset$. Then $\Phi := \Phi(\Upsilon, S, T) \subseteq \Sigma^*$ is an (S, T)-phase class for Υ starting with S and terminating with the first occurrence of any $t \in T$ if*

- *Φ is a phase class for Υ,*
- *$\bigcup_{v \in \Phi} pre(v) \cap \Sigma = S$, and*
- *for all v maximal in Φ the following holds: For $\omega, u \in \Upsilon, z \in \Sigma^*$ with $\omega = uvz$ it follows $(\omega)^{-1}(\Upsilon) = \emptyset$ or $t := suf_1(v) \in T$ and $card(t, v) = 1$.*

We can now define the property that we will use for our formal verification: After having observed an action b in ω, agent P believes that in any sequence that can have happened, an action in Γ must have happened within a specific phase class:

Definition 5 (Authenticity within a phase). *Let $B \subseteq \Sigma^*$ be the behavior of a system, $\omega \in B, b \in alph(\omega)$, and $\Phi(W_P) \subseteq \Sigma^*$ a phase class for W_P. A set of actions $\Gamma \subseteq \Sigma$ is authentic for agent $P \in \mathbb{P}$ after ω within $\Phi(W_P)$ and with respect to b if it is authentic for P after ω and for all $x \in \lambda_P^{-1}(\lambda_P(\omega)) \cap pre(W_P)$ for which exists $u, z \in \Sigma^*$ and $v \in \Phi(W_P)$ such that $x = uvz$ and $b \in alph(v)$ it follows $alph(v) \cap \Gamma \neq \emptyset$. If the property holds for all $\omega \in B$ we denote this property shortly by* auth-wi-phase$(\Gamma, b, P, \Phi(W_P))$.

5.2 The Formal Model

Our formal model uses the agent set $\mathbb{P} = \{ECU_A^1, ECU_A^2, ECU_B^1, ECU_B^2, Eve\}$ and two buses $\{bus_A, bus_B\}$. The agents in $\mathcal{ECU}_A := \{ECU_A^1, ECU_A^2\}$ are connected to bus_A, those in $\mathcal{ECU}_B := \{ECU_B^1, ECU_B^2\}$ are connected to bus_B, and Eve is connected to both buses but not member of any group. We further use the action names $\mathtt{A} = \{send, recv, read, loseCnt\}$ and the parameter set $\{aname, ecu, ecukey, ecucnt, prevcnt, bus, mackey, msgid, msg, cnt\}$ with $aname \in \mathtt{A}, ecu \in \mathbb{P}, ecukey, mackey \in \{key_A, key_B\}, ecucnt, cnt \in \mathbb{N}, bus \in \{bus_A, bus_B\}, msgid \in \{\mathtt{sync}, \mathtt{fmsg}\}, msg \in \mathcal{M}$. The set of actions Σ_{bCnt} is then given as a subset of the cartesian product of action names and other parameters' values. Due to page limitations we forgo the formal definition. The concrete actions of our model are then specified as follows:

$(send, ecu, ecukey, ecucnt, prevcnt, bus, mackey, msgid, msg, cnt)$: ecu sends a complete message on bus. The message's MAC is generated with $mackey$ and covers $msgid, msg, cnt$. ecu may or may not have generated the MAC. The parameters $ecukey$ and $ecucnt$ denote ecu's MAC generation and verification key, and its local busCnt value, respectively, $prevcnt$ denotes the busCnt value used in ecu's previous action. An honest ECU sets cnt to prevcnt-1 but leaves its local busCnt value unchanged (see Prop. 7).

$(read, ecu, ecukey, ecucnt, prevcnt, bus, mackey, msgid, msg, cnt)$: ecu reads a message without processing it afterwards. This action includes the decrement of ecu's previous busCnt value resulting in $ecucnt$.

$(recv, ecu, ecukey, ecucnt, prevcnt, bus, mackey, msgid, msg, cnt)$ denotes the successful reception and processing of a message by ecu. ecu decrements its local busCnt value (i.e. the one used in the previous action) and verifies that the result is equal to cnt (in case $msgid = \mathtt{fmsg}$) or bigger ($msgid = \mathtt{sync}$), and sets $ecucnt = cnt$. Note that all agents including the sender perform either a $read$ or a $recv$ action.

$(loseCnt, ecu, ecucnt, prevcnt, bus)$ represents ecu losing its local busCnt value for some reason (e.g. caused by technical problems), resulting in a bigger busCnt value, modeled by $ecucnt > prevcnt$.

Introducing a Phase Class into the Model. The idea of the busCnt system is that counter values included in the messages are strictly monotonically decreasing. From the viewpoint of an agent receiving a message (action b), the action that "activated" the busCnt value contained in the message's MAC is the respective $send$ (action a). So each send action starts a new phase class, and each phase class ends with a new send action, hereby invalidating the counter of the previous phase class.

Considering the characteristics of a CAN bus as described in Sect. 3.2, there cannot be any other send action between a and b on this bus. Hence for each $read$ and $recv$ action b the corresponding send action a, denoted by $\sigma(b)$, is unique. These considerations give rise to the phase class definition below (with the function $\widehat{\kappa}_{par}(a)$ extracting the parameter par of action a).

Definition 6 (Active Phase). *Let $W_{bCnt} \subseteq \Sigma^*_{bCnt}$ denote the agents' initial knowledge, $b \in \Sigma_{bCnt}$ with $\widehat{\kappa}_{aname}(b) \in \{read, recv\}$. Then we define the phase class active at b with respect to W_{bCnt} as follows:*

$$\Phi(b) := \Phi(W_{bCnt}, \{\sigma(b)\}, \{a \in \Sigma_{bCnt} \mid \widehat{\kappa}_{aname}(a) = send \\ \wedge \widehat{\kappa}_{bus}(a) = \widehat{\kappa}_{bus}(b)\})$$

Agents' Local View and Initial Knowledge. All agents see their own actions completely and all messages sent on a CAN bus they are connected to but cannot see who sent them nor the values of parameters stored locally by the sender. Agents cannot see messages sent on a bus they are not connected to and cannot see actions $read, recv$ and $loseCnt$ performed by other agents. We forgo the formal definition of agents' local view.

With specifying the agents' initial knowledge we capture the characteristics of our system and in particular those of a CAN bus. We assume that the initial knowledge of all agents $P \in \mathbb{P}$, denoted by W_{bCnt}, is identical and satisfies all properties described verbally below.

Prop. 1 A $read$ and $recv$ action b, respectively, on a specific bus is always preceded by the corresponding send action $\sigma(b)$: $prec_{W_{bCnt}}(\sigma(b), b)$ (because of page limitations we forgo the formal specifications of the subsequent properties).

Prop. 2 A $recv$ action performed by an honest ECU must be preceded by the respective send action of an agent owning the key used for MAC generation.

Prop. 3 Only members of ECU_X ($X \in \{A, B\}$) own and can use key_X. Since Eve does not own a key and honest ECUs use their key to generate and verify a MAC, the MAC key contained in a send or receive action being equal to the ECU's key is equivalent to the ECU being member of the respective group.

Prop. 4 The parameter $prevcnt$ of an action performed by an honest ECU contains the local busCnt value of the ECU's previous action.

Prop. 5 When an honest ECU receives and accepts a message, its local busCnt is equal to the message's cnt value. This can be equal to the agent's previous local busCnt value decremented by 1 or smaller (in case the message is a synchronization message and contains a smaller counter).

Prop. 6 When an honest ECU reads a message without accepting it, it decrements its previous busCnt value by 1 and uses the result as its new local busCnt value.

Prop. 7 An honest ECU sends a message including its local busCnt decremented by one but does not change its local busCnt value.

Prop. 8 In a phase class starting with a particular $send$ action on a specific bus and terminating with the next send action on this bus, all honest ECUs connected to the bus are either inactive or perform one action $read, recv$ or $loseCnt$.

Prop. 9 If an honest ECU performs two *recv* actions with its local busCnt value of the first one being less or equal to the local busCnt value of the second one, then it must have performed a *loseCnt* action in between.

Prop. 10 A synchronization message always contains the correct counter corresponding to the number of messages that have been written to the bus.

5.3   Verification of the Formal Model

The property we want to prove is that whenever an ECU receives a message, the respective action that writes the message to the bus is performed by an honest ECU connected to the same bus. Our formal proof shows two issues: First, if the same key is used for messages on more than one bus, what can be proven at most is that one of the ECUs connected to one of these buses has generated the message. Second, we can only prove the desired property for an honest ECU that has not lost its local busCnt value and that does not receive a synchronization message in time.

Theorem 1. *Let B_{bCnt} denote the system's behavior, $\omega \in B_{bCnt}$ and $b :=$ (recv, ecu, ecukey, ecucnt, prevcnt, bus, mackey, msgid, msg, cnt) $\in alph(\omega)$ with $ecu \in ECU_X, X \in \{A, B\}$. Then the following property is satisfied:*

$$\text{auth-wi-phase}(\{(send, ecu', ecukey', ecucnt', prevcnt', bus, mackey, msgid, msg,$$
$$cnt) \,|\, ecu' \in ECU_X\}, b, ecu, \Phi(b))$$

Proof. Assume the MAC keys for both buses are identical, i.e. $key_A = key_B$. Assume further without loss of generality $ecu = ECU_A^1 \in ECU_A$ performs a *recv* action b. By definition, $\lambda_{ECU_A^1}$ keeps b, thus $b \in alph(x)$ for all $x \in \lambda_{ECU_A^1}^{-1}(\lambda_{ECU_A^1}(\omega)) \cap W_{bCnt}$. By Prop. 2, there exists a *send* action $a_1 \in alph(x)$ performed by ecu_1 with the same $mackey, msgid, msg, cnt$ and the sender's key equal to $mackey$. Since $ecu = ECU_A^1$, Prop. 3 implies $ecukey = mackey = key_A = key_B$ which in turn implies $ecu_1 \in ECU_A \cup ECU_B$. We cannot locate the set ecu_1 belongs to any further, thus the desired property cannot be proven.

Assume now $key_A \neq key_B$, i.e. we can conclude $ecu_1 \in ECU_A$. By Prop. 1 b is preceded by $\sigma(b) = (send, ecu', ecukey', ecucnt', bus, mackey, msgid, msg, cnt)$ that starts the phase class active at b. By definition, ECU_A^1's local view does not reveal the sender, hence assume $ecu' \neq ecu_1$ and $\sigma(b) \neq a_1$. Assume that with action a_2 by ecu_1 and a_3 by ECU_A^1 directly before a_1, both ECUs are synchronized and own the correct busCnt value k. By Prop. 7, $\widehat{\kappa}_{cnt}(a_1) = k-1 = \widehat{\kappa}_{cnt}(b)$. Prop. 8 implies that ECU_A^1, assuming it is active, performs a *read, recv* or *loseCnt* action a_4 before $\sigma(b)$, assume it is no *loseCnt* action. If $\widehat{\kappa}_{aname}(a_4) = recv$, Props. 4 and 5 imply $cnt = \widehat{\kappa}_{ecucnt}(a_4) = \widehat{\kappa}_{prevcnt}(a_4) - 1 = \widehat{\kappa}_{ecucnt}(a_3) - 1 = k - 1$, and $\widehat{\kappa}_{aname}(a_4) = read$ leads to $\widehat{\kappa}_{ecucnt}(a_4) = k - 1 = cnt = ecucnt$ by Props. 5 and 6. Now Prop. 9 implies that ECU_A^1 performs a *loseCnt* action a_5 between a_4 and b with $\widehat{\kappa}_{ecucnt}(a_5) > \widehat{\kappa}_{prevcnt}(a_5)$ and Prop. 4 implies $\widehat{\kappa}_{prevcnt}(a_5) = \widehat{\kappa}_{ecucnt}(a_4) = k-1$. Assume $\widehat{\kappa}_{ecucnt}(a_5) = k$ and that ECU_A^1 does not perform any other actions before b. Then Props. 4 and 5 imply $ecucnt =$

$prevcnt - 1 = \widehat{\kappa}_{ecucnt}(a_5) - 1 = k - 1 = cnt$. Thus ECU_A^1 may very well receive and accept the message sent by $ecu' \notin ECU_A$.

This result meets our expectations: In case an ECU loses its busCnt value and the next regular synchronization message takes too long, message replay can in principle not be avoided.

If between a_5 and b, ECU_A^1 performs more recv actions with $msgid = \texttt{fmsg}$, the situation is equivalent to ECU_A^1 performing b. Consider on the other hand the case where ECU_A^1 receives one or more synchronization messages (i.e. with $msgid = \texttt{sync}$) between a_5 and b with a_6 the last of these actions. Then by Prop. 8 a_6 happens before $\sigma(b)$ and by Prop. 1 it must be preceded by another send action $\sigma(a_6)$. Since cnt is sent in a_1, Prop. 10 implies $\widehat{\kappa}_{cnt}(\sigma(a_6)) = \widehat{\kappa}_{cnt}(a_6) = \widehat{\kappa}_{ecucnt}(a_6) < cnt$ and by Props. 4 and 5 it follows $cnt = ecucnt \le prevcnt - 1 = \widehat{\kappa}_{ecucnt}(a_6) - 1 < cnt - 1$ which in turn implies that b is not a recv action, a contradiction to our assumption.

This part of our proof shows that even if an ECU loses its counter, as long as it receives a synchronization message "early enough", a replay is not possible.

Assume now that ECU_A^1 does not perform a loseCnt action. b being a recv action, Prop. 5 implies $ecucnt = cnt \le prevcnt - 1$ which is by Prop. 4 equal to $ecucnt_4 - 1 = cnt - 1$, i.e. $cnt \le cnt - 1$. Since this is always false, b cannot be a recv action but is a read action, again a contradiction to the assumption we started with.

Finally, assuming that before ecu_1's send action ECU_A^1 and ecu_1 are not synchronized is equivalent to assuming that one of them has lost its local busCnt value which we have already discussed. This concludes our proof.

Our proof shows that as long as no honest ECU loses (for whatever reason) its local busCnt value, or, if so receives a synchronization message in time, our approach prohibits message replay. Note that our Theorem does not state that the sender is necessarily different from the recipient. By the very nature of symmetric cryptoalgorithms, the replay of a message to the sender must be prohibited by information incorporated into the message, e.g. adequate message ids.

6   Discussion and Conclusions

In this paper we have introduced a new hardware based approach for provision of freshness to messages sent over in-car networks via a CAN bus. In current approaches, (truncated) counter or time stamp values are transmitted in messages from sender to recipient. A synchronization master regularly provides the current freshness value to all ECUs, hereby allowing them to be switched off at times in order to save electric power. By assigning to the transceiver the additional functionality of counter maintenance and MAC generation and verification, we accomplish the same effect: Only the transceiver needs to be continuously running, while the power consuming main ECU processors can be inactive at times. Continuously active transceivers open up the possibility to use the physical characteristics of messages sent on a CAN bus as the basis of our counter mechanism. The fundamental difference between the established approaches that are currently considered and ours is that in ours the pulse generator is integral component of the system itself: The very writing onto a bus causes a change of the counter values of all ECUs connected to this bus as they inevitably read the message (even if not accepting it) and decrement their counters. By this read action, the counter contained in the message that is being read and thus the message's MAC is invalidated. Any subsequent message written onto the bus must include a smaller counter in order to be accepted. Hence it is impossible for an attacker to circumvent the change of the ECUs' counter values.

Nevertheless, ECUs may lose their counter values, caused e.g. by technical problems or attacks. In order to cope with this situation, should it occur, our approach includes a synchronization mechanism. Again, by taking advantage of the physical characteristics of a CAN bus that allows any ECU to overwrite a 1-bit by a 0, the mechanism ensures that it is always the smallest (i.e. correct) counter value that is actually sent, corresponding to the actual number of sent messages, provided at least one ECU per bus owns the correct counter value.

Compared to other approaches our counter mechanism offers several practical advantages: First, it only uses one counter per bus and thus reduces the memory capacity necessary to store counters compared to multi counter approaches. Second it reduces message payload as in contrast to time stamp or other counter based approaches there is no need to send (part of) the busCnt value as part of the messages. A Real Time Clock as pulse generator is equivalent to our approach in the sense that the clock signal cannot be manipulated. However, it is considered costly and thus software based clocks are mostly used. These in turn diverge and thus require synchronization to adjust the clock base which is therefore susceptible to manipulation. Further, clock based approaches always call for acceptance intervals since between MAC generation and verification some time passes, even if it is only a couple of milliseconds. This induces points of attack, allowing the replay of synchronization messages within inappropriately chosen acceptance intervals and thus manipulation of software clocks. On the other hand, using counters as pulse generator avoids the need for acceptance intervals but exhibits the attack point of slowing down the pulse since a counter is not related to a specific point in time and thus ECUs have no possibility to detect replay of previously blocked messages.

In contrast, our proof presented in Sect. 5.3 shows that as long as no honest ECU loses (for whatever reason) its local busCnt value, our approach prohibits these types of attack. Only in case an ECU's local counter value is corrupted and the next regular synchronization message takes too long, message replay is possible. This issue is inherent in any approach that cannot prohibit unnoticed loss of the freshness values. Thus the synchronization frequency has to be chosen adequately. Yet what is adequate depends on the transmission speed of the bus, the functionality of ECUs connected to the bus and other factors that are beyond the scope of this paper.

Regarding synchronization, compared to other approaches our solution has the advantage that it is independent of functional disruptions of a synchronization master since all ECUs send synchronization messages simultaneously. As long as there is always at least one ECU that owns the correct counter, only the message with the smallest (and correct) counter is actually sent and received, ensuring that all active ECUs connected to the bus are properly synchronized. The concrete hardware and software realization must ensure the validity of this assumption. Since any message sent on the bus changes the counter value, in contrast to other approaches, ours does not allow relaying of synchronization and other messages. An attacker's possibilities for message replay are thus restricted to waiting for an ECU to be unsynchronized (or causing this state by some means) and invalidating all subsequent regular synchronization messages sent on the bus. This attack possibility is inherent in any approach requiring synchronization and demands for additional measures.

Finally, an attacker can accelerate the pulse generator by inserting messages onto the bus. Independent of being accepted, they will cause the connected ECUs to decrement their counters faster than they normally would. However, a high message frequency will not cause counter overflow as long as the counter size is chosen big enough (we suggest 64 bits, see Sect. 4).

Our proof additionally shows another issue that applies to all approaches: In order to enable a fine grained verification of message origin that allows to distinguish senders of different buses or even cars, an appropriate number of different MAC keys needs to be used, in particular different cars should be equipped with different sets of keys.

We are currently implementing our approach in order to evaluate its practicability. The evaluation on an FPGA will show that the system works in real world scenarios and help us improve the idea presented. It will further support us in determining the exact complexity of our hardware extensions. Finally experiments will help to identify synchronization intervals that do not cause inappropriate message delay.

References

1. AUTOSAR: Specification of Module Secure Onboard Communication, Classic Platform, December 2017
2. Chavez, M.L., Rosete, C.H., Henriquez, F.R.: Achieving confidentiality security service for CAN. In: 15th International Conference on Electronics, Communications and Computers, CONIELECOMP 2005, pp. 166–170, February 2005
3. Elend, B., Adamson, T.: Cyber security enhancing CAN transceivers. In: Proceedings of the 16th International CAN Conference (2017)
4. Grimm, R., Ochsenschläger, P.: Binding cooperation, a formal model for electronic commerce. Comput. Netw. **37**, 171–193 (2001)
5. Groza, B., Murvay, S., van Herrewege, A., Verbauwhede, I.: LiBrA-CAN: a lightweight broadcast authentication protocol for controller area networks. In: Pieprzyk, J., Sadeghi, A.-R., Manulis, M. (eds.) CANS 2012. LNCS, vol. 7712, pp. 185–200. Springer, Heidelberg (2012). https://doi.org/10.1007/978-3-642-35404-5_15

6. Gürgens, S., Ochsenschläger, P., Rudolph, C.: Authenticity and provability — a formal framework. In: Davida, G., Frankel, Y., Rees, O. (eds.) InfraSec 2002. LNCS, vol. 2437, pp. 227–245. Springer, Heidelberg (2002). https://doi.org/10.1007/3-540-45831-X_16

7. Road vehicles - Controller Area Network (CAN). Standard, International Organization for Standardization, Geneva, CH, December 2015

8. Koscher, K., et al.: Experimental security analysis of a modern automobile. In: 2010 IEEE Symposium on Security and Privacy, pp. 447–462, May 2010. https://doi.org/10.1109/SP.2010.34

9. Lu, S.: Vehicle Survivability and Travel Mileage Schedules. NHTSA's National Center for Statistics and Analysis, Washington, DOT HS 809 952 edn. (2006)

10. Miller, C., Valasek, C.: A survey of remote automotive attack surfaces. In: Black Hat USA (2014)

11. Nilsson, D.K., Larson, U.E., Jonsson, E.: Efficient in-vehicle delayed data authentication based on compound message authentication codes. In: 2008 IEEE 68th Vehicular Technology Conference, pp. 1–5, September 2008

12. Nürnberger, S., Rossow, C.: – vatiCAN – vetted, authenticated CAN bus. In: Gierlichs, B., Poschmann, A.Y. (eds.) CHES 2016. LNCS, vol. 9813, pp. 106–124. Springer, Heidelberg (2016). https://doi.org/10.1007/978-3-662-53140-2_6

13. Radu, A.-I., Garcia, F.D.: LeiA: a lightweight authentication protocol for CAN. In: Askoxylakis, I., Ioannidis, S., Katsikas, S., Meadows, C. (eds.) ESORICS 2016. LNCS, vol. 9879, pp. 283–300. Springer, Cham (2016). https://doi.org/10.1007/978-3-319-45741-3_15

14. Schweppe, H., et al.: EVITA deliverable D3.3: secure on-board protocols specifcation. Technical report, EVITA, July 2011

15. Siddiqui, A.S., Gui, Y., Plusquellic, J., Saqib, F.: Secure communication over CAN bus. In: 2017 IEEE 60th International Midwest Symposium on Circuits and Systems (MWSCAS), pp. 1264–1267, August 2017

16. Szilagyi, C., Koopman, P.: Flexible multicast authentication for time-triggered embedded control network applications. In: 2009 IEEE/IFIP International Conference on Dependable Systems Networks, pp. 165–174, June 2009

17. Ueda, H., Kurachi, R., Takada, H., Mizutani, T., Inoue, M., Horihata, S.: Security authentication system for in-vehicle network. SEI Tech. Rev. **81**, 5–9 (2015)

18. Zou, Q., et al.: The study of secure CAN communication for automotive applications. In: SAE Technical Paper. SAE International, March 2017

Enhancing Usage Control for Performance: An Architecture for Systems of Systems

Vasileios Gkioulos[1]([⊠]), Athanasios Rizos[2,3]([⊠]), Christina Michailidou[2,3]([⊠]),
Paolo Mori[2], and Andrea Saracino[2]

[1] Department of Information Security and Communication Technology,
Norwegian University of Science and Technology, Gjøvik, Norway
`vasileios.gkioulos@ntnu.no`
[2] Istituto di Informatica e Telematica, Consiglio Nazionale delle Ricerche, Pisa, Italy
`{athanasios.rizos,christina.michailidou,paolo.mori,`
`andrea.saracino}@iit.cnr.it`
[3] University of Pisa, Pisa, Italy

Abstract. The distributiveness and heterogeneity of today's systems of systems, such as the Internet of Things (IoT), on-line banking systems, and contemporary emergency information systems, require the integration of access and usage control mechanisms, for managing the right of access both to the corresponding services, and the plethora of information that is generated in a daily basis. Usage Control (UCON) is such a mechanism, allowing the fine-grained policy based management of system resources, based on dynamic monitoring and evaluation of object, subject, and environmental attributes. Yet, as we presented in an earlier article, *a number of improvements can be introduced to the standard model regarding its resilience on active attacks, the simplification of the policy writing, but also in terms of run-time efficiency and scalability.* In this article, we present an enhanced usage control architecture, that was developed for tackling the aforementioned issues. In order to achieve that, a dynamic role allocation system will be added to the existing architecture, alongside with a service grouping functionality which will be based on attribute aggregation. This is structured in accordance to a risk-based framework, which has been developed in order to aggregate the risk values that the individual attributes encapsulate into a unified risk value. These architectural enhancements are utilized in order to improve the resilience, scalability, and run-time efficiency of the existing model.

Keywords: Access control · Internet of Things ·
Security architecture · Systems of systems · Usage control

1 Introduction

Modern interconnected systems of systems, require scalable and efficient security mechanisms, for controlling a very large number of access requests in a

S. K. Katsikas et al. (Eds.): CyberICPS 2018/SECPRE 2018, LNCS 11387, pp. 69–84, 2019.
https://doi.org/10.1007/978-3-030-12786-2_5

future with billions of heterogeneous devices connected to the Internet. The evaluation of requests for access to certain pieces of information and services commonly relies on dedicated policies [9], which incorporate object, subject, and environmental attributes. Such policies are based on predefined rules, while access control is *a process by which use of system resources is regulated according to a security policy and is permitted only by authorized entities (users, programs, processes, or other systems) according to that policy* [15]. A multitude of access control policies can be defined, corresponding to distinct criteria for what should be allowed and what not [13].

As presented in detail in our earlier study [3], a limitation of access control is that the access request is only checked once, at the initiation, which highlights the lack of capabilities related to checking alterations on the values of attributes during a session so as to re-evaluate the conformance to the policy. This type of continuous control is a feature that Usage Control (UCON) [6] can provide. UCON enhances Attribute-Based Access Control (ABAC) models [2] in two novel aspects [11]: continuity of control, and mutability of attributes. Continuity of control is the evaluation of access decisions not only at request time, but also when the requester executes access rights on the resource. Further, mutability of attributes means that if changes occur in attribute values while a session is in progress, and the security policy is not satisfied anymore, UCON can revoke the access, terminating the usage of the resources [16]. Yet, the examined environments carry inherent limitations in terms of both computational and communications capacity. Accordingly, corresponding optimizations must be implemented to the original UCON design, seeking to maintain operational efficiency at run-time, but also further security objectives related to resilience. Such optimizations must be initially integrated architecturally, and further enhanced within the components of the deployed policy based management systems.

In this article, we build on the results of the aforementioned articles in order to mitigate the limitations of the original UCON which have been presented earlier [3]. Namely, the current UCON architecture, requires the complete re-evaluation of access permissions per user-asset-session triplet, both at the initiation and at runtime. This, have been experimentally proven in the aforementioned articles to require excessive computational resources, especially as the users, assets, sessions and policy attributes increase. Accordingly, we describe the developed architectural optimizations to the original UCON, seeking to positively affect run time efficiency, scalability, and resilience against active attacks. In order to achieve that, a service group functionality is introduced to the existing model alongside with a dynamic role allocation sub-system, both based on risk aggregation. Thus, the right of access will be granted to a user, based on his allocated role for each group of services and not for one service at a time. The integrated optimizations improve the performance of the model, while increasing its resilience by allowing the mitigation of specific types of active attacks that are based on request flooding.

Architectures of this nature can be described in three abstraction levels, maintaining consistency and completeness. These levels are the (i) architectural model and components, (ii) protocol and interface, and (iii) implementation. In this article, we present and discuss the suggested architecture in all three levels (see Sect. 3), highlighting the integrated optimizations to the original UCON and the corresponding affects. The rest of this paper is organized as follows: In Sect. 2, we report related work and background information on the existing UCON mechanisms. Section 3 describes the developed architecture in the aforementioned abstraction levels. Further, Sect. 4 presents our initial results from a small-scale test-case based validation, while Sect. 5 concludes by proposing future directions which stem from our preliminary work and validation results.

2   Background and Related Work

In this section we will review the theoretical background of the most commonly used access control models, the Role-Based Access Control (RBAC), the Attribute-Based Access Control (ABAC) and the Usage Control. Furthermore, we provide a brief explanation of the risk-based aggregation process, which will be used in the upcoming sections of this study.

2.1   RBAC - ABAC

Role-Based Access Control (RBAC) is a widespread approach for regulating the access to information and resources [14]. The principal idea of this model is that a set of roles is created based on the application environment, where as an example, these roles can arise from the hierarchy of an organization or a company. Each subject is assigned to a role, depending on which, he/she also is entitled to a set of privileges. Hence, subjects that are higher in the hierarchy have the possibility to perform more actions over the resources, whilst subjects belonging in the base of the hierarchy have limited access. The RBAC model can be characterized as flexible, since subjects can be reassigned to roles if needed and also privileges can be given to roles or taken from them considering the current state of the application environment. Another positive aspect of this model is that subjects can be also organized in groups based on their role or some common characteristics, while each group has its own permissions. As an example, a group can be the IT department of a company with permissions to modify user-names/passwords, but no permissions on changing data related to the salary of the employees.

Notwithstanding the benefits in efficiency [10], RBAC also comes with a certain amount of limitations. The inability to take into account time and location constraints, and the fact that in order to change the privileges of a user the role must be also changed, are a only a few examples commonly discussed in bibliography. Thus, to overcome these limitations, a new model came to fill the gap. Attribute-based Access Control (ABAC) [4] considers many different attributes related both to the subject and the object, in order to grant or deny access to a resource. The sets of attributes that can be evaluated by ABAC include both static attributes such as the name or the role of a subject, and dynamic such as the current position of the subject, the time of the day, the age etc. The right of access is regulated by the security policy, which is defined in accordance to the attributes that need to be evaluated and their permitted ranges. Policies of this type can be expressed in formal languages such as XML [2].

The proposed enhancements in the existing UCON model, arise by the combination of the benefits provided by these two approaches, where attribute based aggregation is utilized both for subject roles and object groups. Consequently, these aggregated values are incorporated within the predefined security policies, reducing the required resources for policy evaluation and accordingly increasing the scalability potential of such deployments.

2.2   Usage Control

The original UCON model is based on the ABAC model. It introduces mutable attributes and new decision factors besides authorizations; these are obligations and conditions. Mutable attributes represent features of subjects, objects, and environment that can change their values as a consequence of the system's operation [11]. Since mutable attributes change their values during the usage of an object, the UCON model allows the definition of policies which are evaluated both at the initiation and during a session. In particular, a UCON policy consists of three components: authorizations, conditions and obligations. Authorizations are predicates which evaluate subject and object attributes, and also the actions that the subject requested to perform on the object. Obligations are predicates which define requirements that must be fulfilled before the access (Pre-Obligations), or that must be continuously fulfilled while the access is in progress (Ongoing-Obligations). Finally, conditions are requirements that evaluate the attributes of the environment. The continuous evaluation of the policy when the access is in progress aims at interrupting the access when the execution right is no more valid, in order to reduce the risk of misuse of resources.

Hence, in UCON it is crucial to be able to continuously retrieve the updated values of the mutable attributes, in order to perform the run-time evaluation and promptly react to the changes by revoking access when necessary. The main blocks of UCON are the Usage Control System (UCS) surrounded by the Controlled Systems and the Attribute Environment. The Controlled Systems are those components on which the UCON policy can be enforced. Each Controlled System communicates with the UCS issuing the request to access a resource by performing a specific operation on it. For more information about UCON, readers can refer to [6].

Earlier studies on UCON, highlight that in large-scale heterogeneous systems, such as an IoT application [5], the number of attributes can grow exponentially, increasing the demand for resources but also limiting scalability, and run-time efficiency. Accordingly, in this article, enhancements presented have been developed, towards mitigating these limitations and improving the operation of UCON under such constraints.

2.3   Risk Aggregation

Large-scale applications create a challenging field in regard to access and usage control. The number of the attributes which need to be evaluated grows continuously and hence, the possibility of mistakes and conflicts during the policy development increases. Therefore, a model has been proposed earlier [8], which considers the risk level that each attribute encapsulates, and aggregates these values for policy decisions. For example, if a subject wants to access a classified document and the policy takes into account the role of the subject, then it is possible to assign different level of risk to different roles, e.g. the administrator of the system comes with a low level of risk while a new-hired employee with a high level of risk.

The aforementioned model is a qualitative risk model for systems that make use of UCON, and its goal is to aggregate the risk values of the attributes into one single value, that will characterize the total risk of a given request. In order to achieve the aggregation, the model exploits the Analytic Hierarchy Process (AHP) [12]. Having the total risk value the security administrator has the possibility to define policies which are based only on this value or, as it will be explained later in this section, policies of any other granularity level. In order to make the functionality of the model clearer a set of definitions must be given [8].

- *Full Policy*: A policy considering the attributes as they are extracted when acquiring the attribute values but not yet aggregated.
- *RA-Policy*: A risk aware policy is a policy which is written by considering the risk level of aggregated attributes. It has generally a smaller number of attributes with respect to the correspondent Full-Policy, hence it is easier to define and evaluate.
- *Initial Request*: A generated request enriched with the related attributes extracted.
- *Aggregated Request*: A request automatically computed by our framework, starting from an initial request, translating it to the aggregation level required by the current RA-Policy.

The framework is based on a reverse tree structure which is depicted in Fig. 1. The total risk value, which was calculated by the aggregation of the attributes' risk values, forms the root of the tree. The upper levels consist of several blocks which represent groups of attributes that are related to each other. For example, a possible group could be the attributes related to environmental factors, such as the location or the time of the request. The leaves of the tree represent the attributes that participate in the Full Policy, whilst the Total Risk value is the one being considered by the RA-Policy.

As stated above, the method used for the aggregation of the risk values of the attributes is the AHP. This method demands the definition of three elements: the *goal*, the *criteria* and the *alternatives*. Regarding the risk-aware model the *goal* is to characterize the total risk of the given request, the *criteria* are the various attributes and the *alternatives* are the possible risk levels (i.e. Low Risk,

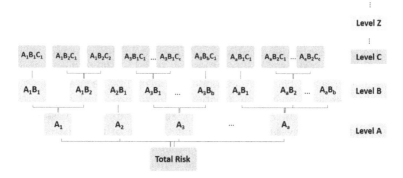

Fig. 1. Total risk reverse tree [8]

Medium Risk, High Risk). A set of comparison matrices is created, where an expert on the specific field of the usage control application environment, defines a level of preference among the criteria, stating by this way the relevance of each criterion with respect to the goal.

A comparison matrix is $N \times N$, where N is the number of the alternatives. Each element of the matrix takes a value in the interval $[1, \ldots, 9]$ which defines the importance of an element in comparison with another one. Let us consider the previous example of accessing a classified document. Regarding the attribute of the role of the subject, it is reasonable to assume that the administrator of the system can be assigned with a lower level of risk than a new employee. The comparison matrix which represents this statement is shown in Table 1. The meaning of this matrix is that if the value of the role is the *administrator* then the value of *Low Risk* is considered to be 7 times more relevant than the *Medium* and 9 times more relevant than the *High* or *Unacceptable Risk*. On the contrary, if the value of the role is *new employee* then the *High Risk* alternative will be valued more than the others as shown in Table 2.

Table 1. Comparison matrix of the alternatives for the administrator

Administrator	Low	Medium	High	Unacceptable
Low	1	7	9	9
Medium	$1/7$	1	3	5
High	$1/9$	$1/3$	1	1
Unacceptable	$1/9$	$1/5$	1	1

Finally, regarding the integration of the risk-aware framework to UCON, there is no need for any modification of the original model. The only requirement is the addition of a set of PIPs, which will acquire the risk values from the AHP blocks. The proposed architecture is shown in Fig. 2, where the attributes are

Table 2. Comparison matrix of the alternatives for new employee

New Employee	Low	Medium	High	Unacceptable
Low	1	$1/4$	$1/9$	$1/9$
Medium	4	1	$1/9$	$1/9$
High	9	9	1	1
Unacceptable	9	9	1	1

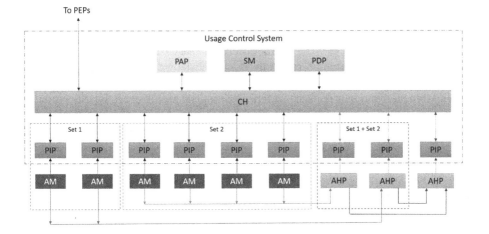

Fig. 2. Risk aware UCON architecture [8]

grouped into two sets. Each one of the sets will be aggregated using AHP and the results of these aggregations will be the input to a final AHP problem which will compute the single total risk value.

Having this architecture, it is also possible to define policies of different granularity levels, although it must be noted that excessive aggregation levels can affect the expressivity of the policy, as discussed earlier [8]. For example, a policy can be defined by using only the single value of total risk, such as *"Subject can access object if the total risk of the request is at most medium"*, or combine this value with attributes either coming directly from the AMs or coming as outcome from any AHP block, such as *"Subject can access object if the total risk is at most medium and the time of the request is within the working hours"* or *"Subject can access object if the total risk is low and the risk of the environmental group of attributes is medium"*. Thus, this model is totally configurable and adjustable to the requirements of the application environment.

3   The Proposed Architecture

In this section, we present the architecture for enhancing the UCON model, in two abstraction levels, namely: (i) the architectural model and its components, (ii) protocol and interface. The aim of this architectural enhancement is to improve the existing UCON model in terms of performance and efficiency. To this end, a service group functionality has been introduced in the current architecture. Alongside the dynamic user role allocation, this functionality gives the possibility for a faster access evaluation and response. Policy attributes are aggregated integrating criticality and risk metrics, allowing for the mapping of service groups but also for the allocation of distinct roles across these groups to every subject. Accordingly, the extraction of the service groups and the current user role (for each group) at run-time is achieved by the Group Handler, and in accordance to the current attribute values. For example, considering that an application environment consists of ten services, the architecture for the enforcement of UCON policies proposed in [7], has to evaluate the subject's request for each one of them. On the contrary, the proposed architecture, after grouping the services, will grant access to these groups in accordance to the predefined policies, and the dynamically allocated user roles, which are independently calculated for each group. Hence, if a user has access to a group, in accordance to his role for this group, and makes a request for a service belonging in this group the evaluation will be faster, improving the run-time efficiency.

3.1   The Architectural Model and its Components

The suggested architecture remains unaltered in comparison to the one proposed in [7], which was based on U-XACML [1], with the exception of the introduction of a Group Handler (GH) as an internal sub-component of the Context Handler (CH), for the purpose of providing high-level compatibility with prior studies and implementations. The components of the architecture and their interconnections are presented in Fig. 3. The actions used by the PEP to interact with the UCS in order to perform an access request, a start/end of usage of resources are the same as in the UCON model described earlier. The same applies for the actions used by the UCS to interact with the PEP in order to revoke access when needed.

The proposed architecture consists of six distinct components. The discrete services provided by these components are:

1. **PEP-Policy Enforcement Point:** The PEP enforces usage control policies by mediating requests from the subscribers to the UCS, and enforcing the corresponding policy decisions. The PEP incorporates functionalities which ensure that no subscriber can register (or remain registered) to a service, without the continuous enforcement of the corresponding usage control policies. Further, the PEP is responsible for the appropriate translation of subscription requests and decisions among the subscribers and the UCS. The communication between the PEP and the UCS is performed via the following actions:

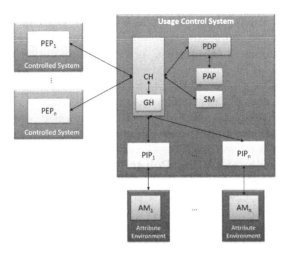

Fig. 3. The proposed architectural model.

TryAccess: Request by the PEP to the UCS to perform an action or access on a resource. The UCS will respond with a Permit or Deny decision.

StartAccess: This is the actual start of using the service requested. There is again evaluation from the PDP and after an affirmative response from the UCS the session actually starts.

EndAccess: This action is invoked when the usage of the resource terminates by a request of the PEP to the UCS.

RevokeAccess: If a mutable attribute changes its value and a violation of the policy occurs, the access has to be revoked. UCS informs the PEP that this session is revoked.

A detailed description of the previous interactions can be found in [7].

2. **SM-Session Manager:** The SM is a database of the ongoing sessions. Accordingly, this component is crucial for the (i) session initiation process, (ii) re-evaluation of active sessions process, and (iii) protection against active DoS (Denial of Service) attacks that are based on request flooding. In particular, a new entry, called Tryaccess entry, is created in the SM database every time the initiation of a new access is permitted, as a result of a successful TryAccess. As soon as a StartAccess action is received, the TryAccess entry is updated to ActiveSession entry.

3. **CH-Context Handler:** The CH operates as the controller of the other components, and is responsible for the management and supervision of the session initiation and session re-evaluation processes.

   – **GH-Group Handler:** This sub-component of the CH is responsible for the computation of both the service groups and subscriber roles that correspond to a session, in accordance with the risk aggregation model describer earlier, where the aggregated values of the corresponding attributes, are mapped into such roles and groups. In respect to the services, this computation can be done apriori and in the simplest form integrated as a Look up Table, although the GH can also incorporate the capacity for empirical environmental observation for dynamic service group management at run-time. As for the computation of the user roles, this is done at runtime in two occasions, the initiation of a session for a specific service group and the re-evaluation of access for a specific service group, but not on a per-session basis as in the original model.

4. **PIP-Policy Information Point:** The PIP is the entity which retrieves policy specific attributes from the operational environment, and provides them to the UCS upon request from the CH.

5. **PAP-Policy Administration Point:** The PAP is the entity which is utilized by the system administrators for the development and integration of policies. Moreover, the PAP is in charge of providing the proper policy when necessary.

6. **PDP-Policy Decision Point:** The PDP is the entity, which is responsible for the evaluation of the policy upon request from the CH, and the computation of pertinent decisions.

3.2   Protocol and Interface

In this subsection we provide the sequence diagrams for the session initiation and re-evaluation processes, discussing the operations and providing corresponding examples. For the rest of this Section *Consecutive steps* refer to Figs. 4 and 5, which provide the sequence diagrams during the initiation and operation phases in the following scenarios.

1. **Session establishment:** *Consecutive steps: 1-3-4-5:*
   In the initial steps of every session establishment request, the PEP translates the request into a TryAcceess message towards the CH, which includes the unique identifier (Service ID) of the service that the subscriber requests access to. Consequently, the CH extracts the service group which corresponds to the given identifier, in accordance with the service grouping established during deployment, based on the risk aggregation method described earlier. Furthermore, the CH seeks to establish whether the subscriber has initiated similar request for this service, by querying the SM for active TryAccess entries. Provided that the SM replies negatively, therefore this request is not part of an active DoS attack, in step-3 the CH requests from the SM a notification about active sessions for the examined subscriber within the same service group. Given that no such sessions are identified, in step-4 the CH retrieves the required attributes from the PIP, extracts the subscriber's role that corresponds to the examined service group, and requests a policy evaluation from the PDP, based on the service group and extracted subscriber role. Further, in step-5, given that the permission is granted, the CH requests from the SM to initiate a corresponding session and send a permission notification to the dedicated PEP.

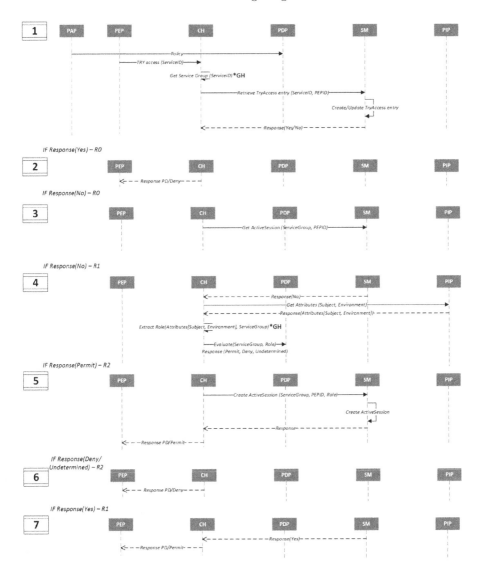

Fig. 4. Initiation phase-sequence diagram.

2. **Denial of Service avoidance:** *Consecutive steps: 1-2*:
   In this scenario the activities executed for step-1 are identical with those described for the *session establishment* scenario. Yet, given that the SM reports that TryAccess entries are still active for the same subscriber-service pair, (i.e. the time to live has not expired) this request is recognised as part of a DoS-Request-flooding attack, and the request is immediately denied in step-2. This improves the resilience of the usage control architecture, in comparison to the original UCON [7].

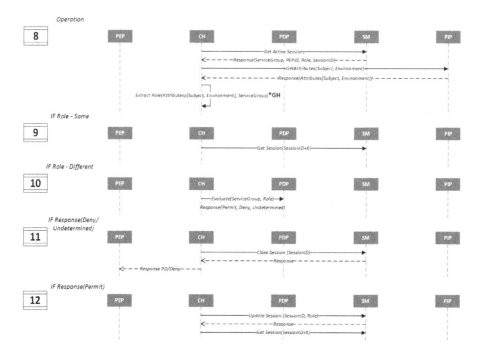

Fig. 5. Operation phase-sequence diagram.

3. **Initial session denial:** *Consecutive steps: 1-3-4-6:*
   In this scenario the activities executed for step-1, step-3, and step-4 are identical with those described for the *session establishment* scenario. Yet, given that the request is evaluated as "Deny" by the PDP, the PEP is notified accordingly by the CH. It must be noted that in this scenario, the TryAccess entry in the SM remains active for the corresponding time to live, leading to the previously described *Denial of Service avoidance* scenario, if an identical request is delivered within this time to live.

4. **Request for the same service group:** *Consecutive steps:1-3-7:*
   In this scenario the activities executed for step-1 and step-3 are identical with those described for the *session establishment* scenario. Yet, given that the requesting subscriber has and active/permitted session for the examined service group, the CH immediately evaluates the request as "allow" notifying the corresponding PEP in step-7. This improves both the efficiency and scalability of the usage control architecture, in comparison to the original UCON.

5. **No attribute change:** *Consecutive steps: 8-9:*
   During the session re-evaluation phase, the CH requests the ActiveSessions entry from the SM. Accordingly, the CH requests from the SM the specific information for the first-in-queue session. Based on these information, and the timely values of the corresponding attributes from the PIP, the role of

the subscriber is re-evaluated. Given that the role has not been changed, no further action is taken and the CH proceeds to the next-in-queue session, as described in step-9.

6. **Attribute change with permission:** *Consecutive steps: 8-10-12*
   In this scenario the activities executed for step-8 are identical with those described for the *No attribute change* scenario. Given that a change occurred in the subscriber's role, the CH requests and new access evaluation from the PDP, in step-10, and updates the corresponding session entry of the SM in step-12, given that permission is granted by the PDP.

7. **Attribute change with denial:** *Consecutive steps: 8-10-11*
   In this scenario the activities executed for step-8 and step-10 are identical with those described for the *Attribute change with permission* scenario. Yet, given that the policy evaluation result by the PDP is *Deny*, the session in the SM is closed and the corresponding PEP is notified, as described in step-11.

4 Test Case

The test case which has been utilized for the initial evaluation of the proposed architecture, and its comparison with the original UCON, is presented in Fig. 6. The test case refers to the cloud service deployment of a state owned airport operator, which is distinguished between a global deployment (with three groups of services, whose instances are available across all the managed airports) and a local deployment (with three groups of services in dedicated local instances per airport). The grouping of the services is achieved utilizing the developed risk aggregation method which has been presented in Sect. 2. A set of object, subject, and environmental attributes have been defined for the definition of the corresponding policies, while four distinct types (roles) of users have also been established in accordance to the aforementioned risk aggregation method.

In this section we present the results from one of the executed scenarios within this test case. In this, one of the operators' employees registers and seeks to obtain access for services S1, S2, and S3 of service group 1G. We executed the registration process for this scenario with the original UCON, and the Enhanced-UCON architecture presented in this article, for policies with 1, 5, 10, 15, 20, 25, 30, 35, and 40 attributes. Each test was conducted for ten repetitions, and the average times for the evaluation are presented in Table 3 and Fig. 7. The table presents the elapsed time, in milliseconds, for each of the services, the total time, and the percentage of improvement. The test environment for this scenario was a virtual machine installing Ubuntu 16.04 64 bit, equipped with an Intel i7-6700HQ with 8 cores enabled, 8 GB DDR4 RAM.

The results highlight a significant improvement in terms of run-time efficiency, as both the number of micro-services and attributes (incorporated within the security policy) increase. This improvement is not affected by the type or complexity of the service towards which the access request is directed, as the services belong to the same group, for which the users role remain unaltered. A small degradation is noticeable for the initial service registration in low attribute

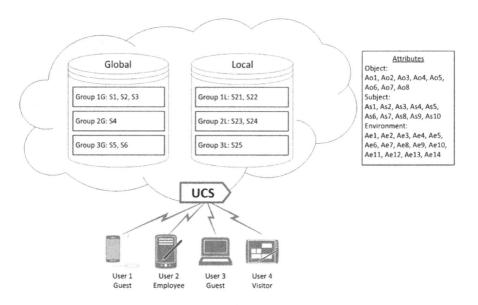

Fig. 6. Exemplified test case scenario.

policies, but this is quickly replaced by significant improvement of up to approximately 85%. In total the average performance, across all tests and repetitions, decreases by 1.346% for the first service, while for the second it improves by 77.195%, and for the third by 77.785%. The overall average improvement for three services, across all tests and repetitions, has been 39.154%.

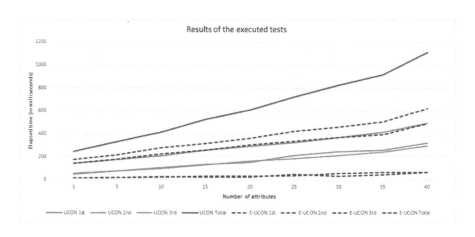

Fig. 7. Results of the executed tests

Table 3. Results of the executed tests

Number of attributes	1	5	10	15	20	25	30	35	40
Original UCON-times in milliseconds (ms)									
1st service	141.1	175.3	210.6	256.9	291.2	322.9	367.5	415	493.9
2nd service	56.6	76.9	105.6	134.8	153	211.8	245.7	256.3	318.8
3rd service	48.1	77.6	96.1	132.1	162.4	185.6	211.3	242	294.7
Total time	247.8	331.9	414	525.5	608.9	721.9	827.3	915.7	1110.4
Enhanced UCON-times in milliseconds (ms)									
1st service	142.7	179	223.4	259	303.1	335.2	368.3	394.8	487.6
2nd service	16.7	17.8	23.4	30.1	34	37.3	57.2	63.3	64.7
3rd service	14.4	19.4	28.2	24.2	24.1	48.9	33	44.3	65.5
Total time	175.4	216.9	277.1	315.3	362.5	422.2	461.1	504.2	618.9
Optimization percentage-%									
1st service	1.134	2.111	6.078	0.817	4.087	3.809	0.218	−4.867	−1.276
2nd service	−70.495	−76.853	−77.841	−77.671	−77.778	−82.389	−76.720	−75.302	−79.705
3rd service	−70.062	−75.000	−70.656	−81.681	−85.160	−73.653	−84.382	−81.694	−77.774
Total	−29.217	−34.649	−33.068	−40.000	−40.466	−41.515	−44.264	−44.938	−44.263

5 Conclusion

In this study an Enhanced-Usage CONtrol (E-UCON) architecture is proposed, where the standard functionality of the model is extended in order to support groups of services and users. This extension aims to improve the model in terms of performance and run-time efficiency, but also to provide the scalability required from the application domain. The mentioned improvements, result from the fact that the right of access will be assigned to user roles towards groups of services and not only in one service at a time, which reduces the evaluation time and the computational requirements. Furthermore, the proposed architecture improves the standard model in terms of security, as it gives the possibility of recognizing and preventing active attacks, such as specific types of Denial of Service based on request flooding. Finally, in this paper a method of simplifying the writing of security policies through the aggregation of the risk values related to individual attributes, is also integrated in the Usage Control model.

The experiments show that the aforementioned enhancements result in significant improvements in performance and evaluation time, especially in realistic deployments with multiple micro-services governed by complex or semi-complex policies. As future work, we intent to develop an extended and heterogeneous test-bed for experimentation, which will be utilized in order to evaluate the performance of the proposed model in different and more demanding use cases. Moreover, further enhancements will be integrated and tested within E-UCON, initially related to (i) credential management, (ii) trust, and (iii) task delegation.

Acknowledgments. This work has been partially funded by EU Funded project H2020 NeCS, GA #675320.

References

1. Colombo, M., Lazouski, A., Martinelli, F., Mori, P.: A proposal on enhancing XACML with continuous usage control features. In: Desprez, F., Getov, V., Priol, T., Yahyapour, R. (eds.) Grids, P2P and Services Computing, pp. 133–146. Springer, Boston (2010). https://doi.org/10.1007/978-1-4419-6794-7_11
2. De Capitani di Vimercati, S., Samarati, P., Jajodia, S.: Policies, models, and languages for access control. In: Bhalla, S. (ed.) DNIS 2005. LNCS, vol. 3433, pp. 225–237. Springer, Heidelberg (2005). https://doi.org/10.1007/978-3-540-31970-2_18
3. Gkioulos, V., Rizos, A., Michailidou, C., Martinelli, F., Mori, P.: Enhancing usage control for performance: a proposal for systems of systems. In: The International Conference on High Performance Computing and Simulation, HPCS 2018 (2018, To Appear)
4. Hu, V.C., et al.: Guide to attribute based access control (ABAC) definition and considerations. National Institute of Standards and Technology (NIST) Special Publication, 800(162) (2013)
5. La Marra, A., Martinelli, F., Mori, P., Rizos, A., Saracino, A.: Improving MQTT by inclusion of usage control. In: Wang, G., Atiquzzaman, M., Yan, Z., Choo, K.-K.R. (eds.) SpaCCS 2017. LNCS, vol. 10656, pp. 545–560. Springer, Cham (2017). https://doi.org/10.1007/978-3-319-72389-1_43
6. Lazouski, A., Martinelli, F., Mori, P.: Survey: usage control in computer security: a survey. Comput. Sci. Rev. **4**(2), 81–99 (2010)
7. Lazouski, A., Martinelli, F., Mori, P., Saracino, A.: Stateful data usage control for android mobile devices. Int. J. Inf. Secur. **16**(4), 1–25 (2016)
8. Martinelli, F., Michailidou, C., Mori, P., Saracino, A.: Too long, did not enforce: a qualitative hierarchical risk-aware data usage control model for complex policies in distributed environments. In: Proceedings of the 4th ACM Workshop on Cyber-Physical System Security, CPSS@AsiaCCS 2018, 04–08 June 2018, Incheon, Republic of Korea, pp. 27–37 (2018)
9. Moore, B., Ellesson, E., Strassner, J., Westerinen, A.: RFC 3060: Policy Core Information Model - Version 1 Specification, February 2001
10. O'Connor, A.C., Loomis, R.J.: 2010 economic analysis of role-based access control. NIST, Gaithersburg, MD (2010)
11. Park, J., Sandhu, R.: The UCONabc usage control model. ACM Trans. Inf. Syst. Secur. **7**(1), 128–174 (2004)
12. Saaty, R.W.: The analytic hierarchy process - what it is and how it is used. Math. Model. **9**(3), 161–176 (1987)
13. Samarati, P., de Vimercati, S.C.: Access control: policies, models, and mechanisms. In: Focardi, R., Gorrieri, R. (eds.) FOSAD 2000. LNCS, vol. 2171, pp. 137–196. Springer, Heidelberg (2001). https://doi.org/10.1007/3-540-45608-2_3
14. Sandhu, R.S., Coyne, E.J., Feinstein, H.L., Youman, C.E.: Role-based access control models. Computer **29**(2), 38–47 (1996)
15. Shirey, R.: RFC 4949: Internet Security Glossary - Version 2, August 2007
16. Zhang, X., Parisi-Presicce, F., Sandhu, R., Park, J.: Formal model and policy specification of usage control. ACM Trans. Inf. Syst. Secur. **8**(4), 351–387 (2005)

Comparative Study of Machine Learning Methods for In-Vehicle Intrusion Detection

Ivo Berger[1], Roland Rieke[2,3(✉)], Maxim Kolomeets[3,4],
Andrey Chechulin[3,4], and Igor Kotenko[3]

[1] TU Darmstadt, Darmstadt, Germany
[2] Fraunhofer Institute SIT, Darmstadt, Germany
`roland.rieke@sit.fraunhofer.de`
[3] ITMO University, St. Petersburg, Russia
[4] SPIIRAS, St. Petersburg, Russia

Abstract. An increasing amount of cyber-physical systems within modern cars, such as sensors, actuators, and their electronic control units are connected by in-vehicle networks and these in turn are connected to the evolving Internet of vehicles in order to provide "smart" features such as automatic driving assistance. The controller area network bus is commonly used to exchange data between different components of the vehicle, including safety critical systems as well as infotainment. As every connected controller broadcasts its data on this bus it is very susceptible to intrusion attacks which are enabled by the high interconnectivity and can be executed remotely using the Internet connection. This paper aims to evaluate relatively simple machine learning methods as well as deep learning methods and develop adaptations to the automotive domain in order to determine the validity of the observed data stream and identify potential security threats.

Keywords: Machine learning · Automotive security ·
Internet of vehicles · Predictive security analysis ·
System behavior analysis · Security monitoring · Intrusion detection ·
Controller area network security

1 Introduction

Each modern vehicle can be regarded as a system of interconnected cyber-physical systems. When vehicles are to take over tasks which are up to now the responsibility of the driver, an increasing automation and networking of these vehicles with each other and with the infrastructure is necessary. In particular, autonomous driving requires both a strong interconnectedness of vehicles and an opening to external information sources and services, which increases the potential attack surface. An indispensable assumption, however, is that the vehicle can not be controlled unauthorized externally. Thus, IT security and data protection

S. K. Katsikas et al. (Eds.): CyberICPS 2018/SECPRE 2018, LNCS 11387, pp. 85–101, 2019.
https://doi.org/10.1007/978-3-030-12786-2_6

are enabling factors for the newly emerging Internet of Vehicles (IoV). Practical experiments [17] have already demonstrated that an attacker can gain remote access to an in-vehicle Electronic Control Unit (ECU) and recent advisories such as [10] also mention that public exploits are available.

This work now examines various methods by which activities of an attacker already inside a vehicle could be detected. The Controller Area Network (CAN) bus is the standard solution for in-vehicle communication between the ECUs of the in-vehicle cyber-physical systems. Whilst offering high reliability the CAN bus lacks any kind of built-in security measures to prevent malicious interference by an outside party. This makes it easy for an attacker with access to one ECU to take over other critical cyber-physical systems within a vehicle. This could be done by broadcasting forged commands on the network, to gain the required knowledge, e.g. by running a fuzzing attack or to impair bus performance by performing a simple Denial of Service (DoS) attack.

In this work, we implemented and analyzed anomaly detection methods which can be applied to existing vehicle architectures as well as new designs by a software update or plug-in module as proposed in [19] without the adoption of new communication standards. The main contribution of this work is a comparative assessment of different Machine Learning (ML) methods with respect to usability for intrusion and anomaly detection within automotive CAN networks.

Section 2 introduces data sets from two different cars with and without attacks that have been used to evaluate the compared methods. Section 3 provides the background on four different ML technologies used in this work including training, validation and performance assessments. Section 4 presents the results of various experimental setups, while Sect. 5 discusses these outcomes and gives recommendations on feasible approaches for the domain of in-vehicle networks. Section 6 describes related work, and Sect. 7 concludes this paper.

2   Data Sets

On the CAN bus every attached device broadcasts messages. At the same time, devices listen for relevant information. We mapped the relevant data of CAN messages to the following tuple structure: $(time, ID, dlc, p_1, \ldots, p_8, type)$, where $time$ is the time when the message was received, ID comprises information about the type and the priority of the message, dlc (data length code) provides the number of bytes of valid payload data, $p1, \ldots, p8$ is the payload of 0–8 bytes, and $type$ marks the message (attack versus no attack). In cases where $dlc < 8$ we inserted dummy content in order to have a fixed tuple structure. For the experiments in this work we used five different data sets, namely, ZOE, $HCLR_{DoS}$, $HCLR_{Fuzzy}$, $HCLR_{RPM}$, and $HCLR_{Gear}$. The ZOE data set has been collected from a 10 min drive with a Renault Zoe electric car in an urban environment. It contains about 1 million messages and has been used before in [22] to perform behavior analysis by process mining. This data set contains no attack data. The other four data sets that we used have been published by the "Hacking and Countermeasures Research Labs" (HCRL) [7]. These data sets are fully labeled and demonstrate different attack types. The $HCLR_{DoS}$ data set contains DoS attacks. For this attack, every 0.3 ms a message with the ID "0000" is injected. Conversely, in the $HCLR_{Fuzzy}$ data set every 0.5 ms a completely random message is injected, whereas $HCLR_{RPM}$ and $HCLR_{Gear}$ contain spoofing attacks. In these data sets every millisecond a message with an ID related to gear respectively engine revolutions per minute is injected. The ID and message does not change. The linear charts of the ZOE, $HCLR_{DoS}$, and $HCLR_{Gear}$ data sets depicted in Fig. 1 show the composition of legal data and attacks. Figure 1a shows that in the $HCLR_{DoS}$ data set DoS messages decrease the number of legal packets, whereas Fig. 1b unveils a big gap in the traffic time-line of the $HCLR_{Gear}$ data set which could probably be a consequence of the spoofing attack. The linear charts of $HCLR_{Fuzzy}$ and $HCLR_{RPM}$ not shown here are similar to $HCLR_{Gear}$.

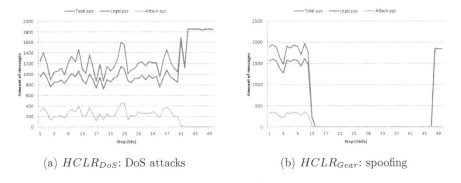

(a) $HCLR_{DoS}$: DoS attacks   (b) $HCLR_{Gear}$: spoofing

Fig. 1. Attack influence analysis by linear graphs

In order to get some more insight into the contents of the CAN data sets, we have visualized them by radial time-intervals using the method described in [12]. Figure 2 shows differences between ZOE and $HCLR_{DoS}$ traffic. The significantly higher number of bars in Fig. 2a is due to a higher number of different IDs in the ZOE traffic. In Fig. 2a the traffic without attacks has no outstanding bars whereas in Fig. 2b solid orange bars are outstanding in comparison to other bars. These bars represent DoS attacks which are decreasing the number of legal messages in the first three intervals during the attack. The radial visualizations of the other HCRL data sets with fuzzing and spoofing injections not shown here did not provide more insights.

3   Machine Learning Methods

This section introduces the compared algorithms including training, validation and performance assessments. The problem of detecting anomalies and attacks in CAN data differs from most ML applications as it does not present a clear

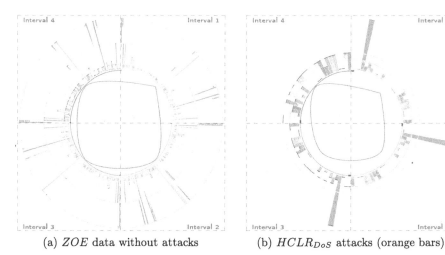

(a) *ZOE* data without attacks   (b) $HCLR_{DoS}$ attacks (orange bars)

Fig. 2. Attack influence visualization by radial time intervals, each summarizing one quarter of the period represented by the data set; traffic is separated in four radial time intervals that consist of bars; each ID is represented as a bar whose height equals the number of messages; bars consists of arcs which represent payload – the more messages with same payload the higher is the arc; so solid (or almost solid) arcs depict messages with few different payloads; transparent bars depict messages with big payload variety. (Color figure online)

classification problem. Anomalies and attacks are by nature unpredictable and thus it is not possible to obtain representative data to train a classifier. Thus, the approach taken in this work is to fit a model for the regular system behavior which can detect deviations from the norm. One aspect of system behavior is the range of values for the IDs and the payload of CAN messages, another aspect is the temporal behavior, resulting in a novelty detection problem and a time series analysis task. Some ECUs send messages periodically and thus are relatively easy to validate. Even though the collection of a representative set of anomalies and attacks is not possible it is beneficial to be able to detect and prevent known types of attacks such as DoS or fuzzing attacks. This presents a standard classification task where a model is trained to differentiate between regular and anomalous CAN communications. Another aspect is the practicality of possible solutions in real-world scenarios. For the deployment in vehicles the trained models need to be able to validate the incoming data steam in real-time, requiring efficient models and thus restricting their complexity.

The training of all models was done using the data sets introduced in Sect. 2 or subsets thereof in order to achieve reasonable training times. The data was split into training and validation sets to get a realistic performance estimate for each model. The validation of the Support Vector Machine (SVM) and standard neural network models use accuracy and confusion matrices. The Long Short Term Memory (LSTM) network was validated by predicting the next message ID based on a window of preceding messages and comparing it to the actual message. All experiments in this paper are written in `Python 3.6`. They utilize the `pandas` [16] library to read and transform the data and `scikit-learn` [21] and `keras` [6] with the `tensorflow` [1] back-end for the ML itself. For visualization `matplotlib` [9] and `seaborn` [28] were used. We now give a short introduction on how each of the methods operate.

3.1 One-Class Support Vector Machines

For anomaly detection One-Class Support Vector Machines (OCSVM) were used, which are an adaption of classic SVMs to be trained with one class with the goal of learning a border which encompasses the training data. OCVSMs are linear classifiers but can make use of nonlinear kernels to represent more complex data structures. They were used with success in [4,27] and this work used the hyper-parameters suggested in [4]. For OCSVMs the `sklearn.svm.OneClassSVM` and `numpy` [20] packages were used to filter out anomalous data from the training set. The `scikit-learn` [21] metrics `accuracy_score` and `confusion_matrix` were used to calculate scores from the predictions on the test set. To visualize the results the metrics for all data sets were saved and displayed using a `seaborn` [28] heat-map for the confusion matrices (Fig. 4) and a simple line graph for the accuracy per subset size (Fig. 3).

3.2 Support Vector Machines

SVMs are linear "max-margin" classifiers as they try to find a hyper-plane separating the data with the greatest possible margin to the closest entry of each class. They are linear but can use kernels to model nonlinear data structures whilst maintaining low hardware requirements when classifying. As they are very similar to OCSVMs the hyper-parameters from [4] were used here as well. Our implementation of the regular SVMs is almost identical to the OCSVM, except that `sklearn.svm.NuSVC` was used instead of `sklearn.svm.OneClassSVM`.

3.3 Neural Networks

Neural networks are the standard for deep-learning and can model very complex nonlinear relationships. The most basic version is the fully connected neural network. It utilizes an arbitrary number of layers with each layer supporting an arbitrary number of neurons. Data is propagated from the input to the output layer using weighted connections between the neurons of these layers, resulting in very complex structures and thus a large amount of trainable parameters and thus flexibility even for relatively small networks. They are usually trained using some form of gradient descent and are prone to overfitting due to their great flexibility. In consequence, the goal was to find the smallest possible network to achieve a good accuracy. Therefore, the anomalous class was set to 0 to work properly for binary classification and all features of the complete set were scaled using the `MinMaxScaler` from `scikit-learn` [21] before training.

The neural networks were implemented using `keras` [6] `Sequential` model from the `keras.models` package and `keras.layers.Dense` as its fully connected layers. From initial test it was found that one hidden layer and one epoch is sufficient for these data sets. For easier testing both layers used the same number of neurons. Binary Crossentropy, Adam and Accuracy was used as loss, optimizer and performance metric (see Listing 1.1).

Listing 1.1. Neural Network: Model and Training

```
def train(x: np.ndarray, y: np.ndarray, split, batch_size,
    neurons):
    # define and compile the model
    model = Sequential()
    model.add(Dense(neurons, activation='relu', input_shape=(x
        .shape[1],)))
    model.add(Dense(neurons))
    model.add(Dense(1, activation='sigmoid'))
    model.compile(loss='binary_crossentropy', optimizer='adam'
        , metrics=['accuracy'])
    # train model
    model.fit(x, y, epochs=1, batch_size=batch_size, shuffle=
        True, verbose=0)
    return model
```

Due to the good optimization of the `tensorflow` [1] back-end the model wasn't tested with different subset sizes but different neuron counts.

3.4   Long Short Term Memory Neural Networks

LSTMs are a derivation of recurrent neural networks for time sequence classification and prediction. They differ from standard neural networks by keeping previous states and thus are able to capture temporal relationships. LSTMs in particular keep a very recent as well as a long-standing state and are able to detect relationships between relatively distant events as well as directly consecutive ones opposed to simpler recurrent neural networks which only remember recent states. LSTMs are trained with time sequences, requiring to pre-process the data sets into message sequences with the window size as a configurable parameter. Furthermore, they are not trained to classify a message as anomalous or non-anomalous but to predict future messages or validate if new messages concur with the learned behavior.

Training a LSTM to predict or validate new messages requires the time series that is the training data to be transformed into a supervised learning problem. This is achieved by using message sequences of a certain window size with the message ID that followed it instead of single messages with a binary label. This enables the LSTM to learn the behavior and temporal relationships between data points. The original version of the code used was taken from [2] and has been adapted and simplified for this work. The next pre-processing step is the transformation of the time stamps to time deltas per ID, i.e. that the time column

gives the seconds since the last occurrence of that ID instead of a comparatively arbitrary time stamp. This is done using `pandas` [16] split-apply-combine
`pandas.DataFrame.grouby` and `apply` functions. To make the problem easier to
solve and thus the training times shorter the predictions were limited to the message IDs instead of predicting/validating whole messages. To achieve good results
the IDs had to be transformed from simple numbers to categories `keras` [6] and
`tensorflow` [1] can properly handle. This process utilizes the `scikit-learn` [21]
`LabelEncoder` and `keras` [6] `to_categorical` functions which first encode the
IDs as labels and then transform them into a one-hot encoded `numpy` [20] array.
The last step before applying the time series transformation is a `MinMaxScaler`.
For usage with `keras` [6] the result of the time series transformation has to be
reshaped into a three-dimensional array containing the original data point, the
following ten steps and the corresponding label.

Listing 1.2. LSTM: Training

```
def train(x, y, batch_size, neurons=10):
    # define and compile the model
    model = Sequential()
    model.add(LSTM(neurons, input_shape=(x.shape[1], x.shape
        [2])))
    model.add(Dense(y.shape[1], activation='softmax'))
    model.compile(loss='categorical_crossentropy',
                  optimizer='adam', metrics=['accuracy'])
    # train the model
    model.fit(x, y, epochs=5, batch_size=batch_size, shuffle=
        False, verbose=0)
    return model
```

Listing 1.2 shows the actual training process which is quite similar to that of
a regular neural network. Differences are in the used loss function (categorical vs.
binary crossentropy) and that the data isn't shuffled for LSTMs as that would
destroy any temporal relationships in the data.

The scoring is essentially the same as for the neural networks with the exception that the predictions are given as probabilities per category which have to
be transformed to the one-hot encoding in the test set by setting the category
with the highest probability to one and all others to zero.

4 Results

This section presents the results of all methods mentioned in Sect. 3. It will
introduce the metrics used and discuss the performance of each method with
regard to the nature of the data sets and validation methods.

4.1 One-Class Support Vector Machines

The OCSVMs were validated with subsets of the data sets described in Sect. 2
of different sizes between 5,000 and 300,000 messages using two different

approaches: The *ZOE* data set consists of non-anomalous data only, resulting in a validation error that is equivalent to the false negative rate, i.e. it was
tested which percentage of the validation data was misclassified as anomalous.
The training portion of the HCRL data set was cleaned of anomalous data and
the trained model tested with both classes using the accuracy for performance
assessment as well as confusion matrices where appropriate with the true label
on the y-axis and the predicted label on the x-axis.

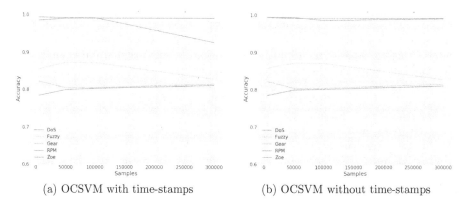

(a) OCSVM with time-stamps   (b) OCSVM without time-stamps

Fig. 3. OCSVM results

The high accuracy on the $HCLR_{DoS}$ data set is expected as the anomalous
entries are easily detectable for any subset of the data. Figure 3a, however, shows
a slight worsening with increasing subset sizes. As the model was trained with all
fields, including the timestamps, the result suggest that the OCSVM is detecting messages with a timestamp outside of the learned boundaries as anomalous.
Excluding the timestamps from training and testing confirms this as it results
in almost perfect accuracy for all subset sizes (see Fig. 3b). As seen in Fig. 3, the
OCSVMs accuracy on the *ZOE* data is almost perfect. Considering that this
data set only consists of regular data the good result comes from a too great
similarity of the training and test data sets. The result thus lacks informative
value about the effectiveness of OCSVMs in anomaly detection. The performance
on the $HCLR_{Fuzzy}$ data set is pretty high on a subset of 50,000 messages and
declines with increasing message count. This can be explained with the random-
ized generation of the anomalous data in this set. With increasing subsets the
amount of completely random data increases as well, which in turn increases the
amount of anomalous data that looks like regular data by chance, resulting in
deterioration of the results. This is confirmed by the confusion matrix in Fig. 4.
The model predicts the regular class almost exclusively and the performance
changes are a result of changes in the test set rather than changes in the model.

The accuracy for the spoofing data sets first shows a slight dip for 50,000 samples and then recovers with larger subsets. The confusion matrices in Fig. 4 show that this is purely due to changes in the test data set as the model only predicts the regular class. The anomalous data in these sets only differ in the timestamp. There is nothing in the ID or payload of these entries that makes them distinct from other non-anomalous messages, making it impossible for a SVM to separate between classes. The confusion matrices (Fig. 4) show heavy bias towards the regular class for all data sets except $HCLR_{DoS}$ and thus that all changes in the performance of the models are due to changes in the composition of the test data and not an improvements of the models itself. We also observed that the removal of the timestamps only has a noticeable effect on the $HCLR_{DoS}$ results. This can be explained with the mentioned bias as well as any potential changes are shadowed by the almost exclusive prediction of the regular class for all other data sets.

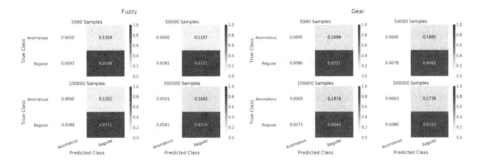

Fig. 4. OCSVM confusion matrices

4.2 Support Vector Machines

SVMs are very similar to OCSVMs as described in Sect. 3.2, hence the method of validation is as described for OCSVMs in Sect. 4.1 with the important difference that SVMs are classifiers and thus were trained with regular and anomalous entries. As SVMs don't support training on data sets with only one class the ZOE data set is excluded from these results. Furthermore, the SVM implementation in scikit-learn [21] is not multithreaded and had very long training times when training with timestamps. For these reasons only results without timestamps are presented. The results in Fig. 5a show that knowledge about the anomalous entries significantly improves accuracy on the impersonation data sets, achieving perfect classification on all but the $HCLR_{Fuzzy}$ data set even with the smallest subset. Looking at the very obvious distinction between regular and anomalous data points in these sets (see Sect. 2) the good performance is as expected as the continuously worsening performance on the $HCLR_{Fuzzy}$ data set.

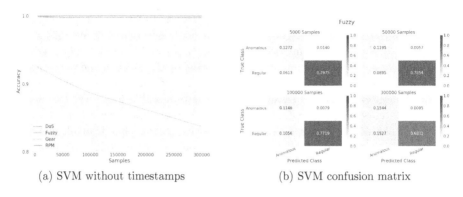

(a) SVM without timestamps   (b) SVM confusion matrix

Fig. 5. Results from support vector machines

Considering that all anomalous entries for this set are random and the resulting possibility of entries falling within the value range of regular entries there are no support vectors that can describe the difference comprehensively. Thus, the accuracy declines with increasing subset size as more and more false negatives are introduced which is shown in the corresponding confusion matrix in Fig. 5b. Despite the clear decline the classification is still surprisingly good considering the simple linear kernel and the random nature of the anomalous entries.

4.3   Neural Networks

The validation of the neural network was done with a standard train/test split of the original data and the performance of networks with different amounts of neurons compared in order to find the simplest possible network to solve the problem. As neural networks are very flexible and even small ones already have a good amount of variables this paper examines a network with only one hidden layer for neurons counts of 2, 5, 10 and 20, going from extremely simple to fairly complex models. The deep learning results are presented as confidence intervals which are obtained using the bootstrap method with 50 iterations and a sample size of 800.000 per iteration.

The very good to perfect results in Fig. 6 for all used data sets show the great flexibility of neural networks. For all data sets the intervals reach 99% even for the simplest network. The explanation for the good performance can be found in the very simple structure of the anomalous entries for the $HCLR_{DoS}$, $HCLR_{Gear}$ and $HCLR_{RPM}$ data sets: in each case there is one exact value combination that has to be detected. Whilst the OCSVMs had problems (cf. Sect. 4.1) with the $HCLR_{Gear}$ and $HCLR_{RPM}$ data sets as their anomalous entries values are within range of regular ones a neural network can learn to single out this exact combination as being anomalous and thus achieve the seen results. The intervals and the outliers in particular show that the networks performance depends greatly on the samples used.

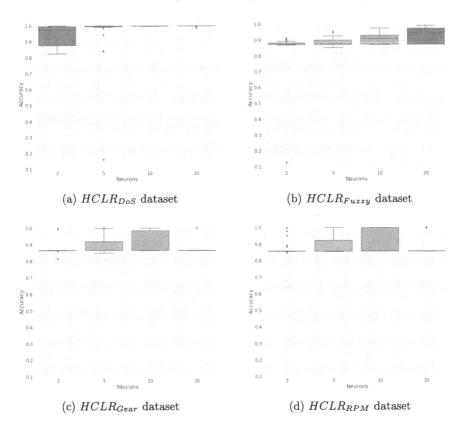

(a) $HCLR_{DoS}$ dataset

(b) $HCLR_{Fuzzy}$ dataset

(c) $HCLR_{Gear}$ dataset

(d) $HCLR_{RPM}$ dataset

Fig. 6. Neural network confidence intervals

The case where the very good results are not as obvious is the $HCLR_{Fuzzy}$ data set, as it has randomly generated anomalous entries which can not be as easily differentiated from the regular ones, which is supported by the need of at least 5 neurons to surpass the 99% accuracy threshold. In this case the great flexibility of the network enables it to learn which value combinations, for example in which range an ECU's payloads are, are valid and thus to distinguish them from the random entries very well. Another observation is that the intervals are generally larger then for the other data sets. As we didn't use stratified splits this suggests that a certain minimum of both regular and random data is required for the network to learn a good model.

The outliers seen in most results illustrate the general importance of having the right data. Out results show that with a proper amount of data to train the model neural networks are capable of detecting complex anomalies reliably.

4.4   Long Short Term Memory Neural Networks

To validate the LSTMs the whole data set was transformed to message sequences as explained in Sect. 3.4 from which the first 80% were used to train bootstrap networks while the remaining 20% validated the message ID predictions the LSTM made. The results graphs (Fig. 7) show the networks performance for a window size of 10 and each individual graph plots confidence intervals on accuracy against neuron count of the LSTM layer. The LSTMs were trained and tested without anomalous entries in order to measure their capability to model the regular data stream.

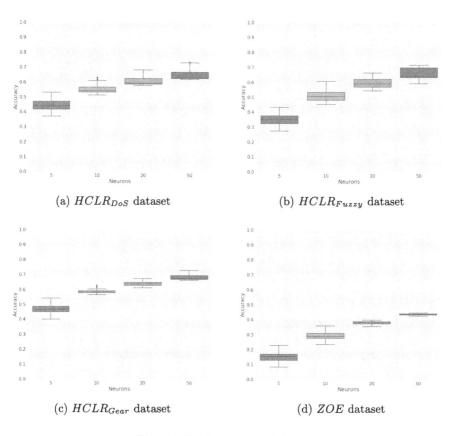

(a) $HCLR_{DoS}$ dataset
(b) $HCLR_{Fuzzy}$ dataset

(c) $HCLR_{Gear}$ dataset
(d) ZOE dataset

Fig. 7. LSTM confidence intervals

For the $HCLR_{DoS}$ and the spoofing data sets the accuracy is quite good considering the relatively small samples and networks used as well as the complexity of the problem. On all of these data sets the network achieves an accuracy up to 50% with only 5 neurons and up to 60% on the DoS data set with 20 neurons. The very similar and good performance is due to equal and relatively low number of regular message IDs in the sets at only 26. Performance on the $HCLR_{Fuzzy}$

data set is noticeably but not significantly worse for the simplest LSTM and very similar to the other HCRL sets for 10 or more neurons. The lower accuracy on the LSTM with 5 neurons is due to the higher number of IDs at 38. The *ZOE* data set with its considerably higher number of message IDs at 110 performs by far the worst at a maximum accuracy just above 40%. Considering that random performance for 110 IDs is at only 0.9% an accuracy over 40% is more than 42 times better than random and thus still quite good. As the data set is from a different source than the others (see Sect. 2) it suggest that the Renault Zoe has more complex internals than the vehicles used to acquire the HCRL data sets.

For all tested data sets there is a clear correlation between message ID frequency and the LSTMs categorical accuracy on that ID. The periodic occurrence of these highly frequent IDs and the possible triggering of reactions to certain periodic IDs explains the good predictions. Consequently, the worst performance can be observed on infrequently occurring IDs, especially as they contain IDs triggered by outside events and thus are simply unpredictable.

5 Discussion

The OCSVM results show very clearly that this comparatively simple method of novelty detection only works for very basic anomaly detection. As OCSVMs try to find a boundary which contains all or most of the seen data it can only detect anomalies which differ significantly from the normal data in terms of raw field values. Considering the observed heavy bias towards the regular class it can still be useful: if it does classify a message as being anomalous there is a high chance that it's correct. Theissler [27] has also conducted a more sophisticated approach. He used Support Vector Data Descriptors, a derivation of OCSVMs, trained with message sequences instead of individual messages with better results and very low to no false anomalies. The low false negative rate and the ability to train them without anomalous data is a quite important aspect. Combined with their relatively simple and thus fast classification makes them a good practical choice for real-time classification in a vehicle.

Regular SVMs share the good results and speed of OCSVMs but require anomalous data for training. Practical use would only come from the classification of attacks which cannot be easily specified such as the fuzzing attack. For any simple specification violating these specifications could be used directly to verify the data stream without the need to train a model. Because of that and the significant decline on performance of SVMs on the $HCLR_{Fuzzy}$ data set the real-world applicability of SVMs for the here evaluated use case is very limited.

Neural networks share the major drawback of needing anomalous training data to be of any use but show impressive performances on all tested data sets. The results suggest that they are able to learn the ECU behavior very well and thus detect diverging data points. Even on the randomly generated fuzzing attack their accuracy was close to perfect. Considering that only a very simple network with one hidden layer and two neurons per layer is needed to achieve this performance and thus classifying very fast, even without a graphics processing unit, they could be a powerful tool to simplify automated specification checking. In practice, they can be trained with regular and randomly generated data and automatically derive specifications for non-anomalous data. This would require additional testing on more diverse data sets in order to generalize this approach.

LSTMs are by far the most complex and thus computationally intensive of the here presented learning algorithms. Our results show their ability to learn the behavior at least partially and they have been applied to the more difficult problem of prediction complete messages with success in [4]. The performance shows diminishing returns when using more than 20 neurons and further simplification might be possible by excluding messages triggered by external events. This opens the possibility of improving the network's performance while reducing its complexity as in the present experiments the accuracy is clearly linked to the number of message IDs. Considering all of the above points LSTMs present a practical and potentially the most powerful approach of anomaly detection out of the methods analyzed in this work.

It is interesting to note that none of the ML methods indicated the big gaps in some of the data sets found by the visualization technique (cf. Fig. 1b).

6   Related Work

A collection of possible intrusion points together with proposals for countermeasures such as cryptography, anomaly detection and ensuring software integrity by separating critical systems are presented in [25, 30]. Whilst the proposed measures should prove effective most of them require hardware changes, conflicting with backwards-compatibility. CAN intrusion detection methods can be grouped into four categories: (1) Work on detection of ECU impersonating attacks such as [3, 5] in most cases uses some kind of physical fingerprinting by voltage or timing analysis with specific hardware. This work seeks to mitigate the general problems of missing authenticity measures in CAN bus design and thus is complementary to the work presented in this paper. (2) Work on detection of specification violations assumes that the specification of normal behavior is available and thus there is an advantage that no alerts based on false positives will be generated. The specification based intrusion detection can use specific checks, e.g. for formality, protocol and data range [13], a specific frequency sensor [8], a set of network based detection sensors [18], or specifications of the state machines [24]. (3) Work on detection of message insertions can be based on various technologies like analysis of time intervals of messages [23] or LSTM [29]. (4) Work on detection of sequence context anomalies comprises process mining [22], hidden Markov models [14, 19], OCSVM [27], neural networks [11], and detection of anomalous patterns in a transition matrix [15]. In most cases the authors of the above mentioned papers described experiments with one specific method. However, because the authors use different data sets for their experiments the results of their work are not directly comparable.

Therefore, we compared different ML algorithms with the same data sets. The closest work to our paper is [4] and [26] which also provides results on method comparison. OCSVM, Self Organizing Maps, and LSTM are used in [4] and LSTM, Gated Recurrent Units (GRU), as well as Markov models are used in [26]. However, in [4] only one small training set of 150,000 packets from the Michigan Solar Car Team was used, and [26] is more focused on attack generation.

7   Conclusion

In conclusion this study has shown the potential of ML for anomaly detection in CAN bus data. Even simple linear methods like OCSVMs can yield good results when detecting simple attacks while more complex neural networks are capable to learn "normal" message content from CAN data. The most sophisticated models, namely LSTMs, are able to learn ECU behavior adequately. Even the deep learning approaches can be kept relatively simple meaning all analyzed methods should be able to detect anomalies in real-time even on low-end hardware. Combined with the existing research ML promises to be an effective way to increase vehicle security. The injected attacks are relatively trivial in nature requiring additional research with more diverse and complex intrusions as well as the comparison of methods used in other research to the here present ones. Focused tests, potentially in cooperation with vehicle manufacturers, have to provide further insights in the prediction capabilities of LSTMs. Furthermore, real-world tests on practical hardware are needed to confirm that real-time detection is indeed possible. Based on reliable anomaly detection, appropriate reactions such as simple notifications or automated prevention measures need to be investigated.

Acknowledgements. This research is partially supported by the German Federal Ministry of Education and Research in the context of the project secUnity (ID 16KIS0398) and by the Government of Russian Federation (Grant 08-08), by the budget (project No. AAAA-A16-116033110102-5).

References

1. Abadi, M., Agarwal, A., Barham, P., et al.: TensorFlow: large-scale machine learning on heterogeneous distributed systems. In: 12th USENIX Symposium on Operating Systems Design and Implementation, OSDI 2016, pp. 265–284 (2016)
2. Brownlee, J.: How to convert a time series to a supervised learning problem in Python. https://machinelearningmastery.com/convert-time-series-supervised-learning-problem-python/ (2018). Accessed 28 June 2018
3. Cho, K., Shin, K.G.: Fingerprinting electronic control units for vehicle intrusion detection. In: Holz, T., Savage, S. (eds.) 25th USENIX Security Symposium, USENIX Security 16, 10–12 August 2016, Austin, TX, USA, pp. 911–927. USENIX Association (2016)
4. Chockalingam, V., Larson, I., Lin, D., Nofzinger, S.: Detecting attacks on the CAN protocol with machine learning (2016)
5. Choi, W., Joo, K., Jo, H.J., Park, M.C., Lee, D.H.: Voltageids: low-level communication characteristics for automotive intrusion detection system. IEEE Trans. Inf. Forensics Secur. **13**(8), 2114–2129 (2018)

6. Chollet, F., et al.: Keras. https://github.com/keras-team/keras (2015)
7. Hacking and Countermeasure Research Lab (HCRL): Car-hacking dataset for the intrusion detection. http://ocslab.hksecurity.net/Datasets/CAN-intrusion-dataset (2018). Accessed 28 June 2018
8. Hoppe, T., Kiltz, S., Dittmann, J.: Security threats to automotive CAN networks - practical examples and selected short-term countermeasures. Reliab. Eng. Syst. Saf. **96**, 11–25 (2011)
9. Hunter, J.D.: Matplotlib: a 2D graphics environment. Comput. Sci. Eng. **9**(3), 99–104 (2007)
10. ICS-CERT: Advisory (ICSA-17-208-01). https://ics-cert.us-cert.gov/advisories/ICSA-17-208-01, July 2017. Accessed 17 Sept 2018
11. Kang, M.J., Kang, J.W.: A novel intrusion detection method using deep neural network for in-vehicle network security. In: 2016 IEEE 83rd Vehicular Technology Conference (VTC Spring) (2016)
12. Kolomeets, M., Chechulin, A., Kotenko, I.: Visual analysis of CAN bus traffic injection using radial bar charts. In: Proceedings of the 1st IEEE International Conference on Industrial Cyber-Physical Systems, ICPS-2018, Saint-Petersburg, Russia, pp. 841–846. IEEE (2018)
13. Larson, U.E., Nilsson, D.K., Jonsson, E.: An approach to specification-based attack detection for in-vehicle networks. In: 2008 IEEE on Intelligent Vehicles Symposium, pp. 220–225, June 2008
14. Levi, M., Allouche, Y., Kontorovich, A.: Advanced analytics for connected cars cyber security. CoRR abs/1711.01939 (2017)
15. Marchetti, M., Stabili, D.: Anomaly detection of CAN bus messages through analysis of ID sequences. In: 2017 IEEE Intelligent Vehicles Symposium (IV), pp. 1577–1583, June 2017
16. McKinney, W.: Data structures for statistical computing in Python. In: Proceedings of the 9th Python in Science Conference 1697900(Scipy), pp. 51–56 (2010)
17. Miller, C., Valasek, C.: Remote exploitation of an unaltered passenger vehicle. Technical report, IOActive Labs, August 2015
18. Müter, M., Asaj, N.: Entropy-based anomaly detection for in-vehicle networks. In: 2011 IEEE Intelligent Vehicles Symposium (IV), pp. 1110–1115, June 2011
19. Narayanan, S.N., Mittal, S., Joshi, A.: OBD SecureAlert: an anomaly detection system for vehicles. In: IEEE Workshop on Smart Service Systems, SmartSys 2016, May 2016
20. Oliphant, T.E.: Guide to NumPy. Methods **1**, 378 (2010)
21. Pedregosa, F., Varoquaux, G., Gramfort, A., Michel, V., et al.: Scikit-learn: machine learning in Python. J. Mach. Learn. Res. **12**(Oct), 2825–2830 (2012)
22. Rieke, R., Seidemann, M., Talla, E.K., Zelle, D., Seeger, B.: Behavior analysis for safety and security in automotive systems. In: 2017 25nd Euromicro International Conference on Parallel, Distributed and Network-Based Processing (PDP), pp. 381–385. IEEE Computer Society, March 2017
23. Song, H., Kim, H., Kim, H.: Intrusion detection system based on the analysis of time intervals of CAN messages for in-vehicle network, pp. 63–68. IEEE Computer Society, March 2016
24. Studnia, I., Alata, E., Nicomette, V., Kaâniche, M., Laarouchi, Y.: A language-based intrusion detection approach for automotive embedded networks. In: The 21st IEEE Pacific Rim International Symposium on Dependable Computing, PRDC 2015, November 2014

25. Studnia, I., Nicomette, V., Alata, E., Deswarte, Y., Kaâniche, M., Laarouchi, Y.: Security of embedded automotive networks: state of the art and a research proposal. In: ROY, M. (ed.) SAFECOMP 2013 - Workshop CARS of the 32nd International Conference on Computer Safety, Reliability and Security, September 2013
26. Taylor, A., Leblanc, S.P., Japkowicz, N.: Probing the limits of anomaly detectors for automobiles with a cyber attack framework. IEEE Intell. Syst. **PP**(99), 1 (2018)
27. Theissler, A.: Anomaly detection in recordings from in-vehicle networks. In: Proceedings of Big Data Applications and Principles First International Workshop, BIGDAP 2014, 11–12 September 2014, Madrid, Spain (2014)
28. Waskom, M., Meyer, K., Hobson, P., Halchenko, Y., et al.: Seaborn: v0.5.0, November 2014
29. Wei, Z., Yang, Y., Rehana, Y., Wu, Y., Weng, J., Deng, R.H.: IoVShield: an efficient vehicular intrusion detection system for self-driving (short paper). In: Liu, J.K., Samarati, P. (eds.) ISPEC 2017. LNCS, vol. 10701, pp. 638–647. Springer, Cham (2017). https://doi.org/10.1007/978-3-319-72359-4_39
30. Wolf, M., Weimerskirch, A., Paar, C.: Security in automotive bus systems. In: Proceedings of the Workshop on Embedded Security in Cars (July), pp. 1–13 (2004)

SDN-Enabled Virtual Data Diode

Miguel Borges de Freitas, Luis Rosa, Tiago Cruz$^{(\boxtimes)}$, and Paulo Simões

Department of Informatics Engineering, Centre of Informatics and Systems,
University of Coimbra, Coimbra, Portugal
{miguelbf,lmrosa,tjcruz,psimoes}@dei.uc.pt

Abstract. The growing number of cyber-attacks targeting critical infrastructures, as well as the effort to ensure compliance with security standards (e.g. Common Criteria certifications), has pushed for Industrial Automation Control Systems to move away from the use of conventional firewalls in favor of hardware-enforced strict unidirectional gateways (data diodes). However, with the expected increase in the number of interconnected devices, the sole use of data diodes for network isolation may become financially impractical for some infrastructure operators.

This paper proposes an alternative, designed to leverage the benefits of Software Defined Networking (SDN) to virtualize the data diode. Besides presenting the proposed approach, a review of data diode products is also provided, along with an overview of multiple SDN-based strategies designed to emulate the same functionality. The proposed solution was evaluated by means of a prototype implementation built on top of a distributed SDN controller and designed for multi-tenant network environments. This prototype, which was developed with a focus in performance and availability quality attributes, is able to deploy a virtual data diode in the millisecond range while keeping the latency of the data plane to minimal values.

Keywords: Data diode · Unidirectional gateways ·
Software Defined Networks · Industrial and automation control systems

1 Introduction

Industrial Automation and Control Systems (IACS) encompass a broad range of networks and systems used to monitor, manage and control cyber-physical processes in critical infrastructures, such as the power grid or water distribution facilities. The growing number of cyber-attacks against today's highly distributed IACS is raising awareness towards the need for in-depth cyber-security strategies, somehow leading to a shift back to these system's origins with the use of data diodes. When SCADA systems first appeared in the 1960's they were implemented as air-gapped islands restricted to the process control perimeter and specially isolated from corporative networks. Security was granted due to intrinsic isolation and the use of proprietary and poorly documented protocols [9].

© Springer Nature Switzerland AG 2019
S. K. Katsikas et al. (Eds.): CyberICPS 2018/SECPRE 2018, LNCS 11387, pp. 102–118, 2019.
https://doi.org/10.1007/978-3-030-12786-2_7

In the 1990's, business requirements to increase productivity and performance, together and the massification of ICT technologies, broke with the previous isolated generation of IACS. Organizations began to adopt open TCP/IP connections to link their process control and Enterprise Resource Planning (ERP) systems. Corporate management layers took advantage of this real-time data to manage plant inventories, control product quality and monitor specific process variables. It is estimated this network interconnection lead to 3–8% cost savings at large facilities [15] – however, it also brought a drastic increase on the inherent cyber-security risks, by contributing to expand the exposed IACS attack surface.

To mitigate unwanted accesses to the IACS network, middleboxes such as firewalls started to be implemented as digital barriers in the perimeter of both process and organizational networks, sometimes sitting behind a DMZ. Firewalls are often prone to configuration mistakes and are relatively accessible for exploit development by skilled individuals. In the long-term, firewalls are known to have considerable operating costs as firewall rules have to be continuously audited and maintained while firmware updates must be installed as soon as they are available [16]. The use of firewalls on IACS networks also contradicts some of their fundamental requirements: the need for real-time access to plant data, high availability and service continuity. As middleboxes, commercial off-the-shelf (COTS) firewalls introduce latency and jitter in the network, also introducing a point-of-failure (e.g., when subject to flooding attacks, throttling policies may cause service disruption).

Unlike firewalls, data diodes provide a physical mechanism for enforcing strict one-way communication between two networks. They are also known as *unidirectional gateways* since data can be securely transferred from an restricted access network (such as a process control network) to a less secure network (the corporate zone) with no chances of reverse communication. Data diodes are often built using fibre optics transceivers, through the removal of the transmitting component (TX) from one side of the communication and the respective receiver component (RX) from the opposite side [11]. This makes it physically impossible to compromise such devices to achieve reverse connectivity. Moreover, they usually do not contain firmware, requiring minimal or no configuration at all, or have minimal software supported by micro-kernels that can be formally verified [5].

Data diodes allow organizations to retrieve valuable data generated at the process level, while guaranteeing the trustworthiness and isolation of the critical infrastructure. They are the only devices receiving the Evaluation Assurance Level 7 (EAL7) grade in the Common Criteria security evaluation international standard. As a result, NIST recommends the adoption of data diodes [17].

Despite its advantages, from a security standpoint, data diode implementations come with high capital expenditure for organizations: it is estimated that for a typical large complex facility such costs can reach $250,000 while recurring support costs may ascend to values circa $50,000/year per data diode [19]. Furthermore, most data diode solutions are vendor-dependent, with the range of supported protocols strongly depending on the specific implementation – this means that many protocols on which some organizations rely upon may not be supported at all. Moreover, like any middlebox, data diodes need to be physically placed at a specific point in the network topology to be able to block network traffic, eventually requiring multiple deployments to secure dispersed network segments. Considering such shortcomings, many organizations may not be willing to invest in devices that are not future-proof or lack flexibility, fearing they may become outdated by the time their break-even point is reached.

To deal with the inherent limitations of existing solutions, we propose using Software Defined Networking (SDN) and Network Function Virtualization (NFV) to implement a cost-effective data diode. SDN aims at shifting the network equipment control plane functionality to a logically centralized entity – the network controller. In SDN, network switches are turned into "dumb" devices whose forwarding tables are updated by the network controller, using open protocols such as Openflow [13]. NFV provides a way to decouple network equipment functionality in several chained Virtual Network Functions (VNFs), which may be hosted in dispersed infrastructure points-of-presence.

SDN can be leveraged to implement innovative network security approaches: the network controller has a global view of the network topology graph, has real-time state awareness over all allowed network flows and can modify the network state by means of a proactive (preinitializing flow rules) or reactive (deciding upon packet arrival) approach. For such reasons, an SDN-based data diode could provide an alternative to both firewalls and conventional appliances. Note that to efficiently forward network packets, general purpose network switches contain forwarding tables called TCAMs (*ternary content-addressable memory*) which are able to perform an entire table lookup in just one clock cycle [18]. Hence, an SDN-enabled virtual data diode could effectively block traffic at Layer 2, avoiding the typical latency imposed by firewall middleboxes. Vendor lock-in, management complexity and deployment issues are also mitigated due to the use of open protocols, the existence of a single managing interface to control the overall network and the removal of placement restrictions imposed by hardware appliances. SDN also helps future proofing virtual data diode implementations: the data diode application can be easily adapted to support new protocols, and/or new network functions can be added to the network via NFV.

The remainder of this paper is organized as follows. Section 2 provides a review of the major COTS data diode products, together with an overview of the main challenges for protocol support in unidirectional communications. Section 3 explains how SDN can be leveraged to implement a functional data diode. Section 4 presents our proof-of-concept (PoC) prototype: a simple SDN data diode that is able to support the UDP protocol, implemented in a distributed network controller environment and geared towards performance and availability. Finally, Sect. 6 provides a wrap-up discussion and concludes the paper.

2   Data Diodes for IACS Security

Data diodes are devices that restrict the communication in a network connection so that data can only travel in a single direction, having borrowed their name from electronic diode semiconductors. Although different hardware implementations exist, supporting different physical layers (e.g. RS-232, USB, Ethernet), most make use of optical couplers to guarantee physical isolation. The transmitter side of a data diode converts electrical signals to optical form using light emitting diodes (LEDs), while at the receiving end photo-transistors convert the optical data back to electrical form [8]. It is the physical air-gap in the optical-coupler that makes data diode devices so secure and appealing in the critical infrastructure context.

In IACS, data diodes are often deployed to isolate specific network domains or between corporate and process control networks, to support the unidirectional transfer of historian data, HMI screen replication, or for one-way telemetry (operational data, security events, alarms and syslog). Data diodes are commercially available in two different form factors: single-box solutions and PCI express cards [10]. The former category may also encompass single-box or split-device variations, in which a component is deployed at each side of the connection.

Despite the similarities in the key isolation mechanism, commercially available solutions differ significantly in terms of supported services and protocols. Data diodes have to make use of additional software components for each side of the unidirectional link to be able to support TCP/IP-based SCADA protocols, such as MODBUS/TCP, Ethernet/IP and DNP3. Such protocols were designed for bidirectional operation, relying on a three-way handshake and requiring continuous acknowledgments between communication peers. In [6] the TCP workflow in unidirectional links is explained along with the presentation of a design for a unidirectional gateway for IACS applications (Fig. 1).

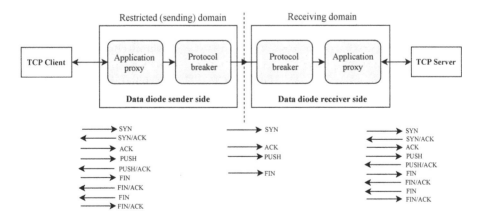

Fig. 1. TCP workflow in uni-directional gateways (adapted from [6]).

The architecture includes two different components at the edge of the unidirectional link: (i) an application proxy and (ii) a protocol breaker. The former is responsible for acting as a proxy for TCP connections. In the sender side of the data diode, the application proxy operates as a TCP server, automatically responding with SYN/ACK, PUSH/ACK and FIN/ACK to any SYN, PUSH or FIN packets sent by the TCP client. Any packet generated by the TCP client is forwarded by the application proxy to the unidirectional link. On the receiving end, the application proxy simply emulates the TCP client forwarding any received packets. The protocol breaker component acts as a middleware for packet encapsulation for protocols that do not require acknowledgments (e.g. UDP). It can also be used to provide confidentiality within the unidirectional link or to apply forward error correction to the data transfer.

2.1 Data Diode Products

There are diverse commercial data diode solutions in the market, depending on the specific use case and protocol support. Table 1 provides a summary of the three most notorious products in the context of IACS. Next, we provide a brief review of those products, based on publicly available documentation.

Table 1. IACS commercial data diodes.

Company	Owl CyberDefense	Fox-IT	Waterfall
Form factors	1U rack mount, DIN rail, PCIe cards	1U rack mount	Modular designs: gateway pairs (1U), single box(1U), DIN rail
Bandwidth	10 Gbps	1.25 Gbps	1 Gbps
IACS applications	Rockwell, OSIsoft PI, Schneider Electric	OSIsoft PI	OSIsoft, GE, Schneider Electric, Siemens, Emerson, Areva, Honeywell, AspenTech, Scientech, Rockwell
IACS protocols	Modbus, OPC	Modbus, DNP3, OPC, ICCP	OPC DA/HDA (backfill)/UA, A&E, DNP3, ICCP, Siemens S7, Modbus, Modbus Plus, IEC 60870-5-104, IEC 61850
CC certification	EAL4	EAL7+	EAL4+

Owl CyberDefense provides the DualDiode^{TM} technology as part of the company cross domain solution portfolio. Owl's data diodes make use of a hardened Linux kernel, providing optical separation and a protocol breaker that converts all packets to non-routable Asynchronous Transfer Mode (ATM) cells, also supporting data transfers up to 10 Gbps [14]. Protocol support includes TCP/IP connections, UDP, Modbus and the OPC family, as well as historian solutions from Rockwell Automation, Schneider Electric and OSIsoft. Latest revisions of DualDiode^{TM} Network Interface cards received CC EAL4 certification.

Fox-IT's DataDiode^{TM}, is compliant with the highest level of CC certification: EAL7+ [3]. It implements full protocol break capabilities and uses a single optical fiber strand, together with custom optoelectronics designed for one-way operation. Being a firmware-less device, it has no configuration or local state, relying on proxy servers deployed on each side of the connection. These proxies implement several techniques for error detection and increased reliability, using metadata for lost packet detection (supported by proxy-level logs, for manual retransmission), forward error correction codes and heartbeat mechanisms [4]. In government editions, the device includes an anti-tampering mechanism [3]. The Fox-IT data diode is able to achieve 1.25 Gbps in the link layer, although the actual speed is lower due to the proxy servers. It claims to support Modbus, DNP3, OPC and ICCP protocols along with file transfers, SMTP, CIFS, UDP and NTP [7]. The OSIsoft PI Historian is also supported.

Waterfall Security Solutions provides data diode appliances in multiple form-factors, including split-pair, single-box and DIN rail versions, based on a modular combination of hardware and software [22]. Such unidirectional gateways include a TX-only module (containing a fiber-optic laser), a fiber optic cable, an RX module (optical receiver), together with host modules that gather data from industrial servers and emulate different protocols and industrial devices. The latter are provided either as standalone physical modules or virtual machines. Popular industrial applications/historians are supported (e.g. Osisoft PI System, GE iHistorian, Schneider-Electric Instep eDNA), as well as a long list of industrial protocols (e.g. Modbus, DNP3, OPC, Modbus Plus [20]). Devices support up to 1 Gbps data transfers and are certified EAL4+. The company recently announced a reversible hardware-enforced unidirectional gateway whose direction can be controlled by software, using a schedule or exception-based trigger mechanism [21].

3   Leveraging SDN to Virtualize the Data Diode

The OpenFlow protocol is a Layer 3 network protocol that gives access to the forwarding plane of a network switch over the network. It enables network controllers to determine the path of network packets across the switch fabric. The protocol works on top of TCP/IP although the communication between the controller and the switch can also be configured to make use of the Transport Layer Security (TLS) protocol. The protocol works in a *match-action* manner: when a packet arrives at a switch port, the switch starts by performing a table lookup in the first flow table to match the packet headers against the set of flow rules installed in the switch. If a match is found, the switch applies the instruction set configured in the flow rule. In case of a table miss, the corresponding packet action depends on the table configuration: the packet can be forwarded to the controller for further processing (using *Packet-In* messages), can be moved further on the flow table pipeline, can have header fields re-written or can simply be dropped [13]. The match fields in an OpenFlow flow table comprise fields ranging from Layer1 to Layer4 (Table 2) permitting a fine-grained control over the packet identification and ultimate destination.

Table 2. The OpenFlow flow table match fields [13].

Match field	Description
IN_PORT	Ingress port (physical or a switch defined logical port)
ETH_DST	Ethernet destination MAC address
ETH_SRC	Ethernet source MAC address
ETH_TYPE	Ethertype of the packet payload
IPv4_SRC	Source IP address
IPv4_DST	Destination IP address
IPv6_SRC	Source IP address (IPv6 format)
IPv6_DST	Destination IP address (IPv6 format)
TCP_SRC	TCP source port
TCP_DST	TCP destination port
UDP_SRC	UDP source port
UDP_DST	UDP destination port

Taking into account the workflow of a packet reaching an OpenFlow enabled switch, we identify three different approaches for an SDN-based virtual data diode: proactive; reactive; and NFV-assisted.

3.1 Proactive Data Diode

A proactive data diode is an SDN unidirectional gateway implementation that takes advantage of OpenFlow's proactive flow rule instantiation It is the simplest and most limited implementation since it can only support applications that rely on the UDP protocol. Considering two networks with different degrees of classification (cf. Fig. 3), the network controller installs (in advance) two rules in the restricted (sending) domain uplink switch (cf. Table 3). One of the rules instructs the switch to drop any packets entering the switch and originating at the switch port that is connected to the receiving network uplink switch. The other rule forwards any packets entering the remaining switch ports to the receiving domain uplink switch port.

Further limitations can be applied in the second flow rule to limit the devices from the receiving domain network that are allowed to unidirectionally transfer data, using the IN_PORT, ETH_SRC and IPv4_SRC/IPv6_SRC match fields.

For the proactive data diode to support TCP applications, the sending machine has to encapsulate the packet into an UDP packet. Alternatively, flow rules can be installed on the switch to set the UDP source and destination ports (and replace the TCP source and destination fields) to any TCP packets entering the switch. In both cases, in order to support the TCP protocol, additional software is required in the receiving machine to disassemble the received packets into usable data. For this type of virtual data diode, only the uplink switch in the restricted network domain needs to support OpenFlow. The remaining sections of both networks may still rely on traditional network architectures.

3.2   Reactive Data Diode

Instead of installing rules in the up-link network switch, the reactive data diode instructs the switch to forward any received packet headers to the network controller for further processing (Table 4). The network controller can check if the received packet comes from the receiving domain (by looking up the input port) and simply instruct the switch to drop the packet. Similarly, it can instruct the switch to forward the packet if it originates from the restricted (sending) network domain (Fig. 2).

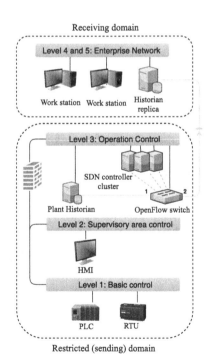

Fig. 2. SDN-enabled virtual data diode.

Table 3. Proactive data diode flow table.

Table	Match fields	Action
0	in_port = 1	output:2
0	in_port = 2	drop

Table 4. Reactive data diode flow table.

Table	Match fields	Action
0	in_port = 1	output:controller
0	in_port = 2	output:controller

Using a reactive approach, the network controller has greater flexibility since it can add support to the TCP protocol. It can behave as *an application proxy* for TCP connections implementing a workflow similar to the one in Fig. 1. TCP acknowledge packets can be faked by the controller and outputted via a switch port to the host establishing the connection. Hence, the TCP protocol can be supported while still only allowing unidirectional communications as long as an application proxy is able to perform the same workflow in the low-priority network. Furthermore, there are some cases in which bi-directional communication between both networks is required or should be temporarily enabled (e.g. an application that relies on TCP for initial connection establishment). The network controller can be programmed in such a way that bi-directional communication is enabled in certain situations. Thus, it is possible to emulate the behavior of the Waterfall's reversible data diode. Despite the provided flexibility, this approach introduces latency in network flows (due to additional packet processing) and the network controller is vulnerable to flooding attacks. Packets originating in the receiving network domain will not be forwarded to the hosts on the restricted domain without the permission of the controller. Nevertheless, hosts on the receiving domain are able to flood the OpenFlow switch with packets destined to the restricted network. Those packets are ultimately redirected to the controller, causing a denial of service which disrupts the unidirectional communication that is expected to happen in the reverse direction.

3.3   NFV-Assisted Data Diode

This approach requires SDN support at the edge of the restricted (sending) network, as well as a virtualization infrastructure containing a virtual Open-Flow switch (e.g. OpenvSwitch). It represents a combined approach where the processing step is supported by virtualized hosts close to the uplink OpenFlow switch and directly accessible to the SDN network. Network traffic originating in the restricted domain with the receiving network as destination is offloaded by the first OpenFlow switch to a dedicated virtual host. This virtual host can either be a virtual machine or an application container with two virtual Ethernet interfaces: one for receiving network packets and another for the output of packets. TCP emulation is performed within the virtual host by automatically generating acknowledgment packets for the three-way handshake and subsequent TCP transfers. Packets that are meant to be sent to the low priority network are chained from the input virtual interface to the output virtual interface (e.g. using IPtables).

Flow rules are proactively installed by the network controller in the uplink switch to: (i) drop any packets coming from the receiving network; (ii) forward any packets from the virtualization host (output port) to the switch port connected to the receiving network; (iii) forward any other packets to the virtualization host input port. In the receiving network domain, a TCP emulation proxy host should also exist and a similar approach can be applied. This data diode implementation avoids flooding attacks against the control plane while keeping the flexibility of the reactive design approach. Protocol support can easily be

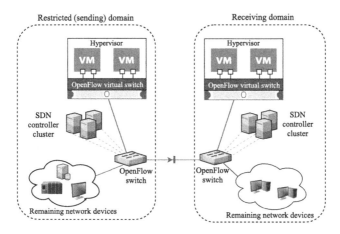

Fig. 3. NFV assisted SDN virtual data diode.

added to the virtual application proxy. The global network topology available at the controller can be used to automatically find the path (sequence of ports) leading to the virtual host. Moreover, if a layer of orchestration is added to the controller, it can continuously monitor the state of the virtual host and request the creation of a new one in case of failure (adjusting the flow rules to respect the new virtual ports).

4   Proof-of-Concept Virtual Data Diode Prototype

In the context of IACS, availability, performance and the need for real-time operation are the key design system attributes. As such, we developed our PoC virtual data diode using distributed SDN controllers, so that the control plane itself does not represent a single point of failure in the overall system operation. Distributed controllers are multi-node architectures where each OpenFlow switch maintains an active connection to one of the controller nodes (the master node) but is configured to use redundant connections to other nodes (slaves), in the case of master node failures. Although many network controller projects exist, only a small minority is distributed [12]. Among those, we selected the Open Network Operating System (ONOS) because it matches well into the critical infrastructure use-cases: high throughput (up to 1 M requests/s), low latency (10–100 ms event processing) and high availability (99.99% service availability) [2]. Our PoC virtual data diode uses a proactive approach regarding flow rule instantiation. Flow rules are installed from a dashboard containing the global topology graph of the network. Using this approach, the OpenFlow switches are still able to virtualize a data diode even in the case of an hypothetical full control plane failure. To increase performance, the data diode does not rely on any controller external interfaces. It was implemented directly in the application (using its OSGi services), extending its external interfaces (REST, command-line and websockets). Figure 4 presents the PoC architecture.

By default there is no connectivity between hosts in the SDN network. The *Proxy ARP* application (ONOS-bundled) proactively installs rules in the switch fabric to forward any ARP packets to the controller so the topology graph and host location can be computed. The developed *Network Manager* application relies on intent-based networking to provide connectivity between a set of hosts in the network. Intents are ONOS high-level abstractions (protocol independent) that allow applications to define generic connectivity policies that are translated internally to flow rules. For each host pair, the host-to-host intent results into two installed rules (with fixed priority) using the *in_port*, *eth_src* and *eth_dst* as match-fields and outputting to a port leading to a path to the host location. ONOS monitors the network state and any installed intents: if a network switch is unavailable and a redundant path between hosts exists, a new set of flow rules is generated and installed, keeping the intent active. By ensuring selected host connectivity, the *Network Manager* application creates logical subsections in the overall topology graph, providing the basis for multi-tenancy.

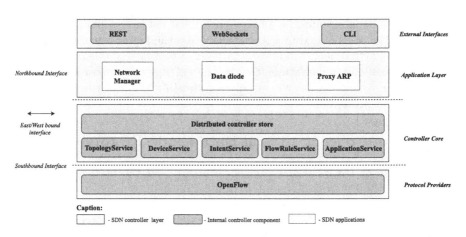

Fig. 4. Architecture of the virtual data diode PoC.

The *Data Diode* application then uses the information stored by the *Network Manager*. When a deployment is requested, given a topology edge link and the network name, the application finds the connection point (host-switch/port) in the graph and requests the *Network Manager* the list of hosts belonging to that network. The application then installs one rule per network host-pair in the edge switch (identical to one of the rules installed by the *Network Manager*) with the action field set to *Drop*. Those flow rules have a higher priority field than the rules defined by the *Network Manager* application superseding them. A workflow similar to the one depicted in Table 3 was not followed in the implemented prototype, in order to avoid binding physical ports to data diode deployments and preserve multitenancy support. Additionally, the *Data Diode* implements a monitor that asynchronously receives any events produced by the network (*Network Manager* application) – its purpose is to install new rules to enforce the diode behavior for each new host.

5   Evaluation

This section discusses the experimental evaluation of our PoC virtual data diode.

5.1   Experimental Testbed

Figure 5 ilustrates the testbed and network topology used for the validation of the virtual data diode prototype. It consists of a single OpenFlow switch controller by a three node ONOS cluster. The OpenFlow switch was running OpenvSwitch (CentOS 7) in a COTS server (Dell Poweredge R210), with six available gigabit Ethernet interfaces. The server was configured with Intel DPDK for increased network performance (bypassing the Linux Kernel and promoting direct memory access using hugepages and the VFIO universal IO driver). The switch configured to use the three controller plane nodes, connects to the master node via an off-band management network not accessible to the hosts in the SDN network. The three controller nodes were CentOS 7 virtual machines, each with 4 GB of RAM. The network hosts are composed by an Environmental Monitoring Unit (EMU) and two Modbus TCP agents. The EMU is an arduino-based board with built-in Ethernet ASIC (Freetonics EthertTen), containing a DTH11 sensor and an electromechanical relay. The temperature, humidity and relay state values are kept updated in three holding registers, and made available in the SDN network via the Modbus TCP protocol.

The Modbus TX and RX hosts are virtual machines with gigabit ethernet configured in passthrough mode. Their role is to emulate the behavior application proxies and protocol breakers found in commercial data diodes (cf. Fig. 1). The TX agent queries the EMU holding registries, serializes the data into the pickle format and sends it through the UDP protocol to the RX agent. This RX agent behaves as the EMU device on the other side of the network. It desserializes the received data, updates the internal registries and exposes a Modbus TCP

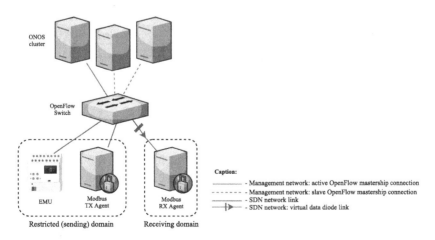

Fig. 5. Experimental testbed.

server. A virtual data diode was deployed (from the SDN controller) in the edge
link connecting the switch to the RX agent. Thus, the connection between both
agents was considered unidirectional (TX → RX only).

5.2 Validation and Lessons Learned

The functional validation of the virtual data diode was achieved recurring to
the Netcat tool: the RX agent was configured as an UDP server while the TX
agent acted as a client and vice-versa. We confirmed that in the former case
packets were able to flow while in the last no communication occurred. The non-
functional validation focused on assessing the prototype performance. Experiments focused on three aspects:

(a) the effect of the data layer on the latency of Modbus TCP readings;
(b) the overall network performance of the data plane;
(c) and the deployment latency of the virtual data diode.

For (a) we designed a test consisting of an increasing number of sequential
reads of ten EMU holding registries. For the TX agent we removed the ability
to process and packetize the obtained data and measured the time immediately
before and after each query. The measured times should be taken as the base
values for reading latency. For the RX readings, the time was recorded right after
data has been desserialized and updated in the agent context. Furthermore, a
counter was increased upon receiving a reading from the TX agent. Total test
duration was computed using the temporal instant before the first query by the
TX agent as starting time. Both machines were synchronized via NTP before
performing the test and each test was repeated five times. Table 5 summarizes
the obtained latencies (and percentage of failed readings). Confidence intervals
were calculated using a t-student distribution with a 95% confidence interval.

Table 5. Latency effect of the data layer on Modbus TCP readings.

Modbus agent	Number of queries	Time (s)	Failed reads (%)
TX	1	0.067 ± 0.139	-
	10	9.889 ± 0.640	-
	100	111.045 ± 0.331	-
	500	566.654 ± 0.558	-
RX	1	0.654 ± 0.344	0
	10	10.185 ± 0.777	0
	100	111.820 ± 0.897	0
	500	567.679 ± 0.549	0.360 ± 0.444

It is possible to conclude that even though the added latencies show a cumulative effect with respect to the number of readings (almost defining a linear
trend) the latency increase is almost negligible. For 500 EMU readings, the

additional processing by the agents and the subsequent network transfer only delays the overall reading time by 1 second. It is also possible to see that, as the number of queries increases, we start noticing a minimal amount of readings not reaching the RX agent – although being reported as sent by the TX agent. This can be explained by the no-guarantee nature of the UDP protocol. While this problem could be mitigated by adding error correction mechanisms to the unidirectional data packets or sending the same packet multiple times, in experiment (b) we analysed the effect of the sender/receiver buffer size on packet loss. This experiment also measured the maximum bandwidth of the data diode link.

For asssessing (b), iPerf was used to limit the TX sender bandwidth at values ranging from 10 Mbps to the maximum theoretical value of the link (1 Gbps) while changing the sender buffer size (100–6000 KB). The virtual data diode was disabled during this test, since Iperf requires an initial TCP connection. Measurements show that the buffer size plays a significant role on the packet loss, since it affects the total number of packets that can be sent in a single transfer (cf. Fig. 6).

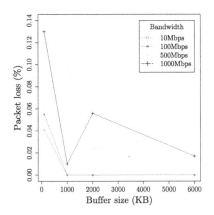

Fig. 6. Percentage of lost packets vs. bandwidth and write buffer size.

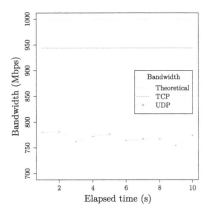

Fig. 7. UDP bandwidth vs. TCP and theoretical bandwidth.

If the bandwidth is known beforehand, both agents can be optimized for minimal packet loss. This is important in IACS scenarios, since SCADA traffic patterns tend to be predictable, with stable network topologies [1]. Regarding the stress test on the data diode link, we started by performing a TCP test. The bandwidth achieved by TCP is expected to be higher than the actual bandwidth of the UDP transfer since it optimizes the transfer window size during the transfer. We took the measured value (944 Mbps) as the reference for the actual bandwidth. The maximum bandwidth using UDP was 769.7 ± 7.4 Mbps (cf. Fig. 7), a value in line with some commercial switches, despite our software-based testbed.

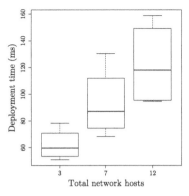

Table 6. Virtual data diode deployment times depending vs number of network hosts

Network hosts	Deployment time (ms)
3	62.188 ± 14.810
7	93.33 ± 33.345
12	122.418 ± 39.790

Fig. 8. Virtual data diode deployment times vs number of network hosts.

For the (c) experiment, we measured how the deployment times of the virtual data diode varied, accordingly to the number of network hosts. Hosts were "faked" by changing the MAC address and the IP address of one of the machines, followed by the generation of ARP packets. Upon detection in the network controller, those fake hosts were added to the previously created network. A controller command-line command was introduced in the *Data diode* application to deploy and remove the virtual-data diode in a loop, while collecting the elapsed time. Table 6 and Fig. 8 present the results. Although the deployment times increase with the number of network hosts, it is in the millisecond range. A small value considering that for n hosts, $n - 1$ flow rules have to be installed and the datastore has to be consistently synchronized between all the controller nodes.

6   Conclusion

Current trends, such as Industry 4.0 and Internet of Things are evolving industrial control networks towards ubiquity, moving away from the traditional monolithic and self-contained infrastructure paradigm, in favor of highly distributed and interconnected architectures. In this perspective, the use of data diodes provides a convenient way to isolate mission-critical network domains, while still allowing for relevant information (i.e., telemetry) to be accessed from the outside. However, as the number of interconnected devices increases, the costs of multiple physical data diodes may become impractical for organizations.

To deal with the inherent limitations of traditional implementations, we proposed the virtual data diode concept, which leverages the benefits of SDN and NFV. This concept was demonstrated and evaluated by means of a proof-of-concept prototype, designed with performance and availability in mind. The use of proactive flow rule instantiation removes the complete dependency on the control plane, allowing the virtual data diode to use the available switch bandwidth. The use of a distributed controller provides reliability and continuous operation in case of controller node failures. Prototype evaluation measurements recorded virtual data diode deployment latencies in the millisecond range, with minimal latency in the link layer. Even stressing the switch to its full rate capacity (with much higher values than the ones typically found in IACS), packet loss in the link was minimal. While not providing the same security levels of physical data diodes (it is a software implementation), the virtualized version still compares favorably with diode alternatives, such as firewalls, while maintaining functional equivalence to its physical counterpart.

Acknowledgements. This work was partially funded by the ATENA H2020 Project (H2020-DS-2015-1 Project 700581) and Mobiwise P2020 SAICTPAC/0011/2015 Project.

References

1. Barbosa, R.: Anomaly detection in SCADA systems: a network based approach. Ph.D. thesis, University of Twente (2014). https://doi.org/10.3990/1. 9789036536455
2. Berde, P., Gerola, M., et al.: ONOS: towards an open, distributed SDN OS. In: Proceedings of the Third Workshop on Hot Topics in Software Defined Networking - HotSDN 2014, pp. 1–6 (2014). https://doi.org/10.1145/2620728.2620744
3. FoxIT: Fox DataDiode Data Sheet (2018). https://www.fox-it.com/datadiode/downloads/
4. FoxIT: Fox IT FAQ. Online (2018). https://www.fox-it.com/datadiode/faq/
5. Genua: Data Diode Cyber-diode. Brochure (2018). https://www.genua.de/fileadmin/download/produkte/cyber-diode-flyer-en.pdf
6. Heo, Y., et al.: A design of unidirectional security gateway for enforcement reliability and security of transmission data in industrial control systems. In: International Conference on Advanced Communication Technology (2016). https://doi.org/10. 1109/ICACT.2016.7423372
7. Jeon, B.S., Na, J.C.: A study of cyber security policy in industrial control system using data diodes. In: 18th International Conference on Advanced Communication Technology (ICACT), p. 1, January 2016. https://doi.org/10.1109/ICACT.2016. 7423373
8. Jones, D.W.: RS-232 data diode - Tutorial And Reference Manual. Technical report, United States (2006)
9. Mckay, M.: Best practices in automation security (2012). https://doi.org/10.1109/ CITCON.2012.6215678
10. Mraz, R.: Data Diode Cybersecurity Implementation Protects SCADA Network and Facilitates Transfer of Operations Information to Business Users. Presentation (2016)
11. Okhravi, H., Sheldon, F.T.: Data diodes in support of trustworthy cyber infrastructure. In: Proceedings of the Sixth Annual Workshop on Cyber Security and Information Intelligence Research, CSIIRW 2010, pp. 23:1–23:4. ACM, New York (2010). https://doi.org/10.1145/1852666.1852692
12. Oktian, Y.E., et al.: Distributed SDN controller system: a survey on design choice. Comput. Netw. **121**, 100–111 (2017). https://doi.org/10.1016/j.comnet.2017.04. 038

13. Open NF: OpenFlow Switch Specification Version 1.5.1 (Protocol v. 0x06) (2015). https://www.opennetworking.org/wp-content/uploads/2014/10/openflow-switch-v1.5.1.pdf
14. Owl Cyberdefense: Learn About Data Diodes. Online (2018)
15. Peterson, D.G.: Air Gaps Dead, Network Isolation Making a Comeback. Online. http://www.digitalbond.com/blog/2011/07/19/air-gaps-dead-network-isolation-making-a-comeback/
16. Scott, A.: Tactical data diodes in industrial automation and control systems. Technical report, United States (2015)
17. Stouffer, K.A., et al.: NIST SP 800–82 rev2. Guide to Industrial Control Systems (ICS) Security: SCADA Systems, DCS, and Other Control System Configurations Such As Programmable Logic Controllers (PLC). Technical report, USA (2015)
18. Sun, Y., Liu, H., Kim, M.S.: Using TCAM efficiently for IP route lookup. In: 2011 IEEE Consumer Communications and Networking Conference, CCNC'2011, pp. 816–817 (2011). https://doi.org/10.1109/CCNC.2011.5766609
19. Waterfall Security: Unidirectional security gateways vs. comparing costs. Technical report, Israel, Firewalls (2012)
20. Waterfall Security: Unidirectional Security Gateways (2018). https://static.waterfall-security.com/Unidirectional-Security-Gateway-Brochure.pdf
21. Waterfall Security: Waterfall FLIP (2018). https://waterfall-security.com/wp-content/uploads/Waterfall-FLIP-Brochure.pdf
22. Waterfall Security: Waterfall WF-500 product datasheet. Product Datasheet (2018). https://waterfall-security.com/wp-content/uploads/WF-500-Data-Sheet.pdf

Realistic Data Generation for Anomaly Detection in Industrial Settings Using Simulations

Peter Schneider$^{(\boxtimes)}$ and Alexander Giehl

Fraunhofer AISEC, Garching, Germany
{peter.schneider,alexander.giehl}@aisec.fraunhofer.de

Abstract. With the rise of advanced persistent threats to cyber-physical facilities, new methods for anomaly detection are required. However, research on anomaly detection systems for industrial networks suffers from the lack of suitable training data to verify the methods at early stages. This paper presents a framework and workflow to generate meaningful training and test data for anomaly detection systems in industrial settings. Using process-model based simulations data can be generated on a large scale. We evaluate the data in regard to its usability for state-of-the-art anomaly detection systems. With adequate simulation configurations, it is even possible to simulate a sensor manipulation attack on the model and to derive labeled data.

By this simulation of attacked components, we demonstrate the effectiveness of systems trained on artificial data to detect previously unseen attacks.

Keywords: Anomaly detection · Cyber-physical systems · Modeling · Security · Simulation

1 Introduction

As industries follow the trend of the internet of things, they connect more and more of their production machines to local networks and the internet. Connectivity from the internet down through sensors and actuators allows for new business models and essentially makes the machines cyber-physical systems. As such, they interface between the virtual world, i.e. the internet, and the real world. As these machines have been constructed assuming they are only accessed locally, this increase in connectivity between them introduces new attack vectors. The examples of Stuxnet and Duqu have shown that the new risks imposed can lead to theft of intellectual property and even cause physical damage [10]. Currently, the industry is adopting the lessons learned from the business IT and uses firewalls to build up demilitarized zones, restricts the physical access to critical components and implements various fingerprinting-based detection mechanisms. While screening for known attack fingerprints can be effective in business IT, industrial networks are also attacked by adapted strategies specific to the asset

© Springer Nature Switzerland AG 2019
S. K. Katsikas et al. (Eds.): CyberICPS 2018/SECPRE 2018, LNCS 11387, pp. 119–134, 2019.
https://doi.org/10.1007/978-3-030-12786-2_8

which cannot be covered. Due to insecure configurations, USB autorun attacks, infected and badly handled private devices, and insecure update processes, all these countermeasures have once failed to prevent attacks [5,11,21]. In addition to that, zero-day exploits and quickly evolving malwares often stay undetected for a long time so that they are referenced as advanced persistent threats [2]. Methods designed to detect specific intrusion codes or signatures fall short of detecting newly emerging highly targeted threats. Additionally, due to availability and safety constraints imposed on industrial systems, modifications and updates to fingerprint databases can be difficult to achieve.

Therefore, relying on signatures of the attack vectors seems inappropriate. As these fingerprinting-based techniques are inferior in this scenario, anomaly detection is a viable solution for security in industrial settings. These systems rely on a model of normal system operation. Attacks are assumed to change the system behavior and can, therefore, be detected.

One major problem in developing anomaly detection systems for this setting is the lack of suitable training data. Nearly all existing approaches do need a lot of data to derive a model of the normal operation or even distinguish between normal behavior and anomalies. However, there is only a limited set of data available. Mostly, because most companies having such data fear to expose their intellectual property with it – maybe even unknowingly. Hence, most of the current research uses either private, handcrafted, or inadequate datasets to evaluate their approach [16]. Additionally, only a few of them are publicly available. This results in state-of-the-art intrusion detection systems which cannot be compared by their performance. Therefore, there is a need for suitable training data for detecting anomalies in industrial networks and enabling big data approaches for IT security in this domain.

This paper presents an approach to develop meaningful but reproducible datasets which are suitable for process- and network-based anomaly detection. By the use of process-based simulations special network data is crafted which can represent data in real-world intrusion detection systems. Our approach is not only capable of generating cyber-physical process data but also of simulating attacks on the underlying processes. Having control over the simulation configuration all the data is labeled in the end and is therefore usable for state-of-the-art anomaly detection systems.

In summary, we make the following contributions:

- We present a workflow to generate cyber-physical process data for anomaly detection systems on a large scale.
- We evaluate that data and investigate its usability for the detection of anomalies.
- We show how to include attacks the simulation and how to detect them in the data using state-of-the-art methods.

2   Related Work

Generating data for anomaly detection in industrial settings requires having a look on available work in different areas. Existing schemes for anomaly detection in this domain need to be considered to understand the requirements of state-of-the-art methods. Already available datasets can be investigated for their flaws and looking on previous attempts of data generation may yield insights in inherent flaws to simulations.

2.1 Anomaly Detection in Industrial Networks

At the moment, current research is investigating two different approaches to anomaly detection in industrial settings. The first tries to adapt business network anomaly detection to the fieldbus protocols used in the industry. Other approaches include more domain-specific knowledge into the systems to detect anomalies based on an altered behavior of the industrial process. The authors of [9] use discrete-time Markov chains to detect alterations in sequences of network communication of a cyber-physical system. As they tested their approach on real-world data of a real plant, the effectiveness of their approach cannot be compared to other solutions without re-implementation. Often, telemetry analysis is used to detect anomalies in industrial network traffic [23,27]. Proposing a clustering approach, the authors of [1] chose a different method to detect anomalies in industrial process data with an accuracy of up to 98%. Several articles already concluded that the integration of process data into intrusion detection systems leads to an increase in accuracy.

According to the authors of [22], neglecting these properties results in inferior attack detection. Further, [26] showed that there are severe risks in the manufacturing of physical parts. Therefore, they argue that there is a need to also focus on the physical parts of industrial processes. First approaches use process data to build a model of the underlying process to detect deviations from that normal state [14,15]. However, they only use specially crafted, non-public datasets.

2.2 SCADA Datasets and Testbeds

There are few datasets which can be used to compare the performance of intrusion detection systems on industrial network data. [19] introduced a first Modbus dataset which originates from simulations. They used self-developed programs, scripts, and different approaches to generate their datasets.

In contrast, the framework proposed in this paper generates almost real industrial data to ensure that the underlying physical data is meaningful and reproducible.

To measure the performance of their detection approach [27] use a custom simulation testbed which is not described in detail. By using a handcrafted featureset they detect intrusions in Modbus traffic. In [16], about 30 Industrial Control System testbeds have been reviewed. However, the authors found that less than half of them actually tried to verify the acquired data. [6] shows one example of an ICS testbed where the authors evaluate different processes. However, as they build up the actual network infrastructure, their approach is not directly transferable to other use cases. [20] found that while ICS testbeds usually address vulnerabilities in one layer, e.g. the field devices, attacks most often target several layers. Therefore, they argue that multilayered ICS testbeds are needed to effectively analyze the vulnerabilities and develop countermeasures. Our framework provides such a multilayered approach by merging two existing frameworks into one.

3 Simulation Framework

The simulation framework proposed consists of three elements. At first, a process simulation generates realistic sequences of process parameters. The foundation for this process simulation is a process model describing the available components and their interaction. The simulation calculates the different process parameters based on mathematical and physical models. Thereby, the process parameters are sampled at specific time intervals.

Afterwards, the physical process model is split into parts and mapped to virtual devices resembling the network components monitored. Furthermore without loss of generality, we assume that those devices are connected in a bus topology, as this mode of operation is currently being adopted in industry connectivity [18].

Finally, the extracted components become the networking nodes in the network simulation. The generated process parameters are embedded in a suitable fieldbus protocol. Figure 1 shows the general workflow for this sequential simulation framework.

If effects of the networking, e.g. latency or jamming, need to be simulated, a co-simulation is required instead of the sequential approach outlined here. In a co-simulation as shown in Fig. 1 also using the dashed line, the simulation stops after each time interval to include the feedback of each other simulation. In this setup, both simulations are executed alternating while an adapter transfers the states between the simulations [13].

In the end, this yields realistic network data very similar to captures in a production site with real data.

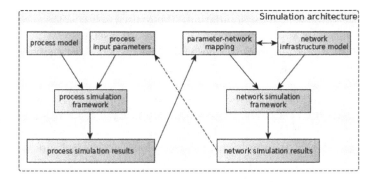

Fig. 1. Simulation framework workflow.

3.1   Industrial Process Simulation Using Modelica

Modelica is a well-known object-oriented programming language used in a variety of simulation frameworks. It is designed to easily model physical processes and control loops. OpenModelica [12] is an open source implementation of that language providing a graphical modeling toolkit as well as interfaces for interaction with the simulations.

Physical processes are modeled in the Modelica language using a variety of building blocks. Unavailable functionality can be added through the addition of external libraries.

The modeled process is then compiled to an executable which generates corresponding time-series data to given initial values. The data generated by Open-Modelica using free models has already been reviewed [8, 24]. Building on these findings, OpenModelica provides the industrial process simulation to the framework.

As Modelica is an object-oriented language, the definition of this simulation starts with its parent element followed by the constituent components. Each of the listed components corresponds to a separate Modelica language model definition. They resemble building blocks as the physical and mathematical model is encapsulated in them. To model the system behavior the components are connected through `equations`.

Additionally, OpenModelica provides means for interfacing with the simulation allowing also the implementation of a co-simulation framework.

3.2   Network Simulation Using NS-3

For the purpose of simulating the underlying network infrastructure, NS-3's python interface is used [7]. It provides the necessary simulation of the physical communication channels as well as the lowest network layers up to TCP. The industrial network data is generated using a custom application layer protocol which is common in proprietary industrial settings. Using this protocol the application simply sends messages containing the parameter name and value to the destination component at regular intervals. That is the same methodology like in common industrial fieldbus protocols. While CAN uses CAN-identifiers transferred along the actual data values, the high-level CANopen protocol uses a known object dictionary (COD) to map bytes into the transferred process data objects (PDO) [4]. In the end, both methods define a static mean to lookup the meaning and interpretation of every data byte transmitted, effectively yielding name-value pairs. The same is true for the widespread modbus protocol which uses function codes transmitted along with the actual data [17].

3.3   Sequential Simulation

To derive a multilayered dataset with realistic process data on the one hand and a realistic embedding in industrial network traffic, on the other hand, we

---

Algorithm 1. ModelSplitting

Input: Modelica model file M
Input: model name m
Output: List of top-level connections L
 1 Let L be a list;
 2 startFound = endFound = False;
 3 **foreach** *line l in M* **do**
 4 $\quad$ $pattern = $ "\s*model " $ + m$;
 5 $\quad$ if $\mathtt{match}$($pattern$, l) **then**
 6 $\quad$ $\quad$ $\lfloor$ $startFound = True$;
 7 $\quad$ **if** $startFound \wedge \neg endFound$ **then**
 8 $\quad$ $\quad$ $pattern = $ "$\mathtt{connect}$\(([^,]*), ([^)]*)\)";
 9 $\quad$ $\quad$ $res = \mathtt{match}$($pattern$, l);
10 $\quad$ $\quad$ **if** $res \neq None$ **then**
11 $\quad$ $\quad$ $\quad$ $\lfloor$ $\mathtt{append}$(L, $\mathtt{group}$(res, 1), $\mathtt{group}$(res, 2));
12 $\quad$ $pattern = $ "\s*end " $ + m$;
13 $\quad$ if $\mathtt{match}$($pattern$,l) **then**
14 $\quad$ $\quad$ $\lfloor$ $endFound = True$
15 **return** L;

---

need to chain these two simulation frameworks as shown in Fig. 1 with the non-dashed lines. Using this combined approach we assume that prepared anomaly detection algorithms will be able to more accurately generate alarms and to detect attacks originating from network manipulation or the manipulation of involved processes.

First, the cyber-physical process under test needs to be modeled in the Modelica programming language. As such models often are part of the engineering and development process, we assume that such a model is detailed enough to allow analyzing the main functionality. For research, there are also several thoroughly tested open source models available which can be used for comparison of IDS performances [3,8,24].

Each of these models requires a reliable initial state. This state is not required to be an equilibrium state for the industrial process. Therefore, it should not be a state which causes the system to diverge.

Using the model and its initial state it is possible to run a simulation with OpenModelica resulting in all process parameters at given time intervals.

3.4 Automatic Infrastructure Derivation

Actually deriving network data from the generated process parameters requires a network infrastructure model corresponding to the cyber-physical model. The framework relies on the assumption that every building block in the Modelica description of the industrial process at the top-most level represents a single network node, i.e. a discrete device.

This allows for a more realistic modeling of real-world scenarios where parts of the functionality of the system are encapsulated within one single complex device. Not all simulated connections from the OpenModelica simulation will show up in the final network trace as in real-world scenarios where the system is only partially visible to an IDS. As the Modelica model also describes the interconnection of blocks, the accompanying data exchange between these follows directly from the model. Algorithm 1 automatically splits the Modelica model at its topmost level into blocks and returns a list of the connections between these blocks.

The expression `\s*model m` (l. 5–7) and the corresponding end with `\s*end m` (l. 13–15) finds the start of the description of model m. Using two capture groups every pair of two connected components and also the direction of the connection can be retrieved with `connect\(([^,]*), ([^)]*)\)` (l. 9).

The referenced function `match` takes a pattern and a string which is searched for the pattern. Concerning the regular expressions, the *-modifier is assumed to be greedy and the function `group(res, i)` returns the content of the i-th capture group in the matching result `res` (l. 10–12).

Data exchange between the network nodes can be modeled either by push or poll paradigms. From our experience, both methods are actually used so that we decided to push the data to the next node as most field busses (e.g. CAN or ProfiNet) are typically used like this. A mapping component splits the simulation results into the desired parts, which generates a list of data packets, their destinations, and timestamps for each identified node. These lists are then passed to a custom application for the NS-3 network simulation which sends out the corresponding network packets at the right time. Being a NS-3 application the network stack handles the underlying protocols, i.e. TCP handshakes and responses, while on the application layer the data is not used any further. By instructing NS-3 to capture the network traffic on each virtual device into packet capture files simulated network traffic traces are generated.

3.5 Sensor Manipulation Attacks

For the creation of suitable test data for anomaly detection systems, it is indispensable to also have malicious examples, i.e. data corresponding to the attacked system state. Therefore, the framework provides a generic algorithm to manipulate the simulation model. The algorithm replaces one connection in the model with a time-triggered switch to model a manipulated sensor or actuator. The given connection between the output value c_1 and input value c_2 gets replaced by a connection from c_1 to the first input of the switch s_1 and the output of that switch s_y to c_2. The value n used for replacement during the manipulation is connected to the second input of the switch s_2. Using an integer step function is, the inputs get switched at a specific point in time t_2.

$$is = \begin{cases} 1, & for \quad t \le t_2 \\ 2, & for \quad t > t_2 \end{cases}.$$

Therefore, the input value of c_2 equals to

$$c_2 = \begin{cases} c_1, & for \quad t \leq t_2 \\ n, & for \quad t > t_2 \end{cases}.$$

Applying this algorithm to an existing Modelica model yields a similar model representing an attacked version of the system starting from the time t_2.

4   Data Usability Validation

The usability of the generated data from such simulations for the purpose of anomaly detection was analyzed by generating a test dataset and training a deep learning network with it. The systems analyzed for validation are a heat recovery boiler (HRB) plant [8] from the *ThermoPower* library (with 1367 simulated equations), a velocity control system for a drive [3] from the *Industrial-ControlSystems* library (258 equations) and a complex waste water treatment system [24] from the *WasteWater* library (3066 equations). In the following, a deeper look is given on the HRB plant, while similar observations and results can be obtained for all tested models.

Figure 2 shows the *ClosedLoopSimulator* for the HRB plant. The system consists of a HRB plant (P), a temperature controller (*TempController*) and the input values for the set point temperature, i.e. the temperature the water leaving the plant shall have, and the valve opening, i.e. a parameter steering how fast the water is running through the boiler.

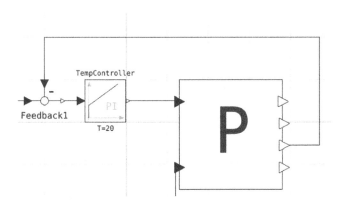

Fig. 2. Original system [8].

This process is comparable to many industry applications where a machine is controlled by a user interface over the network. Simulating this system using OpenModelica yields the temperature curve for the outgoing water shown in Fig. 3. The blue curve shows the desired temperature (in Kelvin), i.e. the input signal over the network, while the red one shows how the simulated boiler control system reacts. At time $t_1 = 50\,\text{s}$ the valve is closed a bit to test the response of the controller to disturbances in the process. The water temperature gets back to the setpoint after a short time.

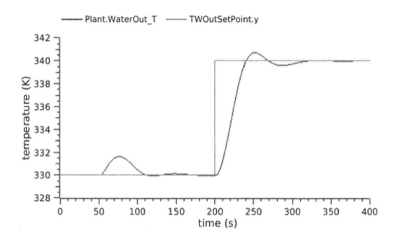

Fig. 3. Temperature curve of original simulation. (Color figure online)

4.1 Introducing Simulated Attacks

Going one step further, we altered the initial model to simulate a manipulated sensor device firmware. Starting from the time $t_2 = 205\,\text{s}$, we exchange the real output temperature of the plant with the actual temperature setpoint. This directly resembles an attack on the temperature sensor of the boiler. This attack can be modeled with the Modelica language by exchanging the input to the feedback unit $f1.u1$ from the water temperature $P.WaterOut_T$ to the actual setpoint temperature $TWOutSetPoint$.

A switch ($extractor1$) is used to choose one of the two incoming signals. The real sensor value is assigned to the first input, the setpoint temperature to the second. The choice of the output is derived from an integer step function yielding the input to the feedback unit as

$$f1.u1 = \begin{cases} P.WaterOut_T, & for \quad t \le t_2 = 205\,\text{s} \\ TWOutSetPoint, & for \quad t > t_2 = 205\,\text{s} \end{cases}.$$

The simulated temperature curve of this modified model is depicted in Fig. 5. As expected, the water temperature now settles at $333K$ instead of the desired setpoint of $340K$. Starting from $t_2 = 205\,\text{s}$ the closed loop controller gets the signal that the desired temperature is already reached and therefore stops further heating. In this case, this leads to an early stop of the heating. If the sensor incorrectly reports a temperature below the setpoint, this results in a diverging system where the temperature controller never stopped heating.

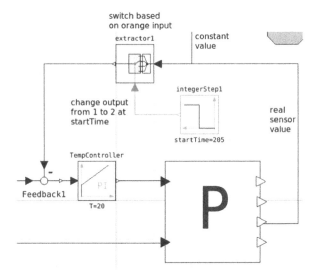

Fig. 4. Faked sensor data model.

4.2 Anomaly Detection on Simulated Data

For the development of machine learning based models, the dataset must be diverse and large enough [25]. To test whether the generated data is not just plausible but also suitable for machine learning we used a neural network to predict the next parameter values given the current ones.

As we are going to strictly evaluate the usability of the cyber-physical process data, we do not include any metadata of the network communication in our analysis but only use the generated process data directly.

From the 1169 process parameters available after the simulation of the HRB plant in OpenModelica, we only use a small subset which may be directly available in network traffic, i.e. the input and output connections of the plant and the two controllable inputs, the setpoint temperature and the valve opening. To automate this we split the Modelica model using Algorithm 1 at its topmost level into building blocks, i.e. the blocks shown in Fig. 2. The connections between these blocks are interpreted as network communication.

The anomaly detection approach for validation is based on a deep neural network (DNN) architecture. The network is used to predict the values of the process parameters at one timestep ahead. By observing the difference between the real and predicted values the state of the industrial process can then be monitored. The DNN uses linear regression layers to predict the values of the process parameters in the future. The neural network consists of one input, one output, and two hidden layers. The input layer has the size of two times the number of parameters being predicted in the output layer. The size of the hidden layers is adapted to each evaluated model. In addition to the original definition of the system model some normal distributed noise was introduced on the valve

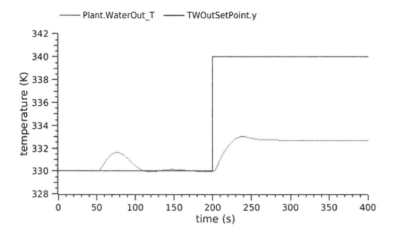

Fig. 5. Temperature curve of attack simulation.

opening input. This leads to a continuous fluctuation in the water outflow of the plant simulating imperfections in the implementation which were missing in the original system model.

With the data from the unmodified operating HRB plant, the network is trained to predict the values of the input connections at the next timestep (t_1) based on the previous (t_{-1}) and the current (t_0) values. So, the network is effectively learning the normal system behavior without the knowledge of how an attack might look like. After training using the gradient descent method, a comparison of the predicted and real behavior results in the blue relative error curve for the out-flowing water temperature in Fig. 6.

The error of the training dataset remains in a constrained band. The only exception is the short peak starting at timestep $20000(=200\,\text{s})$. This is when in the unmodified version of the model the setpoint temperature is altered. Therefore, it is correct to interpret this spike as an anomaly.

4.3 Attack Detection Using Simulated Data

We also investigated whether simulated attacks can actually be detected while the model has been trained only with normal data.

Therefore in a second run, we simulated the manipulated sensor model depicted in Fig. 4. Additionally, we changed the initial setpoint temperature, the time when the setpoint change occurs and the amount of change. Therefore, if the model was overfitted, the relative error should increase already before the manipulation starts because the initial and final setpoint temperatures are different. The configurations of the test and training simulations are shown in Table 1.

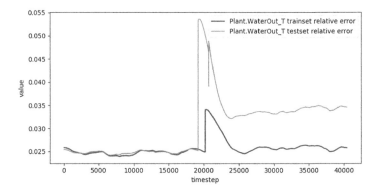

Fig. 6. Relative prediction errors for the normal and attacked dataset of the water outflow temperature. (Color figure online)

Table 1. Simulation setup for the generation of datasets.

Setting	Training data	Test data
Initial setpoint temperature	$330K$	$320K$
t_1, time for setpoint change	$200\,\mathrm{s}$	$190\,\mathrm{s}$
t_2, time for attack	–	$205\,\mathrm{s}$
Final setpoint temperature	$340K$	$350K$

The previously trained model was then used to predict the parameters' values at each next timestamp. The red curve in Fig. 6 illustrates the relative difference in predicted and real values. For the first part, the error is of the same order as for the unattacked (blue) dataset. This verifies that the learned model is actually portable to similar situations as the attack is only carried out after $t_2 = 205\,\mathrm{s}$, i.e. timestep 20500. The spike at timestep $19000(=190\,\mathrm{s})$ corresponds to the change of the setpoint temperature. As expected, the peak on the test dataset occurs earlier than in the training dataset. This indicates that a configuration change of the plant does not alter the prediction capability of the learned model.

While with the unattacked dataset the model comes back to an error near to zero, with the attacked dataset the relative error levels at an about 10 times higher relative error caused by the manipulated sensor. From the time $t_2 = 205\,\mathrm{s}$ the water outflow temperature sensor starts maliciously reporting that it measures the setpoint temperature. Thus, the heating stops too early and the outflow temperature has a significant difference to its actual setpoint. This difference can now also be seen in the right half of the red curve in Fig. 6.

To derive a suitable anomaly detection approach an error threshold can be estimated either by experimental evaluation or by appropriate machine learning strategies. This actually is possible since given the simulation setup each timestep in the data is labeled.

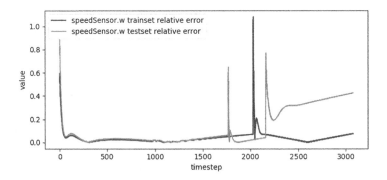

Fig. 7. Relative prediction errors for the normal and attacked dataset of the speed sensor in the *IndustrialControlSystems* VelocityDrive simulation.

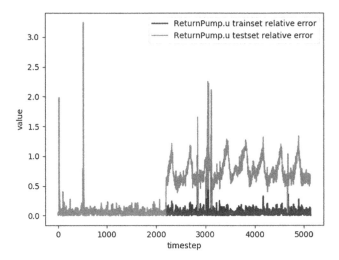

Fig. 8. Relative prediction errors for the normal and attacked dataset of a pump inflow in the *WasteWater* ComplexPlant simulation.

Similar results can also be obtained for other models. Figures 7 and 8 show the relative error curve of one of the parameters in the *VelocityDrive* and *WasteWater* simulations. The simulation configuration for the training and test datasets has been altered in a similar way as shown in Table 1 to verify the model portability. As in the HRB example explained before, the blue curve always represents the relative error on the training data, i.e. with no manipulation, while the red curve shows the error of the test data introduced by model configuration changes and attacks. Also in these two more complex simulations, a sensor manipulation can be detected while the neural network has only been trained on normal operation data.

5   Conclusion

In this paper, we presented a framework and workflow to generate usable industrial anomaly detection data. By using a combination of modeling, simulation
and an infrastructure mapping we are able to create industrial network traffic which reflects the physics of the network transfer as well as those of the
cyber-physical process. Being a simulation, our approach does not require costly
specialized hardware.

Additionally, we showed that the integration of attacks in the simulation
results in labeled data suitable for machine learning. In contrast to solutions
which use hardware or hardware-in-the-loop, we can model an arbitrary complex
system while still having a scalable system. Also, simulation of attacks on the
cyber-physical system can be carried out without interference with production
environments or danger of physical impact.

In our evaluation, we additionally showed that it is actually possible to train
anomaly detection systems to predict cyber-physical systems behavior. Given
that, new possibilities emerge by the integration of this knowledge into existing
intrusion detection systems.

Previous approaches designed the anomaly detection to be suited for the use
case, i.e. the approach has been adapted to the domain's constraints and specific
problems. Instead of that, we used off-the-shelf approaches nearly unmodified to
detect anomalies in the data. Therefore, for the anomaly detection itself, there
is no need of a deep understanding of the underlying cyber-physical process.

Acknowledgements. The presented work is part of the German national security
reference project IUNO (http://www.iuno-projekt.de). The project is funded by the
BMBF and aims to provide building-blocks for security in the emerging field of
Industrie 4.0.

References

1. Almalawi, A., Fahad, A., Tari, Z., Alamri, A., AlGhamdi, R., Zomaya, A.Y.: An
   efficient data-driven clustering technique to detect attacks in scada systems. IEEE
   Trans. Inf. Forensics Secur. **11**(5), 893–906 (2016)
2. Bencsáth, B., Pék, G., Buttyán, L., Felegyhazi, M.: skywiper (aka flame aka
   flamer): A complex malware for targeted attacks. CrySyS Lab Technical report,
   No. CTR-2012-05-31 (2012)
3. Bonvini, M., Leva, A.: A modelica library for industrial control systems. In: Proceedings of the 9th International MODELICA Conference; 3–5 September 2012,
   Munich, Germany, pp. 477–484. No. 076, Linköping University Electronic Press
   (2012)
4. Boterenbrood, H.: Canopen High-Level Protocol for Can-Bus. Nikhef, Amsterdam
   (2000)
5. Brunner, M., Hofinger, H., Krauß, C., Roblee, C., Schoo, P., Todt, S.: Infiltrat-
   ing Critical Infrastructures with Next-generation Attacks. Fraunhofer Institute for
   Secure Information Technology (SIT), Munich (2010)

6. Candell, R., Zimmerman, T., Stouffer, K.: An industrial control system cybersecurity performance testbed. National Institute of Standards and Technology, NISTIR 8089 (2015)
7. Carneiro, G.: Ns-3: network simulator 3, April 2010. http://www.nsnam.org/tutorials/NS-3-LABMEETING-1.pdf
8. Casella, F., Leva, A.: Modelica open library for power plant simulation: design and experimental validation. In: Proceeding of the 2003 Modelica Conference, Linkoping, Sweden (2003)
9. Caselli, M., Zambon, E., Kargl, F.: Sequence-aware intrusion detection in industrial control systems. In: Proceedings of the 1st ACM Workshop on Cyber-Physical System Security, pp. 13–24. ACM (2015)
10. Chen, T.M.: Stuxnet, the real start of cyber warfare? [editor's note]. IEEE Netw. **24**(6), 2–3 (2010)
11. Federal Office for Information Security, Germany: Industrial Control System Security Top 10 Threats and Countermeasures 2014. BSI Publications on Cyber-Security (2014)
12. Fritzson, P., et al.: OpenModelica - a free open-source environment for system modeling, simulation, and teaching. In: 2006 IEEE International Symposium on Intelligent Control Computer Aided Control System Design, 2006 IEEE International Conference on Control Applications, pp. 1588–1595. IEEE (2006)
13. Giehl, A.: Development of a co-simulation framework to analyse attacks and their impact on Smart Grids. Master's thesis, Technische Universität München, July 2013
14. Hadžiosmanović, D., Sommer, R., Zambon, E., Hartel, P.H.: Through the eye of the PLC: semantic security monitoring for industrial processes. In: Proceedings of the 30th Annual Computer Security Applications Conference, pp. 126–135. ACM (2014)
15. Haller, P., Genge, B.: Using sensitivity analysis and cross-association for the design of intrusion detection systems in industrial cyber-physical systems. IEEE (2016). https://doi.org/10.1109/ACCESS.2017.2703906
16. Holm, H., Karresand, M., Vidström, A., Westring, E.: A survey of industrial control system testbeds. In: Buchegger, S., Dam, M. (eds.) NordSec 2015. LNCS, vol. 9417, pp. 11–26. Springer, Cham (2015). https://doi.org/10.1007/978-3-319-26502-5_2
17. IDA, M.: Modbus messaging on TCP/IP implementation guide v1. 0a (2004)
18. Jazdi, N.: Cyber physical systems in the context of industry 4.0. In: 2014 IEEE International Conference on Automation, Quality and Testing, Robotics, pp. 1–4. IEEE (2014)
19. Lemay, A., Fernandez, J.M.: Providing scada network data sets for intrusion detection research. In: 9th Workshop on Cyber Security Experimentation and Test (CSET 16). USENIX Association (2016)
20. McLaughlin, S., Konstantinou, C., Wang, X., Davi, L., Sadeghi, A.R., Maniatakos, M., Karri, R.: The cybersecurity landscape in industrial control systems. Proc. IEEE **104**(5), 1039–1057 (2016)
21. Nohl, K., Krißler, S., Lell, J.: BadUSB-on accessories that turn evil. Black Hat USA (2014)
22. Pasqualetti, F., Dörfler, F., Bullo, F.: Attack detection and identification in cyber-physical systems. IEEE Trans. Autom. Control **58**(11), 2715–2729 (2013)
23. Ponomarev, S., Atkison, T.: Industrial control system network intrusion detection by telemetry analysis. IEEE Trans. Dependable Secure Comput. **13**(2), 252–260 (2016)

24. Reichl, G.: Wastewater a library for modelling and simulation of wastewater treatment plants in Modelica. In: Paper Presented at the 3rd International Modelica Conference, Citeseer (2003)
25. Sommer, R., Paxson, V.: Outside the closed world: on using machine learning for network intrusion detection. In: 2010 IEEE Symposium on Security and Privacy (SP), pp. 305–316. IEEE (2010)
26. Turner, H., White, J., Camelio, J.A., Williams, C., Amos, B., Parker, R.: Bad parts: are our manufacturing systems at risk of silent cyberattacks? IEEE Secur. Priv. **13**(3), 40–47 (2015)
27. Zhang, J., Gan, S., Liu, X., Zhu, P.: Intrusion detection in scada systems by traffic periodicity and telemetry analysis. In: 2016 IEEE Symposium on Computers and Communication (ISCC), pp. 318–325. IEEE (2016)

Security and Privacy Requirements Engineering (SECPRE 2018)

Sealed Computation: Abstract Requirements for Mechanisms to Support Trustworthy Cloud Computing

Lamya Abdullah[1,2]($\boxtimes$), Felix Freiling[1], Juan Quintero[1,2],
and Zinaida Benenson[1]

[1] Friedrich-Alexander-Universität Erlangen-Nürnberg (FAU), Erlangen, Germany
felix.freiling@cs.fau.de, zinaida.benenson@fau.de
[2] Uniscon GmbH, Munich, Germany
{lamya.abdullah,juan.quintero}@uniscon.de

Abstract. In cloud computing, data processing is delegated to a remote party for efficiency and flexibility reasons. A practical user requirement usually is that the confidentiality and integrity of data processing needs to be protected. In the common scenarios of cloud computing today, this can only be achieved by assuming that the remote party does not in any form act maliciously. In this paper, we propose an approach that avoids having to trust a single entity. Our approach is based on two concepts: (1) the technical abstraction of *sealed computation*, i.e., a technical mechanism to confine the processing of data within a tamper-proof hardware container, and (2) the additional role of an auditing party that itself cannot add functionality to the system but is able to check whether the system (including the mechanism for sealed computation) works as expected. We discuss the abstract technical and procedural requirements of these concepts and explain how they can be applied in practice.

Keywords: Security requirements · Trusted computing ·
Trustworthy computing · Cloud computing · Cloud service · Auditor

1 Introduction

Cloud computing has become widespread as it allows for supplying and utilizing computation resources in an on-demand fashion. This reduces cost, increases flexibility and improves infrastructure scalability [19]. Cloud computing is increasingly being adapted for services provided by networks of small devices, commonly referred to as the *Internet of Things* (IoT). IoT Cloud [2] or "Cloud of Things" (CoT) [1] provides resources such as storage, analytics tools and shared configurable computing resources to reduce the cost and complexity associated with the IoT systems.

When the data processing and storage are delegated to a cloud provider, users of cloud services usually have to trust the cloud provider to act as expected.

© Springer Nature Switzerland AG 2019
S. K. Katsikas et al. (Eds.): CyberICPS 2018/SECPRE 2018, LNCS 11387, pp. 137–152, 2019.
https://doi.org/10.1007/978-3-030-12786-2_9

However, in common cloud deployments, there is no technical guarantee that a single malicious insider like a system administrator or a person with physical access to the cloud infrastructure does not tamper with code and data. Hence cloud clients should be provided some technical guarantees and indications that the cloud service is trustworthy.

As an example, consider the scenario of an IoT Cloud implementation for *usage-based insurance* (UBI) [16], a novel car insurance business model, where the insurance company calculates premiums based on drivers' behavior using actual driving data.

In UBI, participating cars are equipped with a telematics devices to collect driving data such as location, speed, acceleration, cornering, and other details. Driving data are processed to get a ranking based on personal driving behavior. Using the driver ranking, the insurance company calculates a customized premium to the policyholder employing a more accurate risk estimate, reducing incurred losses [9,25] and offering a bonus in the case of good driving behavior.

UBI promises many benefits such as, for the insurance companies, reducing incurred losses through accurate risk estimates [9,25] and, for the policyholders (drivers), improving their driving style through feedback and decreasing their premiums. But obviously, UBI also raises concerns, such as user discrimination [16], and consumer privacy [9,25].

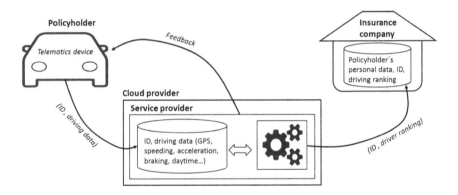

Fig. 1. High-level view of usage-based insurance scenario: The data is processed by the service provider on behalf of the insurance company. Processing is performed by a cloud provider running the service provider's software. The policyholders receive feedback on their driving habits.

Figure 1 depicts an abstract view of UBI: The service provider may actually be the same entity as the insurance company, but in many business implementations (BonusDrive by Allianz [4], SmartDriver by HUK-Coburg [15]) it is a different company. One reason for separation is that insurance companies do not have the corresponding know-how to compute the driving ranking. Another reason is that the insurance companies want to mitigate consumers' privacy concerns by stating that they have no access to the behavioral data, as it is processed by a third party [5].

Users who process sensitive data in the cloud have the following general security requirements:

- Confidentiality of data: Policyholders agree that their ranking is computed, but they want their individual usage data to remain confidential towards the insurance company and the cloud provider.
- Confidentiality of code: Service providers want to protect their intellectual property from other parties, in particular the insurance company and the cloud provider. So the software which is deployed in the cloud should be protected.
- Integrity of data and code: Insurance company, service provider and the policyholders should have a guarantee that the cloud provider does not change data or code in any unauthorized way.

On the one hand, users establish a sense of trust in the cloud provider in practice via contracts over *Service Level Agreements* (SLAs), auditing certificates and reputation.

Unfortunately, even with the most refined SLAs the necessity to place trust in the cloud provider remains.

On the other hand, numerous technical approaches [18] have been proposed to achieve security requirements such as those above using trusted hardware. For example, *hardware security modules* (HSMs) [10, 26], i.e., tamper-resistant physical computing devices, can perform secure and confidential computation of data. Using HSMs, it is possible to deploy specific software modules, create cryptographic keys and process data purely within the hardware device. Returning to our UBI scenario, the HSM can be used to effectively protect the service provider's data and code from the cloud provider. However, in this case the necessity to trust a single entity is not avoided, it is merely shifted from the cloud provider to the trusted hardware provider. This observation is not specific to HSMs but holds also for other such technologies such as Intel SGX [6, 24].

1.1 Contributions

In this paper, we propose a general approach that ensures generic confidentiality and integrity of cloud service and that avoids the necessity of having to trust a single entity.

Our approach is based on the combination of two concepts:

1. *Sealed computation*, an abstract technical mechanism to confine the processing of data within a tamper-proof hardware container (like a HSM), and
2. a procedural mechanism of mutual checking applying the additional role of an *auditing party*, which is necessary to check whether the system works as expected, but cannot modify it.

We describe the abstract technical and procedural requirements of both concepts and argue that they are sufficient to achieve the generic security properties described above. In the spirit of work by Morris Jr. [20], our work is conceptional, avoiding over-formalization but still providing clear definitions and evaluating statements. The main insight is to show how an abstract hardware mechanism (sealed computation, solely defined by its requirements) must be utilized in the cloud service such that the necessity to trust in a single entity is avoided.

Similar to other work [6,24], this paper focuses on integrity and confidentiality properties and do not consider availability. We use the UBI scenario above repeatedly as an example to illustrate our exposition, it generalizes to many other scenarios.

1.2 Outlook

We first define the concept of sealed computation in Sect. 2. Then the system and attacker model is presented in Sect. 3. Section 4 describes the procedural mechanism applying the role of an auditor.

In Sect. 5 we provide a security analysis and argue that general security requirements are satisfied unless two parties act maliciously. Related work is discussed in Sect. 6. Finally, Sect. 7 concludes the paper.

2   Sealed Computation

While data at rest can, typically, be protected by encryption, while protecting data during processing commonly is still an interesting problem to solve. We introduce a definition of sealed computation using abstract roles to keep it general, later, these are mapped to the parties introduced in Sect. 3. The term *sealed computation* is an abstraction that describes a well-defined level of protection against such attackers. Intuitively, this is done by encapsulating the software execution within a physical piece of hardware. We utilize the notion of sealed computation to maintain the integrity and confidentiality requirements of the system.

2.1 Definition

In sealed computation, a party A provides a physical execution container C into which a party B may "seal" its software. The container C ensures that the software is running in an unmodified fashion. Furthermore, C also guarantees that only a restricted set of interactions with the software are possible through a well-defined interface. Apart from that, no information is leaked from within C to the outside, not even to A the provider of the container nor the software provider B.

More formally, let a party A provide a physical execution container C and party B provide a software M which implements some input/output specification via a well-defined interface. The interface can be thought of as a description of input/output signals over wires or the format of incoming or outgoing protocol messages.

Definition 1 (Sealed Computation). *We say that B seals M within C provided by A if the following technical requirements are met:*

- *(Sealing) A and B cannot access the code and data of M after it has been sealed within C, apart from changes allowed by the interface.*
- *(Attestation) As long as M has not terminated and as long as A acts honestly, C can provide evidence which proves that C is running software provided by B in a manner which is unique to the sealing instance, i.e., any change of M, C or any subsequent sealing using the same combination will result in different evidence.*
- *(Black-box) Information flow between M and any other party (including A and B) is restricted by the interface specification of M, i.e., nothing about the internal state of M (code and data) can be learned apart from what is given away via the interface.*
- *(Tamper-resistance) Any usage of M that does not satisfy the interface specification results in termination of M and the destruction of C such that neither code nor data from within C can be retrieved.*

Intuitively, the Sealing requirement of sealed computation binds the execution of a program to a particular hardware environment. The requirements of Black-box and Tamper-resistance limit access to data and code only to interactions given in the functional specification of M: Black-box restricts information flow for expected interactions, while Tamper-resistance does this for unexpected interactions.

The Attestation requirement enables external parties to validate the fact that M has been sealed. It implies that C contains some known unique characteristic that can be validated by checking the provided evidence. This validation, however, depends on the correctness of A. A common realization of this is for A to embed a secret key within C and allow external parties to validate its existence by providing the corresponding public key. The existence of such a unique characteristic implies that it is possible to establish an authentic and confidential communication channel to M once sealing has started.

Similarly, note that B or any user of M still has to rely on A to act honestly because it is not verifiable whether C actually implements sealed computation. However, *if B correctly seals M within C provided by an honest A, even A cannot change M afterwards and the tamper-resistance requirement of C protects all secrets within M that are not accessible via its interface or before sealing.*

2.2 Confidential Software Deployment

The notion of sealed computation is a powerful abstraction that can be used to describe techniques that protect software also during deployment. We now argue that the technical requirements of sealed computation allow to ensure the confidentiality of the code which is sealed.

Intuitively, the idea of confidential software deployment is for B to initially install within the sealed computation a *loader stub* which is able to load the final user program specified by B into C. Within the sealed computation, this software is decrypted, installed and then takes over the final interface operations expected by the users. This loader stub can be part of the sealed computation mechanism from the start. Since it can be easily added to any mechanism that satisfies Definition 1, we did not include it as an additional requirement in that definition.

Observe that M cannot be assumed to remain confidential if A is untrustworthy. However, *if* A is trustworthy, sealed computation can be used to run code that remains confidential even towards A.

3   System and Attacker Model

3.1   Participants

For a general cloud-based application system model, our approach assumes the following main participants - referred to as entities or parties interchangeably:

1. *Data Prosumer* (DP): The DP is a producer and/or consumer of data at the same time, i.e., it produces input data and/or has an interest to consume the computed results. The way in which data is processed by the application is described by the DP in the form of a *functional specification*.
2. *Application Software Provider* (ASP): The ASP develops and maintains the analytics software which processes the data in the cloud and computes desired results according to the functional specification.
3. *Cloud Provider* (CP): The CP provides the cloud service which includes the hardware infrastructure, the software, and all associated configuration, administration and deployment tasks. The CP is also responsible for the security of the system as well as its availability towards the DP.
4. *Auditing Party* (AP): The AP is an independent party that helps to ensure the integrity of the hardware and software before the system becomes operational. We simply refer to the AP as the *auditor*.
5. *Sealed Computation Provider* (SCP): Additional entity to be considered is the SCP provides the sealed computation technology.

To map the sealed computation definition in Sect. 2 to the UBI scenario, it may help to think of the execution container C being a specific HSM provided by party A (the SCP), while party B is the service provider (SP) who wrote software M on behalf of insurance company (DP).

3.2   User Security Requirements

The desired security requirements of the parties are described in more detail here. Every requirement has a name that is prefixed by the corresponding participant role.

Definition 2 (User Security Requirements). *The participants have the following* security requirements:

- *(DP-Privacy) The DP requires that data remains confidential to any other party, i.e., neither CP, nor ASP, nor AP, nor SCP can learn anything about the data.*[1]
- *(DP-Integrity) Results which are obtained from the system by the DP are correctly computed on data as provided according to the functional specification. DP-Integrity covers data storage and processing integrity.*
- *(ASP-Integrity) The analytics software provided by the ASP is executed in an unmodified form within the system. Note that ASP-Integrity does not imply DP-Integrity since the latter refers also to data.*
- *(ASP-Confidentiality) No other party except the AP is able to learn about the analytics software developed by the ASP apart from what is described in the functional specification.*

3.3   Attacker Model

In this section, we formulate the attacker model. First, the ways in which individual participants may maliciously misbehave are described (the *local* attacker assumption). Then we define a condition that restricts the number of parties that may act maliciously (the *global* attacker assumption). The participants may act as follows:

- Application Software Provider (ASP): The ASP could provide an analytics software that leaks information about the processed data, thus violating DP-Privacy. Also, the ASP could violate DP-Integrity by providing software that incorrectly computes the results, i.e., computes the results not according to the functional specification provided by the DP.
- Sealed Computation Provider (SCP): The SCP could provide an incorrect sealed computation mechanism, i.e., a mechanism that has back-doors or vulnerabilities that enable changing code and data, thus violating ASP-Integrity or DP-Integrity, or a system that leaks code or data which violates ASP-Confidentiality or DP-Privacy.
- Cloud Provider (CP): The CP could leak any software that it has access to a malicious party, thereby violating ASP-Confidentiality. The CP has physical access to the mechanism provided by the SCP so it may attempt to access and/or modify data that is stored/processed, thus violating ASP-Integrity, DP-Integrity or DP-Privacy.
  We assume, however, that the CP protects its systems from interference and misuse by external attackers that are not specific to our scenario. Therefore these attacks are excluded from consideration in this work.

---

[1] While privacy has many definitions, here we explicitly use the term Privacy and not Confidentiality to emphasize end users' privacy (as individuals) against the providers and operators of the system (as organizations).

– Auditing Party (AP): During checking, the AP could try to add functionality to the system to leak information about the processed data and/or the software, thereby violating DP-Privacy or ASP-Confidentiality directly.

If any party acts in ways described above we say that this party *acts maliciously*. A party that does not act maliciously is considered *honest*.

For reasons of simplicity, the DP is excluded from our attacker model. Typical misbehavior of the DP can be giving a wrong functional specification, providing false data or to reveal the received results to any other party. Correct behavior in this respect cannot be enforced using a trustworthy cloud service as we envision here. Therefore, the DP is assumed to always be honest.

The *global* attacker assumption, i.e., a restriction on the number of parties that may act maliciously is formulated as follows: either the AP or both SCP and ASP are honest. More precisely, if the identifiers are taken as Boolean predicates of whether they are acting honestly or not, then the global attacker assumption is satisfied if the following condition holds:

$$AP \vee (SCP \wedge ASP)$$

Note that the condition is independent of the actions of the CP, and that it does not state which party exactly acts maliciously (AP, SCP or ASP).

3.4 Availability of Remote Attestation

To establish trust, it is often necessary to use mechanisms for *remote attestation*. Following the terminology of Coker et al. [8], attestation is the activity of making a claim to an appraiser about the properties of a target by supplying evidence which supports that claim. An attester is a party performing this activity. The result of an attestation depends on a mixture of facts that the appraiser can check directly on the evidence provided by the attester (e.g., cryptographic signatures) and trust in the attester itself (the mechanism by which the evidence was generated). Any party being part of a remote attestation has the requirement that the directly checkable part of the attestation works as expected. In practice, this means that the used cryptography (e.g., digital signatures) is secure and that honest parties protect their cryptographic secrets.

4   Combining Sealed Computation with an Auditor

One application of sealed computation in cloud computing would be for the CP to offer a mechanism to its "customers" DP and ASP to perform a sealed computation on the provided cloud hardware. In this case SCP and CP would be the same party. However, note that utilizing sealed computation alone is not sufficient to ensure the participants' security requirements because (1) sealed computation does not guarantee anything before sealing takes place, and (2) the mechanism of sealed computation cannot be trusted without means to verify its function. We will therefore treat CP and SCP as independent parties.

4.1   The Role of Auditor

The sealed computation is combined with the role of an auditing party AP to establish the security requirements described in Definition 2. In general, auditors are known to usually perform independent checks and assess other entities in terms of service, performance, security and data privacy and system operations [14]. We use the AP to both guarantee the functionality of the sealing mechanism provided by the SCP and to verify the functionality of the analytic software provided by the ASP. Once sealing has taken place, the mechanism of sealed computation ensures continued trust in the system without having to interact with the AP anymore.

The auditor is *not* allowed to add or modify functionality in the system. This is ensured by a mutual checking procedure described below. The AP, however, has to enable a possibility of attestation which is independent of the SCP. This can be realized by either providing an independent mechanism or (better) by adequately configuring an attestation technique that is already presented in the sealed computation technology (e.g., by embedding a secret within the physical container of sealed computing).

Figure 2 illustrates the structural model with the roles and responsibilities of each participant. The idea is to base the well-functioning of the system on the assumption that either the auditor or all parties checked by the auditor are honest during critical phases of system operation. While commonly the DP had to trust the CP exclusively, it now must rely on trust *either* in the SCP and ASP *or* the AP (a condition expressed in our global attacker assumption above).

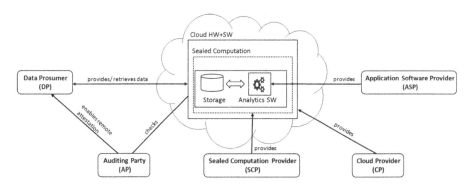

Fig. 2. Refined structural model with participants: the ASP provides software run within a sealed computation, a mechanism provided by the SCP and hosted by the CP. The AP performs an independent verification of the analytic software and the sealed computation container and enables mechanisms for the DP to remotely check its integrity.

To illustrate the different roles using our introductory UBI scenario, the policyholders and the insurance company share the role of the DP. The insurance company defines the functional specification of the driver ranking based on which the ASP develops the analytic software. The SCP could be a provider of the sealed computation container (like a HSM) and the AP would be a company like a certified public accountant, that is able to perform code and security audits on hard- and software. The SCP is assumed to have appropriate security mechanisms in place against attacks by parties not considered above (e.g., hackers and cybercriminals). Regarding remote attestation, the HSM provides certificates with which attestation evidence generated by the HSM can be verified [27].

4.2   Trust Establishment Procedure

For simplicity and comprehension of discussion we distinguish the execution lifetime of the system model into mutually exclusive phases: the *Checking* phase and *Running* phase. During the Checking phase, the trust establishment procedure takes place, while the Running phase begins with the service start-up. During the Running phase, the DP can upload data and get results and the CP operates the cloud system.

The exact actions and obligations of the participants and interplay among each other are described as trust establishment procedure below. This procedure can be regarded as a form of procedural requirement which in combination with the technical requirements of Sealed Computation allows to fulfill the user requirements.

Definition 3 (Trust Establishment Procedure with Mutual Checking). *The participants undergo the following procedure:*

1. *Trust establishment in analytics software:*
   (a) The ASP prepares the analytics software ready to be deployed.
   (b) The AP verifies whether the analytics software satisfies the functional specification and does not leak any information about the processed data.
   (c) At the same time, the ASP ensures that the AP does not change any functionality of the analytics software.
   (d) As a result of this procedure, ASP and AP generate public evidence to be produced by an attestation mechanism by which it can be verified that the checked version of the software is running in the sealed computation (e.g., a hash of the binary code that can be attested).
2. *Trust establishment in sealed computation mechanism:*
   (a) Before the sealed computation system is shipped and deployed, regardless of the deployment model, the SCP prepares the sealed computation mechanism (hardware and software, including the possibility for confidential software deployment).
   (b) The AP verifies (off-line) the integrity of the sealed computation mechanism, i.e., the entire hardware and software system. This includes a physical check for the security measures, policy compliance, data security and data privacy, functional check also of the confidential software deployment mechanism.

(c) At the same time, the SCP ensures that the AP is not adding new functionality during these checks, i.e., that the AP is behaving according to the auditing procedure specifications.

(d) The AP and the SCP generate public evidence that enables attestation of the sealed computation mechanism, e.g., by embedding independent private keys within the sealed computation container to which they possess the corresponding public keys.

3. The sealing mechanism is started in the presence of AP and SCP. At this time the auditing procedure ends and both SCP and AP can leave the deployment site which is run by the CP.

4. Using the confidential deployment procedure, the ASP loads the code that was checked by the AP in Step 1 above.

5. The AP and the SCP must be present any time when the system and/or the sealed computation mechanism is reset/restarted, is under maintenance or shall be changed. In such cases the AP and the SCP must re-check the system and both must re-enable the attestation mechanism as described in the above procedure.

The result of this procedure are two pieces of public evidence that all parties can use to verify their security requirements:

– Public evidence provided by AP and SCP that DP, CP and ASP can use to verify that an instance of sealed computation is running.
– Public evidence provided by AP and ASP that can be used to verify that a particular software is running within the sealed computation.

5   Security Analysis and Discussion

5.1   Security Analysis

To argue that the security requirements from Definition 2 are met, we make the following introductory observation: The sealed computation mechanism defined in Definition 1 will not be in the Running phase if the ASP software or the sealed computation mechanism is not correct.

To see this, we make a case distinction based on the global attacker assumption which states that all parties can act maliciously as long as the global attacker assumption is satisfied, i.e., either the AP or both the ASP and the SCP behave honestly. There are three possible cases for parties to act maliciously during the checking phase when the trust establishment procedure (Definition 3) takes place:

– The ASP is malicious: If the ASP is malicious, then the AP must be honest. So if the ASP acts maliciously and implements an incorrect software then the checking procedure (Step 1b) mandates that the AP checks the software correctness. Since the AP is honest, it will detect the incorrectness of software, the check will fail and the Running phase will not take place.

- The SCP is malicious: If the SCP is malicious, then the AP must be honest. So if the SCP is not honest, the sealing container may not be implemented correctly. However, the checking procedure (Step 2b) requires the AP to check whether the sealed computation requirements are met. Since the AP is honest, it will detect incorrectness and the Running phase will not be entered.
- The AP is malicious: If the AP is malicious, then the ASP *and* the SCP are both honest. In this case, the analytics software and the sealed computation mechanism are correct from the beginning. Furthermore, the mutual checking procedure (Steps 1c and 2c) requires that both ASP and SCP ensure that the AP does not manipulate the functionality of the analytics software or the sealed computation mechanism. So if the Running phase is entered, the sealed computation mechanism and the analytics software are both correct.

Therefore, under the attacker assumption, the establishment procedure guarantees that the system will not enter the Running phase unless it is working properly as defined in the specification.

Subsequently, during the Running phase, the sealed computation mechanism (Definition 1) takes over to guarantee the desired requirements. To argue for the fulfillment of ASP-Integrity and DP-Integrity, the Sealing and Tamper-resistance requirements of the sealed computation ensure that content (data and code) in the sealed container cannot be improperly modified. Furthermore, the Black-box requirement restricts information flow such that DP-Privacy and (assuming confidential deployment) ASP-Confidentiality are maintained.

5.2   Discussion

While our results are conceptual, they provide a preliminary guideline of building a trustworthy cloud computing service in which cloud customers can trust that cloud providers and operators cannot access their data and code. In essence, sealed computation may not be a brand new concept, as sealed storage was defined by Morris [20]. Whereas, to the best of our knowledge, sealed computation was not formally defined comprehensively before. Any computational implementation that satisfies the requirements defined in Definition 1 can be considered a sealed computation mechanism. However, in practice, one may argue that any assumption like the security of cryptography or requirements like Black-box of any hardware device only hold with a certain probability, so the guarantees in practice never hold with 100%. One may also argue that many parts of the procedures described in Definition 3 are also rather hypothetical and cannot be realized fully in practice. For example, the AP is assumed to *perfectly verify* the correctness of the software of the ASP (in Step 1b) against the functional specification. While software verification has come a long way, it still is restricted by the size and complexity of the software system. Another example that appears far from practice is the statement that the AP can verify the correctness of the sealed computation container (hardware and software) provided by the SCP (in Step 2b). It is well-known that the production of hardware is a very complex process involving lots of different technologies. The resulting chips are rather non-transparent and need complex validation equipment to be checked.

Useful insights can be inferred from the proposed approach. While the AP is one party in our model, in practice it can consist of multiple independent auditing actors, e.g., different companies that all check independent parts of the system and mutually certify the results towards each other. The collection of auditors in its entirety then forms the AP, meaning also that *all* "sub-auditors" must behave correctly for the AP to be regarded as honest. In practice, these sub-auditors are even often part of the same company, albeit in different parts that are independent of each others (like software development and testing departments).

Another highlight is, it *is* possible to delegate security enforcement to trusted hardware without having to trust a single entity. However, during the Checking phase, the AP must be *continuously present* until the sealed computation container runs, and it must be possible to establish attestation evidence which is *independently supported* by the AP and the SCP (for the sealed computation container) and by the AP and the ASP (for the analytics software). These points result from the requirement of mutual checking, i.e., not only does the AP verify the actions of ASP/SCP, but also ASP/SCP need to prevent the AP from slipping in new functionality to software and hardware, a detail which is often overlooked or (unconvincingly) excluded by the assumption that the AP is always honest. Being able to embed shared attestation credentials of mutually untrusted parties in a single trusted hardware container is a feature which is—at least to our knowledge—not supported by any currently available trusted computing mechanism [18].

So overall, the proposed approach presents an idealized version of system construction and deployment processes which can serve as an orientation for practice towards achieving a trustworthy service.

6   Related Work

Privacy is a major factor in trusting data and computation outsourcing, such as in a cloud-based application. Hence trust establishment has been discussed in the context of cloud from different perspectives in the literature, we distinguish them into technical and non-technical trust enhancement approaches. Georgiopoulou and Lambrinoudakis [13] reviewed a number of trust models for cloud computing trying to provide a gap analysis in the literature. However, the review considered only a very limited set of models.

Non-technical approaches have been developed and used ranging from SLAs and recommendations for security architecture, risk management and operational teams. For example, Alhanahnah et al. [3] studied a trust evaluation framework to allow cloud customers to choose among set of cloud providers based on trust levels. The authors distinguished trust factors into two sets: SLA-based and non-SLA factors based on the provider's reputation and even financial status.

Rizvi et al. [22] utilized the auditor role to provide an objective trust baseline assessment to enable clients to decide between CP candidates. The proposal delegates the trust assessment to an auditor to calculate trust values. So that clients who need to choose between CPs request the trust values from the auditor based on required service. The auditor role, we present, is not the same as the third party role in these works as shown in the trust establishment procedure 3.

Hence the common trust management model in the Web relies on the binding a domain name and a public key, is not enough for privacy in cloud computing. A number of solutions were presented to enforce trust via technical means that ensure the privacy of the users data. Santos et al. [23] employed attribute-base encryption to provide a policy enforcement protocol based on Trusted Platform Module (TPM) abstraction. Similarly, Li et al. [17] proposed a model to support security duty separation in multi-tenant IaaS cloud between CP and customers based on TPM and they added the auditor role optionally. Moreover, Ge and Ohoussou [11] proposed to build an architecture for IaaS model to give the clients trust to deploy their VMs, that provides sealed storage and relies on remote attestation.

These models [11, 17, 23] were designed for Platform as a Service (PaaS) and Infrastructure as a Service (IaaS) cloud models that require less security responsibilities on the CP [7] as they are shared with the customers, while SaaS model requires more responsibilities from CP [22].

A trustworthy and privacy-preserving cloud may be addressed by the use of cryptographic techniques such as fully homomorphic encryption (FHE) [12]. However, it is still inefficient for most computations [24]. Similarly in verifiable computing [21], it was designed to enable result correctness verification but has not shown support for general purpose cloud computing yet.

7   Conclusions and Future Work

We introduced the sealed computation concept and proposed a mutual checking procedure with an auditor role during setup time to provide an increased level of security and trust in cloud scenarios. The sealed computation concept abstracts from trusted hardware technologies like HSMs, the auditor is an abstraction of policies and procedures that increase trust in a single party.

We believe that the abstract system model using the auditor as an additional role is a good approach for medium-size and large cloud deployments instead of running their own private cloud. While the existence of the role of auditor may be intuitive, on the one hand, it is not clear whether the concept is really *necessary*, i.e., whether any technique that distributes trust can simulate the auditor as described above. On the other hand, practical methods for auditing could be investigated. Furthermore, we wish to attempt more rigid formalization for the attestation verification.

Acknowledgments. The authors would like to thank Nico Döttling, Johannes Götzfried, Tilo Müller and Hubert Jäger for hints and useful comments on earlier versions of this paper. This research is conducted under and supported by the "Privacy&Us" Innovative Training Network (EU H2020 MSCA ITN, grant agreement No. 675730).

References

1. Aazam, M., Khan, I., Alsaffar, A.A., Huh, E.N.: Cloud of things: integrating internet of things and cloud computing and the issues involved. In: 2014 11th International Bhurban Conference on Applied Sciences and Technology (IBCAST), pp. 414–419. IEEE (2014)
2. Alam, S., Chowdhury, M.M., Noll, J.: SenaaS: an event-driven sensor virtualization approach for Internet of Things cloud. In: 2010 IEEE International Conference on Networked Embedded Systems for Enterprise Applications (NESEA), pp. 1–6. IEEE (2010)
3. Alhanahnah, M., Bertok, P., Tari, Z.: Trusting cloud service providers: trust phases and a taxonomy of trust factors. IEEE Cloud Comput. **4**(1), 44–54 (2017)
4. Allianz Deutschland AG: Allianz BonusDrive User Guide (2017). https://www. allianz.de/docs/auto/BonusDrive-UserGuide.pdf. Accessed 28 Jan 2018
5. Allianz Press Release: (in German) Nicht alle jungen Fahrer sind Straßen-Rowdies (2017). https://www.allianzdeutschland.de/-nicht-alle-jungen-fahrer-sind-strassen-rowdies-/id_77853754/index. Accessed 28 Jan 2018
6. Baumann, A., Peinado, M., Hunt, G.: Shielding applications from an untrusted cloud with haven. In: 11th USENIX Symposium on Operating Systems Design and Implementation, OSDI 2014, Broomfield, CO, USA, October 6–8, pp. 267–283 (2014). https://www.usenix.org/conference/osdi14/technical-sessions/presentation/baumann
7. Cloud Security Alliance: Security Guidance for Critical Areas of Focus in Cloud Computing v3.0. Technical report Cloud Security Alliance (2011). https:// downloads.cloudsecurityalliance.org/assets/research/security-guidance/csaguide. v3.0.pdf
8. Coker, G., et al.: Principles of remote attestation. Int. J. Inf. Secur. **10**(2), 63–81 (2011). https://doi.org/10.1007/s10207-011-0124-7
9. Derikx, S., de Reuver, M., Kroesen, M.: Can privacy concerns for insurance of connected cars be compensated? Electron. Markets **26**(1), 73–81 (2016). https:// doi.org/10.1007/s12525-015-0211-0
10. Dyer, J.G., et al.: Building the IBM 4758 secure coprocessor. IEEE Comput. **34**(10), 57–66 (2001). https://doi.org/10.1109/2.955100
11. Ge, C., Ohoussou, A.K.: Sealed storage for trusted cloud computing. In: 2010 International Conference On Computer Design and Applications, vol. 5, pp. V5-335–V5-339, June 2010
12. Gentry, C.: Fully homomorphic encryption using ideal lattices. In: Proceedings of the 41st Annual ACM Symposium on Theory of Computing, STOC 2009, Bethesda, MD, USA, 31 May–2 June 2009, pp. 169–178 (2009). http://doi.acm.org/10.1145/ 1536414.1536440
13. Georgiopoulou, Z., Lambrinoudakis, C.: Literature review of trust models for cloud computing. In: 2016 15th International Symposium on Parallel and Distributed Computing (ISPDC), pp. 208–213, July 2016
14. Habib Mahbub, S., Hauke, S., Ries, S., Mühlhäuser, M.: Trust as a facilitator in cloud computing: a survey. J. Cloud Comput. **1**, 19 (2012). https://doi.org/10. 1186/2192-113X-1-19
15. HUK-Coburg: (in German) Mit Sicherheit fahren und sparen. Unser Smart Driver Programm für junge Fahrer (2017). https://www.huk.de/fahrzeuge/kfz-versicherung/smart-driver.html. Accessed 28 Jan 2018

16. Karapiperis, D., et al.: Usage-based insurance and vehicle telematics: insurance market and regulatory implications. Technical report 1, National Association of Insurance Commisioners (NAIC), CIPR Study Series (2015)
17. Li, X.Y., Zhou, L.T., Shi, Y., Guo, Y.: A trusted computing environment model in cloud architecture. In: 2010 International Conference on Machine Learning and Cybernetics, vol. 6, pp. 2843–2848, July 2010
18. Maene, P., Götzfried, J., de Clercq, R., Müller, T., Freiling, F., Verbauwhede, I.: Hardware-based trusted computing architectures for isolation and attestation. IEEE Trans. Comput. **99**, 1–1 (2017). https://doi.org/10.1109/TC.2017.2647955
19. Mell, P., Grance, T.: Effectively and securely using the cloud computing paradigm. NIST Inf. Technol. Lab. **2**(8), 304–311 (2009)
20. Morris Jr., J.H.: Protection in programming languages. Commun. ACM **16**(1), 15–21 (1973). https://doi.org/10.1145/361932.361937
21. Parno, B., Howell, J., Gentry, C., Raykova, M.: Pinocchio: nearly practical verifiable computation. In: 2013 IEEE Symposium on Security and Privacy, SP 2013, Berkeley, CA, USA, 19 May–22 May 2013, pp. 238–252 (2013). https://doi.org/10.1109/SP.2013.47
22. Rizvi, S., Ryoo, J., Liu, Y., Zazworsky, D., Cappeta, A.: A centralized trust model approach for cloud computing. In: 2014 23rd Wireless and Optical Communication Conference (WOCC), pp. 1–6, May 2014
23. Santos, N., Rodrigues, R., Gummadi, K.P., Saroiu, S.: Policy-sealed data: a new abstraction for building trusted cloud services. In: Presented as part of the 21st USENIX Security Symposium (USENIX Security 12), pp. 175–188. USENIX, Bellevue, WA (2012). https://www.usenix.org/conference/usenixsecurity12/technical-sessions/presentation/santos
24. Schuster, F., et al.: VC3: trustworthy data analytics in the cloud using SGX. In: 2015 IEEE Symposium on Security and Privacy, SP 2015, San Jose, CA, USA, 17 May–21 May 2015, pp. 38–54 (2015). https://doi.org/10.1109/SP.2015.10
25. Soleymanian, M., Weinberg, C., Zhu, T.: Sensor data, privacy, and behavioral tracking: does usage-based auto insurance benefit drivers? Technical report, Sauder School of Business (University of British Columbia) & Krannert School of Management (Purdue University) (2017). https://news.ubc.ca/wp-content/uploads/2017/06/UBI_Paper_Latex_Marketing_Science-with-name.pdf
26. Utimaco IS GmbH: Hardware Security Modules (HSMs) are the core business focus for Utimaco (2018). https://hsm.utimaco.com/products/. Accessed 10 Jan 2018
27. Wagner, S., Krauß, C., Eckert, C.: Lightweight attestation and secure code update for multiple separated microkernel tasks. In: Proceedings of 16th International Conference on Information Security, ISC 2013, Dallas, Texas, USA, 13–15 November 2013, pp. 20–36 (2013). https://doi.org/10.1007/978-3-319-27659-5_2

Understanding Challenges to Adoption of the Protection Poker Software Security Game

Inger Anne Tøndel[1,2]([✉]), Martin Gilje Jaatun[2], Daniela Cruzes[2],
and Tosin Daniel Oyetoyan[2]

[1] Department of Computer Science,
Norwegian University of Science and Technology (NTNU),
7491 Trondheim, Norway
inger.anne.tondel@ntnu.no
[2] Department of Software Engineering, Safety and Security, SINTEF Digital,
7465 Trondheim, Norway

Abstract. Currently, security requirements are often neglected in agile projects. Despite many approaches to agile security requirements engineering in literature, there is little empirical research available on why there is limited adoption of these techniques. In this paper we describe a case study on challenges facing adoption of the Protection Poker game; a collaborative and lightweight software security risk estimation technique that is particularly suited for agile teams. Results show that Protection Poker has the potential to be adopted by agile teams. Key benefits identified include good discussions on security and the development project, increased knowledge and awareness of security, and contributions to security requirements. Challenges include managing discussions and the time it takes to play, ensuring confidence in the results from playing the game, and integrating results in a way that improves security of the end-product.

1 Introduction

Current software development is increasingly based on agile methods. Agile software development aims to reduce development time and prioritise value through an iterative approach to development [6]. Agile methods claim to be risk driven [3] and risk management can be said to be treated implicitly in agile development projects [18,25], e.g. through prioritising tasks in the beginning of the iteration.

Security risk is one type of risk that software products face today. Literature reviews on software security in agile development have found that security requirements are often neglected in agile projects [15,19]. Though several approaches to agile security requirements engineering have been suggested in literature, there has been little empirical work done on evaluating how these security requirements approaches work in real life settings [26]. Studies have

© Springer Nature Switzerland AG 2019
S. K. Katsikas et al. (Eds.): CyberICPS 2018/SECPRE 2018, LNCS 11387, pp. 153–172, 2019.
https://doi.org/10.1007/978-3-030-12786-2_10

however identified security benefits that can be traced back to using an incremental risk analysis approach [2]. Thus, it is important to understand better how agile teams can be supported in analysing software security risks and requirements in an ongoing manner.

This paper presents a study of Protection Poker [32,33] in a capstone development project with six development groups. Protection Poker is based on Planning Poker [10], and is a security risk estimation technique for agile development teams. It is intended to be played as part of every iteration planning meeting, in order to rank the security risk of each feature to be implemented in that iteration, and possibly identify additional security mechanisms that have to be implemented to maintain an acceptable risk level. The full team together identifies assets related to the features and uses the Protection Poker game to rank the features according to their security risk; assessing the value of their assets and the ease of attack.

Protection Poker has been evaluated previously in industry with positive evaluation results [33], however that study did not focus on adoption, but rather on awareness and knowledge raising through using the technique. Furthermore, despite positive evaluation results, the team that was studied stopped using Protection Poker sometime after the study was completed.

Motivated by a need to understand why Protection Poker or similar techniques have not yet gained widespread adoption in industry, the goal of the study presented in this paper was to assess to what extent the Protection Poker game would be accepted as a technique in agile teams, and if possible to determine obstacles to adoption of the game. Our investigation was centered on the following research questions:

RQ1: To what extent is Protection Poker accepted by the players, both short-term and longer term?

RQ2: What lessons learned and improvements are identified by the players?

The rest of this paper is structured as follows: In Sect. 2 we provide an overview of related work on security requirements engineering in agile development, to position Protection Poker related to other approaches in this research area and further motivate why Protection Poker was selected for study. In Sect. 3 we describe the research method used for the study that we conducted, as well as details on the version of Protection Poker used in this particular study. We present the results in Sect. 4, and discuss in Sect. 5. We conclude the paper in Sect. 6.

2   Security Requirements in Agile Software Development

Existing approaches to security requirements in agile software development are by and large in line with findings in a review of lightweight approaches to security requirements engineering [27], that points to three important and commonly recommended activities: identifying security objectives, identifying assets, and analysing threats to the system. To illustrate, Peeters [20] introduced abuser stories by extending the concept *user stories* that is commonly used in agile practices. Boström [4] suggested an approach to introduce security requirements engineering into XP. The approach includes identifying critical assets, formulating abuser stories and assessing their risk, and defining security-related user stories and coding standards. Vähä-Sipilä [29] explained how security requirements can be described as security-related user stories or as attacker stories (abuse cases). Then, in development, security is added to the sprint's Definition of Done, by introducing a security threat analysis into the sprints and by flagging potentially risky tasks. Savola et al. [23] explained that security requirements are translated into negative user stories and into non-functional requirements. Nicolaysen et al. [17] suggest that security threats are identified related to functional requirements that is to be implemented, and that after the risk has been calculated at least one misuse story is created. Pohl and Hof [21] suggest the Secure Scrum approach that includes four components; identification, implementation, verification and definition of done. The identification component consists of two steps; (1) ranking user stories according to their loss value, and (2) evaluating misuse cases and ranking them by their risk. Specific tags and marks are used to link the security issues identified to the user stories in the backlog, and the approach specifies how to use these tags and marks in the development. Renatus et al. [22] suggest to split the task of security requirements into two steps performed by different roles; the security curator and developers. This allows for security curators that do not have in-depth technical expertise on the product that is developed and for developers without in-depths security expertise. The security curator's task is then to pre-model features that is to be implemented, identifying affected parts of the system and performing initial threat modeling. The developer then, during the sprints, *"figures out the details and implements the controls"* [22].

Though some of the above mentioned approaches stem from industry settings [20, 23, 29] or have been tried out in real development projects, the current evidence on how these approaches work in practice is limited. The approach of Renatus et al., which was broader than what is presented above on requirements engineering, was evaluated in one SME [22], however the research method used is not described in detail. The approach suggested by Pohl and Hof was evaluated in small student projects lasting only one week [21]. The approach suggested by Boström has been used in one student thesis project [4]. Thus, there is a need for empirical research that can shed light on how agile security requirements approaches work in practice, and what can be done to improve them and increase their adoption by agile development teams.

As already stated in the introduction, security requirements are often neglected in agile projects [15, 19]. A study of practitioners' posts on LinkedIn [26] shed some light on why this is the case: *"People do care about security, but do not think about it"*, *"Security requirements are often poorly defined and owned"*, *"Security requirements get often delivered in the last minute"* and *"Agile techniques are vulnerable for forgetting things like security."* These problematic aspects point to the need for concrete ways to introduce security into an agile project so that security is not forgotten, but rather considered throughout. Any approaches however need to consider the general lifecycle challenges related to security identified in the review by Oueslati et al. [19]: *"Security related activities need to be applied for each development iteration"* and *"Iteration time is limited and may not fit time consuming security activities"*.

Weir et al. [31] identified, based on interviews with 14 specialists, what they consider the three most cost-effective and scalable security interventions in software development. These were all *"cultural interventions"* that influence the work of the teams rather than the artefacts produced; (1) *"developing a 'threat model'"*, (2) having *"a motivational workshop engaging the team in genuine security problems"*, and (3) having continuing *"'nudges' to the developers to remind them of the importance of security."* Of the security requirements approaches introduced above, all can be said to develop a threat model of some sort. The security requirements can work as 'nudges' that remind developers of security. Protection Poker is however the technique that most clearly engages the whole team in discussing security problems, and does so in a way that is concrete and (hopefully) fun. Additionally, it is specifically designed to be applied for each development iteration, addressing the challenge identified by Oueslati et al. [19]. Though Protection Poker is not a full blown security requirement approach, but rather includes parts of the activities commonly used for requirements engineering, resulting in a ranking of features rather than specific security requirements, we believe that a study of Protection Poker with its focus on assets and ease of attack has the potential to be of use for researchers working on other agile security requirement techniques as well; identifying challenges and lessons learned that can be used to improve approaches in this research domain.

3   Research Method

This section describes the research method used for the case study. Additionally, it describes in detail the version of Protection Poker used for this study as well as the motivation for the adjustments of the original technique [33].

3.1   Case Study Method

The research method in this case study is the same as that of a parallel study[1] [28], thus the text below that describes the method is similar in these two studies.

Regarding the *case context*, the study was performed in the *Customer Driven Project* course (TDT4290) at the Norwegian University for Science and Technology (NTNU), autumn 2016. This course is mandatory for 4th year computer science students. In this course, the students are divided into development

---

[1] In addition to Protection Poker, one other technique (Microsoft EoP) was studied in the course. Groups were assigned to use either Protection Poker or EoP by two researchers in cooperation based on name of the project and name of the customer. In deciding which group should use which technique, the researchers aimed for a balance in size and type of customer and in the type of systems developed so that both games had a mixture of different project types.

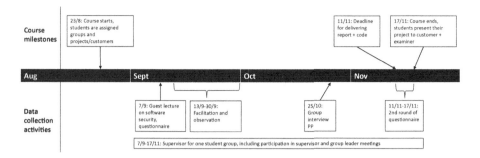

Fig. 1. Overview of data collection activities

teams (5–8 students per team). Every team is given a development project from an external customer (i.e. private companies, public organisations or research institutes). The students are expected to investigate the needs of the customer, develop software, do some testing of this software and document everything in a report and a presentation given to the customer. In general, all student groups use agile methodologies to some extent. Six groups, consisting of 34 students in total, were required to use Protection Poker for their project. This was the first year software security was included as part of the course.

An overview of data collection activities can be found in Fig. 1. As most students had received limited formal training on software security before this course[2], we arranged a lecture where all students were given a short plenary introduction to software security and the Protection Poker game. They played the game on an example project, and responded to a questionnaire that covered the students' acceptance of the technique. Data collection proceeded through facilitation and observations of students playing Protection Poker in their group, and the observations were followed by group interviews towards the end of the course, allowing detailed student feedback on the technique. Additionally, the main author of this paper acted as supervisor for one of the student groups and took part in project leader and supervisor meetings throughout the course. The questionnaire on acceptance was repeated towards the end of the course. The study has been reported to the national Data Protection Official for research. In the following we explain the data collection methods in more detail; the questionnaire, the observations and the group interviews.

The main motivation for using a *questionnaire* was to capture students' immediate and longer term acceptance of the Protection Poker technique (RQ1). A questionnaire could easily reach a large number of the students, and could easily be repeated. We decided to base the questionnaire on the Technology Acceptance Model (TAM) for two reasons. First, TAM, although being criticized [16], is considered a highly influential and commonly employed theory for describing an individual's acceptance of information systems. TAM, adapted from the The-

---

[2] No mandatory training in security, except security being a minor part of some courses that mainly covered other topics.

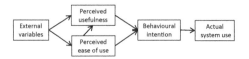

Fig. 2. TAM [30]

ory of Reasoned Action [1] and originally proposed by Davis [7], suggests that
when users are presented with a new technology, a number of factors influence
their decision about how and when they will use it (see Fig. 2), notably:

- *Perceived usefulness:* this was defined by Davis as *"the degree to which a
  person believes that using a particular system would enhance his or her job
  performance"* [8]
- *Perceived ease of use:* Davis defined this as *"the degree to which a person
  believes that using a particular system would be free from effort"* [8].
- *External variables:* include *"system characteristics, training, user involvement
  in design, and the nature of the implementation process"* [30].

Thus, we believed TAM could help us understand the different reasons for acceptance of Protection Poker by the students, and that TAM-based questions could
trigger comments from the students related to acceptance. Second, we were able
to adapt questions from an existing questionnaire [9] to the phenomena we are
studying (the questions used are shown in Fig. 5).

For the *observations*, we created a rota where one of the authors served
as facilitator, and at least one other author participated as observer. After each
observation session, both the facilitator and the observer filled in reflection notes
in a template that contained the following topics: group information; questions
from the students on the technique; suggested changes to the game; participation;
mood; topics discussed; what worked well with the game; challenges with the
game, and; reflections on the observation and how the researchers may have
influenced the process. After playing one session of Protection Poker, all groups
were encouraged to keep on playing by themselves during the project, and we
offered to return and offer support and/or facilitation at a later time, according
to their needs.

Towards the end of the course, all groups were invited to send two to three
participants to an event where the technique would be discussed in more detail.
This event was organised as a *group interview* and was scheduled to last for two
hours. The following topics were covered: students' expectations to the event;
use of the game in the group; brainstorming and discussion on the 4Ls (Liked,
Lacked, Learned, Longed for) [5]; suggestions for improvements to the technique; suggestions for improvements to how software security was handled in the
course, and; feedback on the event. Discussions were recorded and transcribed.
To encourage participation, all participants were served pizza and they had the
opportunity to win cinema gift cards. Non-responding groups were reminded via
email. To promote active participation in the group interviews, each event was
split in two parallel sessions.

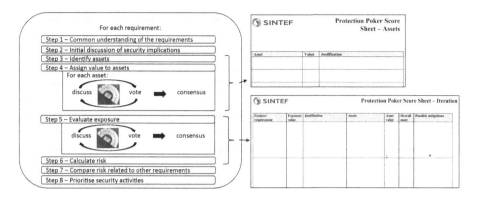

Fig. 3. Playing Protection Poker

3.2   Protection Poker as Used in This Study

The version of Protection Poker used in this study is a variation of the original Protection Poker game [33]. In this section we explain how Protection Poker is played, and the rationale for the modifications made to the game. In addition, we explain what a typical session looked like in this study. A similar but more detailed description of Protection Poker can be found in a previous publication [14]. Playing cards and score sheets to be used during playing are available online[3].

How to Play. Protection Poker is played during an iteration planning meeting, and it is recommended that the full development team participates. One person should have the role as moderator, and this person will be responsible for leading the team through the game, and point the discussions in a good direction. Ideally, a separate person should be tasked with taking notes on important security solutions and ideas that emerge during play. Focus is on the specific requirements the team will likely implement during the next iteration. A basic overview of the steps involved in playing Protection Poker can be found in Fig. 3. The actual playing using the Protection Poker cards is done in steps 4 and 5. Players use the cards to make votes on the risk involved in the requirement they are playing on, and the votes are a basis for further discussions on the risk, and eventually agreeing on a risk value for the requirement. This may require several rounds of voting by using the Protection Poker cards. Below we explain two central concepts of the game, namely risk calculation and calibration.

Protection Poker uses a slight variation of the traditional computation of risk:

$$risk = \left(\sum \text{asset values}\right) \times (\text{the exposure}) \tag{1}$$

---

[3] https://www.sintef.no/protection-poker.

Risk is always related to a requirements that is to be implemented in the next iteration, often this will be some new, enhanced or corrected functionality. *Exposure* relates to how hard or easy the added or changed functionality makes it to attack the system. For *asset value*, one identifies the assets that are related to a requirement and considers their value for various actor types. Assets are typically considered to be *"data stored in database tables or system processes that the new functionality controls"* [33], however in this study we did not use a strict definition of the term asset. In previous work [13], we have defined assets as *"anything of value that needs to be protected"*.

To be able to prioritise between different requirements, it is important to be able to get a spread in the numbers assigned. Thus the highest card (100) should be used for asset values and exposures that are high for this project, and similarly the lowest card (<10) should be given to asset values and exposures that are low for this project. This is to avoid that, e.g., high risk projects rate every requirement with a high number. That would make it very hard to prioritize within the project. As the goal is not to establish a "perfect" and "universal" risk value, but rather to rate the security risk of the requirements in order to be able to better prioritize security effort, it is recommended to perform *calibration* in the beginning in order to arrive at a common understanding of the end-points of the scale, i.e., the team agrees what a <10 or a 100 means for this product. When playing about asset value and exposure, numbers should be assigned relative to these endpoints, as well as the values assigned for previously assessed assets and features.

Modifications. The changes made [14] to the original Protection Poker technique came from initial experiences with playing the game in two EU funded research projects in spring 2015. In the first trial, two of the authors played the game together with one colleague on an incident management tool for cloud service providers that was under development, while another author took part as observer. In the second trial, the technique was tried out in a research project that developed a health app. Four researchers from the project played the game on their project, and two of the authors took part as facilitator and observer. The adjustments made concern two main aspects: terminology and the scale used. On terminology, whereas the original Protection Poker version uses the term "ease of exploitation", we found that this concept was distracting or not properly understood by some pilot players, e.g., leading them to focus too much on threats such as "shoulder surfing" that are easy to perform. In order to focus more on how a feature increases the attack surface of an application, we decided to change it to "exposure". Regarding the scale, the original Protection Poker version uses the same cards as Planning Poker [10], used for effort estimation in agile teams. Planning Poker cards follow a Fibonacci-like sequence, after the rationale that it is easier to have an opinion on whether a task takes 1 or 2 days than whether it takes 40 or 41 days. We argue, however that the same is not true when it comes to relative value of assets or degree of exposure, and since we are less concerned about small risks and more interested in the bigger risks, we opted for a uniform scale instead. This enables us to differentiate between big risks, not just the small ones. Thus, we used Protection Poker cards with the following numbers to determine asset value or system exposure: <10, 20, 30, 40, 50, 60, 70, 80, 90, 100.

What Was a Typical Session Like? When we facilitated the students in playing the Protection Poker game in this study, we covered steps 1–6 in Fig. 3 in addition to calibration. The Protection Poker sessions lasted between 50 and 70 min. The session started by having the students explain their system to the facilitator. Then the facilitator led the students to start identifying assets and calibrate assets. We prioritised calibrating the top end of the scale. The groups played on two to three assets, and spent between one and 17 min per asset played. For most (10 of 14) of the assets, the students were able to agree on a value with two rounds of playing the cards.

Features were identified and calibrated in the same way as assets, however calibration of features was skipped in three of the groups due to limited time left. We prioritised playing about features above identifying and calibrating features. One group did not play on any features, because the nature of their project (creation of an algorithm) made it difficult to come up with features. The other five groups played on one to three features. The students spent between two and nine minutes per feature played. For all but one feature, it was necessary to play two rounds.

Throughout, the facilitator was active in helping the group reach a consensus by suggesting compromise values. This was done to speed up the playing, terminating discussions when it seemed most arguments had been raised. The session ended with reflection about the experience, and the students were asked to provide feedback and suggest improvements.

4   Results

This section presents the results according to the two research questions of the case study. In addition, Table 1 gives an overview of the *observer notes* related to what worked well and what was challenging, and Fig. 4 gives an overview of the students' feedback in the group interviews. In the observations we found that only two of the four groups had obvious security concerns. The group interviews, however, had low participation from those groups; only one participant from only one of those groups, while all the groups with limited security concerns participated with 2–3 people.

4.1   Acceptance of Protection Poker

Acceptance of Protection Poker (RQ1) was mainly studied through the TAM-based questionnaire in the beginning and the end of the course. In this section we provide an overview of the questionnaire responses and explain how observations and group interview responses add to the findings from the questionnaire.

Table 1. Observation notes - count shows for how many groups an aspect was noted by the observer/facilitator.

Issue	Worked well	Challenge
Calibration	• Easy to find the top asset/feature (5) • Calibration resulted in involvement and good discussions (2) • Managed to use the full scale although calibration was not done/only done for highest value (2)	• Did not calibrate the bottom end of the scale (4) • Calibration was skipped for features (3) • Lack of calibration made the scale unclear and this impacted discussion negatively (3) • Few assets or features to calibrate (2) • Took time (1) • Facilitator influence a lot - propose and they agree (1)
Identify features	• Easy to identify features (4)	• Different understanding of features (2) • Few features in the system (2) • Difficult to identify features (1)
Identify assets	• Easy to identify assets (4)	• Some types of assets are difficult (e.g. access rights, reputation, libraries)(4) • Few assets in the system (3) • Confidentiality vs. integrity vs. availability of assets (2)
Discuss and vote on asset value	• Led to good discussions (4)	• Asset value get mixed with exposure (2) • Difficult to relate to and use the whole scale (2)
Discuss and vote on exposure	• Worked well in the group (3) • Clarification, led to common understanding of features (1)	• Exposure and asset value gets mixed up (5) • The term exposure is difficult to explain and understand (2) • Few features (1) • Limited time (1)
Calculate risk level	• Worked well in the group (4) • Triggered security discussions (2) • The score sheet helped progress by making students aware of next asset/feature to discuss (1)	• Questions on how to fill it out (3) • Assets at different levels may lead to skewed risk values (1) • Many scores to assign before calculating the first feature (1) • One feature without an asset (1) • Limited time (1)
Facilitation	• Facilitation ensured progress in the playing (2) • Easy to achieve consensus (2)	• Some participants posed a challenge for the facilitator (3)
Keep track of important parts of the discussion	• The score sheet included a column for "justification" and this triggered students to put something there (3) • Students took additional notes in note books (2)	• Scores are included on score sheet, but important aspects from the discussion are lost (3)

LIKED	LACKED
• Easy to learn and understand results (6) • Good discussions, teamwork (5) • Overview of project, assets, and help to prioritise (4) • New perspectives – the bigger picture (4) • Helped us think about security (3) • Fun to play (3) • Group found new solutions (1) • Independent evaluation in the first round (1) • Relative to the project (1)	• Scale can be improved (4) • Hard to agree (3) • Takes long time (2) • Intuitiveness (1) • Unsure which card to play (1) • Guide of common concerns (1) • Depth (1) • Convincing (1)
LEARNED	**LONGED FOR**
• Make decisions, agree, prioritise (3) • Value of different opinions (3) • Security terms (exposure, asset, attack surface) (3) • What assets we have (2) • Easy to overlook software security risks (1) • How a future version might look like (1) • All is relative (1)	• Improved guides, more help (4) • Project more relevant for security, or different version of the game for projects without many security issues (3)

Fig. 4. Result of 4L brainstorming on Protection Poker

Figure 5 gives an overview of the questionnaire results on the TAM-variables *future use intention, perceived usefulness* and *perceived ease of use*. The results marked *before* refer to responses at the end of the introductory lecture (29 responses), and the results marked *after* refer to responses at the end of the course (30 responses).

Four questions together cover the variable *future use intention*. Though slightly declining throughout the course, the students tend towards being positive to use Protection Poker. One obvious reason for the decline in future use intention, especially concerning questions 1 and 2 where the biggest decline is observed, is the requirement to use Protection Poker in the course, something that will not be the case for any future projects the students encounter. In the end, half (15) of the students agree that they would like to use Protection Poker in the future, while only 5 respond not wanting to use Protection Poker (question 4).

Four questions together cover the variable *perceived usefulness*. In general the students seem to have found Protection Poker to be useful; in the end more students agree (14) than disagree (4) that the advantages of using Protection Poker outweigh the disadvantages (question 8). Expectations on what Protection Poker would deliver was in general high, however, it seems that it did not quite deliver in their current project (question 5). In particular, Protection Poker does not seem to have delivered on security; not improving the security of the product (questions 6) and not reducing security defects (question 7). The open-ended responses on the questionnaire shed some light on these responses. Though students did expect Protection Poker to have benefits, they were divided in their expectations. Ten out of the 28 that responded to the open ended question *"How do you think playing PP will influence the product?"* stated that they did not expect much influence. Of those that did expect an influence, the majority (11) expected it to improve security awareness. Other expectations included identifying the most important parts regarding security (4), a more secure product (3), discussions on security (2) and agreement on security issues in the group (2).

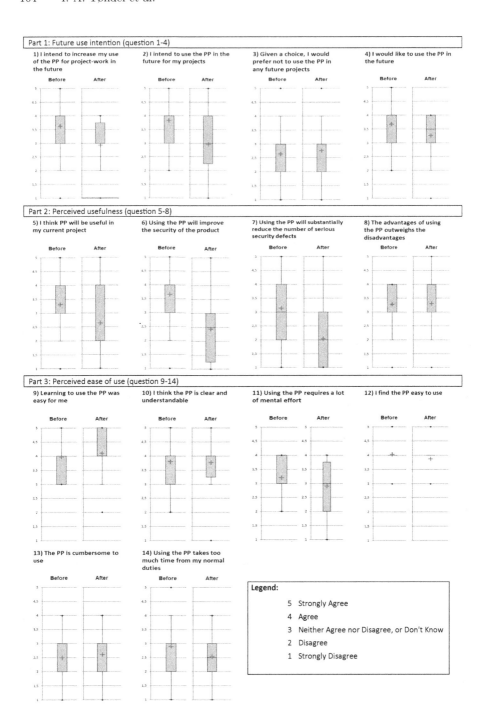

Fig. 5. Result from TAM-based questionnaire

Those that explained why they did not expect an impact from playing the game, explained that this was due to limited security issues in their project. Open ended responses to the question *"How do you believe software security is important to your project?"* confirmed our observations that only two of the six groups had clear security issues that needed to be dealt with, while four groups had very limited attack surfaces or assets of little value, thus having limited security needs. Since it is likely that the limited security needs of projects influenced the usefulness of the technique when it comes to security, we additionally looked at the responses from the two groups that had security issues (10 responses) in isolation. We found that for question 6, all five students that agree that using Protection Poker improved security come from these two groups. When it comes to reduction of security defects (question 7), the students from the groups with security issues are more positive than the others, however, also these students in general do not agree that they experienced such a reduction from playing Protection Poker.

Despite limited need for security, the questionnaire responses indicate that students ended up being quite positive still regarding the usefulness of the game. Positive aspects of the game were discussed in the group interviews, and these can shed some light on what the students found useful. Overall, the students were positive to security and see the need for it in the general case. They explained that they learned many things from playing (see Fig. 4). This included knowledge about security (assets; attack surface; easy to overlook security issues). However, other more general insights were more often pointed out, such as gaining experience in group discussions, making decisions, coming to consensus etc., and that they learned things about their own software projects and how it was understood by other group members.

Six questions together cover the variable *perceived ease of use*. Overall the responses to these questions are positive, and increasingly so towards the end of the course. To illustrate, in the end only one student found Protection Poker to be difficult to learn (question 9), as opposed to 25 finding it easy, and the majority of the students ended up finding Protection Poker to be clear and understandable (question 10, 22 students) and easy to use (question 12, 23 students). The observations and group interviews support these results on perceived ease of use. As can be seen from Table 1, many aspects of the game were observed to be easy to do in most groups. Students in the group interviews responded that the game was easy to learn and that it was easy to understand the results (see Fig. 4). Still, the students we interviewed longed for more help and improved guides to support their playing of the game. Thus, some aspects of the game were still hard. This will be covered in more detail in the following subsection.

4.2   Lessons Learned and Improvements

Lessons learned and improvements (RQ2) were studied through observations and group interviews. We identified two main areas where improvements are needed; the discussions, and the scores and scale used.

Discussions and Speed. Many of the students in the group interviews responded that they liked the discussions they had while playing Protection Poker, and found them useful (see Fig. 4), e.g., that it made everybody participate, and uncovered differences in opinions and understandings of the system. However, discussions proved to be challenging as well, leading to students in the group interviews expressing concerns that: (1) some players end up with too much influence due to their personality; (2) difficulties in reaching consensus results in fighting instead of a common understanding; and (3) it may take a while.

A few students expressed the concern that, when they were not able to agree, this could cause problems later on. In the sessions where we facilitated them when playing Protection Poker, the facilitator was quite active in supporting the students in reaching a consensus. In the group interviews, students stated that they appreciated that the facilitator did this. However, the one group that had played Protection Poker on their own after the session we facilitated explained the following: *"We noticed that when we played the second time (...) we realised that we had to evaluate some things again, because that had either been cut off, because we had some issues where we did not agree and had to stop the discussion."* Students additionally expressed the concern that, although they spent a lot of time discussing, they lacked confidence that they arrived at the "right" result, and were unsure how long their result was valid.

A main difference between student responses in the group interviews and the observation results is that where students were mainly concerned with conflicts and the influence of people with strong personalities, the observation notes additionally contain a concern regarding passive participants. Though Protection Poker requires everybody to participate by putting out cards, this does not require all students to be active in the discussions. Especially in one group, it was very hard to get the discussion going (*"a bit like pulling teeth"* (quote from observation notes)). This group was characterised by both dominating and passive members. The passive member seemed disinterested, did things on the computer while playing, and did not offer input to the discussion although specifically asked by the facilitator about the reasoning behind the card (justification generally referred to as "gut feeling"). From observation notes, half of the groups (3) were characterised either by dominant or passive participants, something that negatively influenced the general mood while playing.

Students did not have any clear suggestions for improvements that directly address the challenges of having both good discussions and ensure the playing of Protection Poker does not takes up too much time. However, one suggestion that addresses this challenge partially is to have fewer cards, and thus a more coarse-grained scale. In addition, students wanted more support on the security, in form of what to discuss and how to ensure they were on the right track. Both the response from the students after the sessions and our own observations suggest that it would have been very difficult for the students to start using Protection Poker without an external facilitator that could help on the game and bring in software security competence. The group interview feedback on need for support included guides, e.g. on finding assets, how to prepare for the session, and examples of what can happen, and ways to ensure the presence of security expertise. Though the need for an external facilitator was clearly expressed by the students, it is important to add that the group that had tried out the Protection Poker technique on their own after the supported session reported that this had gone very well, and in some ways better since they did not have to explain the system to someone external.

Scales and Scores. Both in the observations and the group interviews we identified challenges relating to the scale used. These challenges were of two main types: understanding the relative scale, and understanding the concepts asset value and exposure.

In the group interview, one student expressed that he liked the relative scale as it made it possible to get a prioritisation for the project despite security not being that relevant for them. However, a general feedback from the students in the group interview was that the relative scale was difficult to understand; *"You did not know if a '100' was Armageddon or it was just "we need to look into this".* " When we did observations, the relativity of the scale only seemed to be a major problem in one of the groups. There one student viewed one of the assets (the one we had calibrated as a '100') as so much more important than anything else and thus had the opinion that every other asset would belong in the '<10' category. Thus, the student wanted an exponential scale. Due to time issues, we had decided to skip calibration of the lower end-point of the scale ('<10'), something that may have contributed to their challenges in relating to the scale.

For assets it was sometimes difficult to know how to assess their value, as the value may be different if you consider just confidentiality than if you include other aspects of its value as well. Another challenge is related to how to divide up assets in a way that is consistent and does not impact the scores in a negative way. Students in one group pointed out that if you have assets at different levels of granularity this may skew the scores. One feature with many assets of low granularity may get a higher score, and thus priority, than a feature that has assets with a higher granularity. In the observations, questions on assets and on exposure were common, and these terms were often mixed up in the discussions (e.g. "the exposure of the asset" and "the value of the feature"). Especially the term exposure was found difficult to describe in a good way. Still, students expressed that they found the end result was easy to interpret, that it was predictable due to the process and that it gave them a nice way to prioritise the assets of the project (group interviews, see Fig. 4).

The improvements suggested by students when it comes to the scale goes in two directions: to explain the relativity of the scale better, or to change the scale. The latter suggestion was less common. Additionally, students suggested to take the time to do a full calibration, even though playing Protection Poker without doing a full calibration worked well in many of the groups (see Table 1). Assets were suggested identified in advance, in addition to providing better guidance on this aspect. The challenges related to the term exposure were more an observation than a feedback from the students, and thus students did not suggest any improvements in that respect.

5 Discussion

In the following we discuss the implications of the results of this case study when it comes to adoption of Protection Poker and its effect on the security of the software. Finally, threats to validity are identified and discussed.

5.1 Adoption of Protection Poker and Gaining Impact from Playing

The results of this study show that Protection Poker as a technique has the potential to be adopted by developers. Many of the students would like to continue using the technique, despite its limited usefulness for security in their current project. Students expressed the wish for projects with more security, or a technique that better fit their project, e.g. stating *"now it felt like we took a game that was not meant for our project and tried to play it with our project, even though it didn't fit,"* and *"I think it is a good game, I think it works fine, but I don't think I got that much out of it as I could have, and I could have learned more about the different parts of Protection Poker and software security if I had a game or a project with more security issues."* Based on this, we could state that Protection Poker is not that useful for projects with very limited security issues, either because of very limited attack surface or few assets of any particular value. This type of projects is probably not as prominent in development companies as in our case with student projects. Still, our results point to the need for some kind of criteria to evaluate whether there is enough security issues in a project to justify the effort needed to play Protection Poker.

If adopting Protection Poker, there is the issue of how often Protection Poker should be played in a project. In this study, playing Protection Poker did take quite a lot of time and unless there are important security issues for many of the project's features, the effort needed to play Protection Poker for every iteration may not be justified. Many of the main benefits from the technique as identified in this study, such as new perspectives, increased security awareness, teamwork, etc., is not dependent on playing Protection Poker for every feature.

Identifying and prioritising assets was something that the students in general found useful, however there were challenges associated with doing this as part of playing Protection Poker: it took time and there was the concern that if this was not done at a similar granularity for the whole project this might skew the prioritisation one ended up making through the game. It is an open question whether identification of assets could benefit from being an activity that is decoupled from the actual playing of Protection Poker. It is possible that if asset identification is done beforehand for the project as a whole, this may speed up the playing - especially in the beginning - and help increase confidence in the results. An asset identification task may additionally be useful input to a decision on whether or not Protection Poker is a game that would suit the project.

Due to team-dynamics issues, the teams experienced the playing of Protection Poker quite differently. Protection Poker initially aims to support good discussions, and the voting involved when putting out a card is a way to ensure that all team members' opinions are made visible. However, the goal of reaching a consensus is not realistic in many settings. Teams need to be aware that this is challenging, and not necessarily a strict goal. Though it is not beneficial to have everybody always agree, playing Protection Poker with participants that *never* agree, or always need to be right, is challenging. Based on the results from this study one can assume that how well Protection Poker will perform in a team is highly influenced by the team-dynamics, something that should be considered when deciding whether or not to adopt the technique in a development project. Additionally, since no particularly support in software security is built into the technique, teams that decide to use Protection Poker need to have at least one person that is knowledgeable about software security to have some confidence in the resulting risk estimations.

In this case study, we did not directly measure the impact of playing Protection Poker on the security of the end-product. However, responses from students in the questionnaire and in group interviews show that the students themselves assessed the impact on security from playing Protection Poker to be limited. This is, at least in part, due to limited security needs in four out of the six projects, as projects with security needs seemed to experience more of an impact from playing. Still, also for these groups there does not seem to have been a major impact on the end-product. It is thus important to consider what can be done to increase the security impact of playing Protection Poker.

We do not know what factors that potentially made it difficult to use the results from the game in the development. In this case study, it was up to the students to use the results from playing in any way they found fit. We did not follow up on how they used the results, and provided no specific guidance on how to do this. One potential issue is the limitation pointed out by one student in the group interview that the game does not include anything on *how* something can be attacked and *how* such an attack can be mitigated. If students lack this knowledge it can be difficult to understand what can be done to reduce the risk associated with what they consider high risk functionality in the software. The results of playing Protection Poker is a prioritisation, something the students found to be an important benefit (see Fig. 4), however turning this prioritisation into actual development tasks is not necessarily straight forward, especially if the rationale for the scores is lost due to limited note taking (see Table 1).

5.2   Threats to Validity

The threats to validity (and the following text) is similar to what has been identified in a parallel study previously [28]. In the study it is difficult to separate the effect of the technique itself from other factors, such as motivation, skills, group dynamics, and our influence as researchers. In particular, having researchers act as facilitators constitutes a threat to validity that may influence the process and the results and make the study harder to replicate. We have aimed to be aware of the impact of the context throughout the study. One way we did this is by having the first author be supervisor of one student group. Additionally, we made sure we reflected on our role as researchers and took this into account in the analysis (reflection on our influence as researchers was part of the template for observation notes). As part of this, we made it clear for students that their opinion on Protection Poker would not have any impact on their grade in the course. We as researchers did not have any influence on the grades the students got, except for giving some input to evaluators for the group where the first author acted as supervisor.

This study involves students, and thus not professional software developers. There are studies available that show that students in the later parts of their studies can be used with success in studies instead of professional software developers in some cases, namely for understanding dependencies and relationships in software engineering [11] and for requirements selection [24]. The topic of this study is related to, but not identical to, those studies. We do not claim that the results from our study can be generalised to software developers in general, but believe it to be likely that many of the same issues that we found would apply also in professional settings, in particular since many professionals in small and medium sized development organisations would also be considered novices when it comes to Protection Poker and have limited software security training [12]. However, the context would be different. Although the students in our study did have an external customer and the aim of the course is to have a setting that is as similar as possible to a real development project, the students had some concerns that professionals would not have (e.g. the report and getting a good grade) and this may have impacted the results. Their development projects were also likely to be simpler and with fewer security concerns than what many professional developers would likely encounter.

As explained in Sect. 3.2, we made some changes to the original Protection Poker game before this study regarding terminology (exposure) and scale. The issues that we aimed to address with these changes are however still difficult; students mixed exposure and asset value, and the scale was found to be difficult to relate to for some students. We do not know how the students would have responded to the original version of Protection Poker, but at the same time we do not have the reason to believe it is our changes that is the source of the problem. Rather, it confirms our initial concerns that led to the changes and points to the need for further improvements on these issues.

6   Conclusion

Protection Poker is a technique that includes key security requirements engineering activities in a way that is particularly suited to agile development. This study of Protection Poker has identified both benefits and challenges regarding this particular technique, as used in capstone development projects. The technique led to good discussions on security, increasing awareness and knowledge about security in the team. In this study, however, its impact on the security of the end-product seem to have been limited. Improvements may be needed on the scale and on the terminology used. Having a facilitator that is knowledgeable about security and skilled in team work is likely to be a key to success in use of the game.

Acknowledgment. This work was supported by the SoS-Agile: Science of Security in Agile Software Development project, funded by the Research Council of Norway (grant number 247678). Thanks to the course organizers (Prof. Jon Atle Gulla and Prof. John Krogstie) and the participating students at NTNU. Thanks to Prof. Pekka Abrahamsson and Prof. Laurie Williams for input on the study design.

References

1. Ajzen, I., Fishbein, M.: Understanding Attitudes and Predicting Social Behavior. Prentice-Hall, Upper Saddle River (1980)
2. Baca, D., Boldt, M., Carlsson, B., Jacobsson, A.: A novel security-enhanced agile software development process applied in an industrial setting. In: 10th International Conference on Availability, Reliability and Security (ARES), pp. 11–19. IEEE (2015)
3. Beck, K.: Extreme Programming Explained: Embrace Change. Addison-Wesley Professional, Boston (2000)
4. Boström, G., Wäyrynen, J., Bodén, M., Beznosov, K., Kruchten, P.: Extending XP practices to support security requirements engineering. In: Proceedings of the 2006 International Workshop on Software Engineering for Secure Systems, pp. 11–18. ACM (2006)
5. Caroli, P., Caetano, T.: Fun Retrospectives - Activities and Ideas for Making Agile Retrospectives More Engaging. Leanpub, Layton (2015)
6. Cockburn, A., Highsmith, J.: Agile software development, the people factor. Computer **34**(11), 131–133 (2001)
7. Davis, F.D.: A technology acceptance model for empirically testing new end-user information systems: theory and results. Ph.D. thesis, Massachusetts Institute of Technology (1985)
8. Davis, F.D.: Perceived usefulness, perceived ease of use, and user acceptance of information technology. MIS Q. **13**, 319–340 (1989)
9. Dybå, T., Moe, N.B., Mikkelsen, E.M.: An empirical investigation on factors affecting software developer acceptance and utilization of electronic process guides. In: 10th International Symposium on Software Metrics, pp. 220–231. IEEE (2004)
10. Grenning, J.: Planning poker or how to avoid analysis paralysis while release planning. Hawthorn Woods: Renaissance Softw. Consult. **3**, 22–23 (2002)
11. Höst, M., Regnell, B., Wohlin, C.: Using students as subjects - a comparative study of students and professionals in lead-time impact assessment. Empirical Softw. Eng. **5**(3), 201–214 (2000)
12. Jaatun, M.G., Cruzes, D.S., Bernsmed, K., Tøndel, I.A., Røstad, L.: Software security maturity in public organisations. In: Lopez, J., Mitchell, C.J. (eds.) ISC 2015. LNCS, vol. 9290, pp. 120–138. Springer, Cham (2015). https://doi.org/10.1007/978-3-319-23318-5_7
13. Jaatun, M.G., Tøndel, I.A.: Covering your assets in software engineering. In: The Third International Conference on Availability, Reliability and Security (ARES), Barcelona, Spain, pp. 1172–1179 (2008)
14. Jaatun, M.G., Tøndel, I.A.: Playing protection poker for practical software security. In: Abrahamsson, P., Jedlitschka, A., Nguyen Duc, A., Felderer, M., Amasaki, S., Mikkonen, T. (eds.) PROFES 2016. LNCS, vol. 10027, pp. 679–682. Springer, Cham (2016). https://doi.org/10.1007/978-3-319-49094-6_55

15. Khaim, R., Naz, S., Abbas, S., Iqbal, N., Hamayun, M.: A review of security integration technique in agile software development. Int. J. Softw. Eng. Appl. **7**(3), 49–68 (2016)

16. Li, L.: A critical review of technology acceptance literature. Department of Accounting, Economics and Information Systems, College of Business, Grambling State University (2008)

17. Nicolaysen, T., Sassoon, R., Line, M.B., Jaatun, M.G.: Agile software development: the straight and narrow path to secure software? Int. J. Secure Softw. Eng. (IJSSE) **1**(3), 71–85 (2010)

18. Odzaly, E., Greer, D., Stewart, D.: Agile risk management using software agents. J. Ambient Intell. Hum. Comput. **9**, 823–841 (2017)

19. Oueslati, H., Rahman, M.M., ben Othmane, L.: Literature review of the challenges of developing secure software using the agile approach. In: 10th International Conference on Availability, Reliability and Security (ARES), pp. 540–547. IEEE (2015)

20. Peeters, J.: Agile security requirements engineering. In: Symposium on Requirements Engineering for Information Security (2005)

21. Pohl, C., Hof, H.J.: Secure scrum: Development of secure software with scrum. arXiv preprint arXiv:1507.02992 (2015)

22. Renatus, S., Teichmann, C., Eichler, J.: Method selection and tailoring for agile threat assessment and mitigation. In: 10th International Conference on Availability, Reliability and Security (ARES), pp. 548–555. IEEE (2015)

23. Savola, R.M., Frühwirth, C., Pietikäinen, A.: Risk-driven security metrics in agile software development-an industrial pilot study. J. UCS **18**(12), 1679–1702 (2012)

24. Svahnberg, M., Aurum, A., Wohlin, C.: Using students as subjects - an empirical evaluation. In: Proceedings of the Second ACM-IEEE International Symposium on Empirical Software Engineering and Measurement, pp. 288–290. ACM (2008)

25. Tavares, B., Silva, C., Diniz de Souza, A.: Risk management analysis in scrum software projects. Int. Trans. Oper. Res., 1–22 (2017)

26. Terpstra, E., Daneva, M., Wang, C.: Agile practitioners' understanding of security requirements: insights from a grounded theory analysis. In: 2017 IEEE 25th International Requirements Engineering Conference Workshops (REW), pp. 439–442. IEEE (2017)

27. Tøndel, I.A., Jaatun, M.G., Meland, P.H.: Security requirements for the rest of us: a survey. IEEE Softw. **25**(1), 20–27 (2008)

28. Tøndel, I.A., Oyetoyan, T.D., Jaatun, M.G., Cruzes, D.: Understanding challenges to adoption of the microsoft elevation of privilege game. In: Proceedings of the 5th Annual Symposium and Bootcamp on Hot Topics in the Science of Security (HoTSoS 2018), pp. 2:1–2:10. ACM (2018)

29. Vähä-Sipilä, A.: Product security risk management in agile product management. Stockholm, Sweden (2010)

30. Venkatesh, V., Davis, F.D.: A model of the antecedents of perceived ease of use: development and test. Decis. Sci. **27**(3), 451–481 (1996)

31. Weir, C., Rashid, A., Noble, J.: Developer essentials: top five interventions to support secure software development (2017)

32. Williams, L., Gegick, M., Meneely, A.: Protection poker: structuring software security risk assessment and knowledge transfer. In: Massacci, F., Redwine, S.T., Zannone, N. (eds.) ESSoS 2009. LNCS, vol. 5429, pp. 122–134. Springer, Heidelberg (2009). https://doi.org/10.1007/978-3-642-00199-4_11

33. Williams, L., Meneely, A., Shipley, G.: Protection poker: the new software security game. IEEE Secur. Privacy **8**(3), 14–20 (2010)

An Experimental Evaluation of Bow-Tie Analysis for Cybersecurity Requirements

Per Håkon Meland[1,2]([✉]), Karin Bernsmed[1], Christian Frøystad[1], Jingyue Li[2], and Guttorm Sindre[2]

[1] SINTEF Digital, Trondheim, Norway
{per.h.meland,karin.bernsmed,christian.froystad}@sintef.no
[2] Norwegian University of Science and Technology, Trondheim, Norway
{per.hakon.meland,jingyue.li,guttorm.sindre}@ntnu.no

Abstract. Bow-tie analysis includes a graphical representation for depicting threats and consequences related to unwanted events, and shows how preventive and reactive barriers can provide control over such situations. This kind of analysis has traditionally been used to elicit requirements for safety and reliability engineering, but as a consequence of the ever-increasing coupling between the cyber and physical world, security has become an additional concern. Through a controlled experiment, we provide evidence that the expressiveness of the bow-tie notation is suitable for this purpose as well. Our results show that a sample population of graduate students, inexperienced in security modelling, perform similarly as security experts when we have a well-defined scope and familiar target system/situation. We also demonstrate that misuse case diagrams should be regarded as more of a complementary than competing modelling technique.

Keywords: Bow-tie analysis · Requirements elicitation ·
Controlled experiment · Digital exams

1 Introduction

There is an increasingly tight coupling between the cyber and physical world, which leads to new forms of risks that have not been considered adequately, such that the cyberelement adversely affects the physical environment [2]. This is typically seen in industries that up until now have been running on isolated platforms and networks, but through rapid digital transformations find themselves exposed to hostile cyber attacks from new categories of adversaries, as well as unintentional disclosure of sensitive data. For instance, a *Shodan* search conducted by Trend Micro in 2017 found more than 83,000 industry robots exposed on the Internet, whereas more than 5,000 of these had no authentication whatsoever [20]. These robots were operating in sectors such as automotive, aerospace, defence, food and beverages. Similarly, the increased connectivity and lack of

S. K. Katsikas et al. (Eds.): CyberICPS 2018/SECPRE 2018, LNCS 11387, pp. 173–191, 2019.
https://doi.org/10.1007/978-3-030-12786-2_11

security awareness in the shipping industry are making stakeholders worried that this will become the "the next playground for hackers" [42]. A common trait to all of these industries, is that there are already well-established practices for managing safety concerns. If these practices can be extended to also encompass security, we might have an easier path than introducing a set of security analysis techniques that are unfamiliar to them and must be done in parallel.

Security models provide a useful basis for security analysis and requirements elicitation, e.g. supporting comparative evaluations of threats and intended security properties [3]. Security modelling comes in many different forms and flavours [4], and there is not necessarily one single best or correct way of performing it [34]. In many practical situations, this is a choice depending on factors such as available resources, focus area, domain, level of abstraction and personal preferences, but there is currently little empirical knowledge that can guide us when making these trade-offs. Just as with a number of other phenomena within software engineering disciplines, there are many techniques and methods that are used because "conventional wisdom" suggests that they are the best approaches. As a remedy to this, experiments can investigate the situations in which the claims are true [26]. According to Tichy [39], "experimentation can accelerate progress by quickly eliminating fruitless approaches, erroneous assumptions, and fads. It also helps orient engineering and theory into promising directions".

The purpose of this paper is to present the result of an experiment related to bow-tie analysis applied for cybersecurity. Bow-tie analysis has a long tradition from the safety and reliability domain, where identified preventive and reactive barriers are used as sources for eliciting requirements. We wanted to explore how well the same analysis technique performs in the context of security, and complements to existing security modelling techniques, such as misuse case diagrams [36]. The research hypothesis central to this work is that *the bow-tie notation has a suitable expressiveness for security as well as safety*. There already exists evidence that bow-tie analysis performs well for safety considerations, but if the hypothesis is falsified, then applying bow-tie analysis in assessment where we need to consider both safety and security in combination would make no sense.

This paper is structured as follows. We briefly show related work and explain the history and notation of bow-ties in Sect. 2. The same section also show how bow-tie diagrams compares with misuse case diagrams. In Sect. 3, we explain our research method and the details of the experiment at hand. This is followed by a summary of results in Sect. 4. These results are then interpreted and discussed as a part of Sect. 5, and the paper is concluded in Sect. 6.

2   Background

2.1   Models Covering Safety and Security

There are many examples in the literature of models that allow combinations of safety and security considerations. For instance Johnson [11] shows how to build cybersecurity assurance cases for Global Navigation Satellite Systems (GNSS) using Boolean Driven Markov Processes (BDMP), extending conventional fault trees. Winther et al. [41] include security as part of HAZOP studies, which is a systematic analysis on how deviations from the design specifications in a system can arise, and whether these deviations can result in hazards. Raspotnig et al. [28] make use of UML-based models within a combined safety and security assessment process to elicitate requirements. Kumar and Stoelinga [16] combine fault and attack trees so that both safety and security can be considered in combination. Fishbone diagrams are similar to bow-ties, and are mentioned in Nolan's book on safety and security reviews for the process industries [25], but examples here only focus on safety incidents. FMVEA (Failure Mode, Vulnerabilities and Effect Analysis) [32] is safety and security co-analysis method extended from FMEA (Failure Mode and Effect Analysis), which is a safety analysis method. Like FMEA, FMVEA proposes to use the STRIDE model [35] to identify threat modes first, and then analyze the effect each threat mode. Further examples of methods, models, tools and techniques in the intersection of safety and security can be found in the surveys by Zalewski et al. [43], Piètre-Cambacédès and Bouissou [27], Chockalingam et al. [7], as well as Kriaa et al. [15].

2.2   Bow-Tie History

Bow-tie analysis has since the 1970s been used by organisations world-wide for risk management purposes, but primarily to demonstrate control over health, safety and environmental (HSE) hazards [17]. For instance, Khakzad et al. show this application in safety risk analysis in offshore drilling [12], Trbojevic and Carr [40], as well as Mokhtari et al. [23], do the same for safety assessment in international maritime ports, and Lu et al. [19] apply bow-ties in the context of leakage from natural gas pipelines.

In our modern cybersecurity world, we have to consider the intertwined relationship between safety and security during risk assessment, and make sure that requirements can be traced back to a *source*, such as a barrier. As already described by Bernsmed et al. [4], there have been several efforts at adopting the bow-tie notation for cybersecurity within areas such as engineering environments and maritime operations. This is because these areas are already familiar with the notation from safety assessments, and therefore it is assumed to be easier obtaining community buy-in by evaluating cybersecurity threats in the same way as accident scenarios. However, we are not aware of any empirical evidence from the literature proving that bow-ties are suitable to cover security concepts in addition to safety.

2.3   The Bow-Tie Modelling Notation

A central part of bow-tie analysis is the creation of graphical bow-tie diagrams. A bow-tie diagram is something that resembles a fault-tree on the left hand side with an event-tree on the right [17]. Figure 1 gives an overview of the modelling elements that have been included in our experiment, based on [4]. First of all, the *Hazard* element represents the riskful environment in which one or several

Unwanted events (aka. *top event*) can occur, but which is also necessary to perform business. Note that we only model one top event per diagram. A *threat* is anything that can potentially cause an unwanted event [1], and there can be several types of such threats in a single diagram. To prevent or eliminate threats, we can add *barriers* (aka. *controls*) that interfere between threats and the top event. An *Escalation factor* is a specific type of threat that targets a barrier, opening up for the original threat.

A top event can result in one or several *consequences*. As with threats, we can add *controls/barriers* that can reduce the probability or eliminate the consequences, but these are now of a reactive nature since the top event has already occurred.

Finally, and specifically added for security, an *asset* is anything tangible or intangible with value and should be protected. We allow one or more assets to be modelled per diagram.

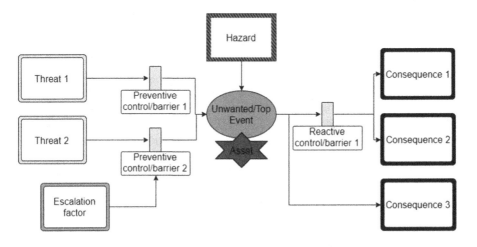

Fig. 1. The basic elements of the bow-tie notation with security extension.

2.4   Bow-Tie and Misuse Case Modelling

Misuse case modelling is a well-known technique for graphical security modelling, and can be summarized as an extension to regular UML use cases [10], adding misuse activities, which can be considered as threats, and mis-actors, who are malicious threat agents instantiating the misuse activities [36]. Misuse cases have been proven useful in different industrial cases when considering security [22] and eliciting requirements [36], and are therefore a good basis for comparison with bow-tie diagrams. Table 1 gives an overview of the main properties of both misuse case and bow-tie diagrams. Based on this comparison, we would argue that misuse case and bow-tie diagrams are more complementary than competing types of security models, something we have exploited in our experiment.

Table 1. A comparison of misuse case and bow-tie diagrams.

Misuse case diagrams	Bow-tie diagrams
[Both] Defined by a simple to understand graphical notation with an open-ended method, allowing for a lot of creativity to the modeller	
Originate from computer security and requirements engineering, based on UML use case diagrams	Originate from the safety & reliability domain, related to fault analysis
Developed to identify malicious actions (misuse) for a given scenario	Developed to investigate accident scenarios and define barriers
The misuse activity element represents an unwanted event (something that threatens regular activities)	The top event element represents an unwanted event
Suitable for describing many different misuse activities in a single diagram	Focus on a single unwanted top event per diagram
Show actors (threat agents) related to misuse activities	Do not represent actors, but in which riskful environment (hazard) the top event can occur
Mitigations are modelled as security activities	Mitigations are modelled as barriers, which are clearly defined as either preventive or reactive
Can depict vulnerabilities that a misuse activity can exploit	Represent threats/causes that can lead to the top event
Consequences are not part of the diagram	Explicitly depict possible consequences following the top event

3   Experiment Method

In order to plan our experiment, we adopted and applied the guidelines by Kitchenham et al. [13], originally designed for empirical studies in software engineering. The form of the study is a *controlled experiment*, which is a scientific method for identifying cause-effect relationships [37], and as a means to "acquire general knowledge about which technology (process, method, technique, language or tool) is useful for whom to conduct which tasks in which environments". The intervention we introduce is the use of the bow-tie notation for security analysis on two sample population that are both working on the same case. Since there are no random assignments, this should be classified as a *quasi-experiment*, and as a formal experiment since we have a high level of control over the variables that can affect the truth of the hypothesis [26].

One of the sample populations consists of students, and therefore it has been important to make sure that they perceive a value from participation [5]. By carefully scoping the case of the experiment and having an approach that is new to the student sample and professionals in general, we expect to get relevant results with external validity [31]. The case in focus and experiment setup is described in the sections below.

3.1 Case: Digital Exams

The security modelling assignment we chose is the use of digital exams, something that is rapidly growing in popularity at Universities and other educational institutions. Here, exams are created, solved and graded using online systems. This is meant to be more efficient than traditional exams done on paper, however, relies on technology and opens up to new types of threats that need to be identified and dealt with. For instance, a survey by Chen and He [6] shows that there is a great diversity of security risks for online exams, nevertheless, security is not considered as a top priority among learning providers and practitioners. Additionally, there is evidence that both digital and "analogue" exams suffer due to new technical ways of cheating. According to the Guardian [21], there has been a 42% rise in cheating cases between 2012 and 2016 involving gadgets such as mini cameras and micro earbuds. London [18] gives an overview of further inventive and not-so-inventive ways that have been used for cheating on online exams. All in all, a case related to digital exams provides an interesting and relevant arena for looking at security issues and possible solutions.

In our case, there are many of students participating in the exam in the same confined room and within the same time frame. This is a bit different to other types of digital exams, which can be done from home and at any given time. Furthermore, the students are allowed to use their own personal computers with internet access through WiFi, but are not allowed to use supporting materials, such as curriculum books and notes. A specific Web browser must be installed on their computers, known as the *Safe Exam Browser*[1] (SEB), which regulates access to websites, search engines, other applications and system calls, also referred to as *browser lockdown*.

3.2 Experiment Setup

Our experiment engaged two types of populations as a basis for comparison; a small sample of security experts and larger sample of computer science MSc graduate students. The characteristics of these groups can be described as follows. The students participated in the experiment as a part of a classroom exercise in a course on secure software engineering, and were motivated to learn security modelling in order to apply such techniques for their exercises and final exam. Before the experiment, the students had taken several lectures including security concepts and principles, OWASP top 10, crypto introduction, multilevel security and multilateral security. The students had limited knowledge of security modelling on beforehand and no experience at all from bow-tie modelling. Moreover, the students had significant practical experience related to digital exams as they had already been exposed to this on several occasions. It is unknown how experienced and reflected they were related to cheating.

The security experts had a great deal of prior knowledge and practical experience in various types of security modelling, and in particular bow-tie for specific

---

[1] This is an open source tool available and further documented at https://www.safeexambrowser.org/.

domains. In contrast to the students, the experts had limited practical experience of participation in digital exams, though one of them was skilled with setting up exams using the online system. The experts were motivated by the research itself, and the desire to create a good reference model that the student results could be compared to.

As an introduction, the students were given a lecture on threat modelling, including the misuse case and bow-tie notations. As we know from prior experiences, one of the challenges of bow-tie diagrams is setting the scope of the unwanted event. Therefore, the students were presented with a misuse case model that we hoped would better define the scope and the relationship between the events. This model is shown in Fig. 2, and depicts a number of actors and typical activities related to digital exams, as well as misuse case activities and associated threat actors. For example, the actor *professor* will need to *log in* to the system and *create exam assignments* prior to the examination day. An external *attacker* actor would possibly want to *steal assignments* and maybe sell this online to students that want to cheat. After the examination day, an additional *external examiner* is involved in the process of *grading exams*. The attacker could at this point in time try to *change the results* of the exam. During the examination day itself, the main legitimate actor is the *student* that needs to *setup* his/her computer, which also involves sub-activities such as *connecting to the network* and *installing the correct SEB software*. In order to *do the exam*, the student must authenticate by *logging in, enter the exam pin* for this particular exam, *solve the assignments* and finally *submit the exam*. On the right side of the diagram, we have depicted a *bad student* actor that inherits all the activities from the legitimate student actor. With the misuse case notation, it is common to use a grey shading for such malicious "insiders" [29]. The bad student has a misuse activity mostly relevant prior to the examination day, which is to *buy the assignments in advance*, and two others that threaten the regular activities during the exam. The first one, *disrupt exam*, is basically a way of sabotaging the examination for everyone, possibly motivated by a wish of cancelling/delaying the exam. The second one is *cheat during exam*, which a student would do to illegitimately improve his/her grade. The *proctor* is a type of examination guard that *supervises the exam* and is there to mitigate cheating attempts and disruptions.

The next step of the introduction was to show how a misuse activity can be detailed as bow-tie top event. This was demonstrated with *disrupt exam* as shown in Fig. 3. In this model, there are a number of threats that can lead to a disruption, such as *tampering with the fuse box* to cause power outage, *jamming the wireless network* or performing some other action to *make the online server unavailable*. The assets that needs to be protected are the *network*, the *SEB software* and the *physical premises* themselves. We added some example preventive controls/barriers, such as *locking the fuse box cabinet* and having a system *mirror site* on hot standby. In terms of disruption consequences, computers can stop working and the bad student can be expelled. The only reactive control/barrier shown here is *switching to paper* in order to complete the exam.

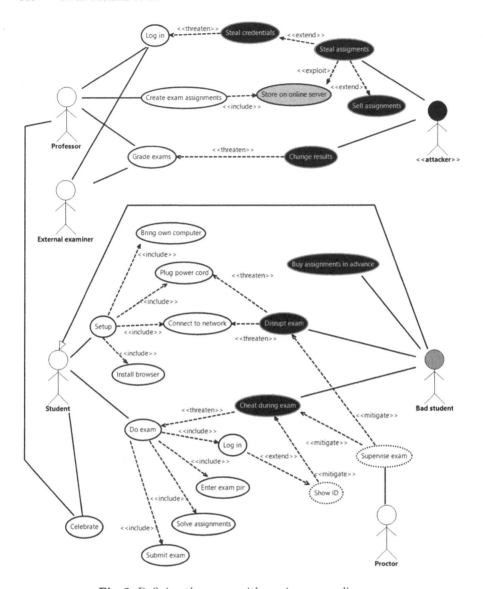

Fig. 2. Defining the scope with a misuse case diagram.

Having introduced the notation, defined the scope and given examples, the populations were now ready to work on their own diagrams. We predefined *digital exam* as the riskful environment, *cheat during exam* as the top event and the asset *answers* as a starting point. Both populations worked on this same case, with access to external information such as SEB documentation and articles about online exams and cheating. The students worked in teams, typically 2-3 persons per model, spending about 30 min on their task, and were observed by two of the authors of this paper. The experts worked independently of each

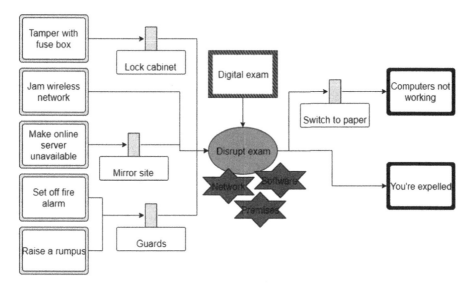

Fig. 3. Example model showed as a preparation.

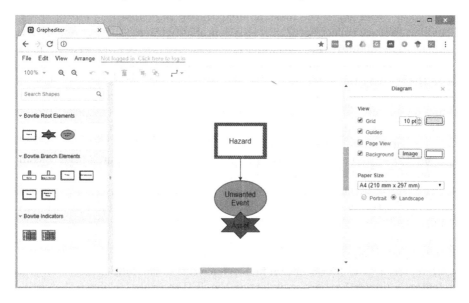

Fig. 4. The online tool used for making the bow-tie diagrams.

other for about one hour. Both populations used an online modelling tool[2] to create their models. The tool itself has an intuitive drag-and-drop interface for the basic bow-tie elements, and runs within any web browser. A screenshot of this tool is shown in Fig. 4.

---

[2] Freely available at https://github.com/KDPRO-SINTEF/BowtieTool.

The students were informed that all participation was anonymous and voluntarily, and that we wanted to make use of the result to evaluate the bow-tie notation for security.

4   Results

4.1   Models Made by Students

A total of 40 students were present in the experiment session, which resulted in 13 different models. Observations from the classroom indicated that approximately 30 students contributed to these models. This estimate is based on the average size of the groups and that we also know that not all models were submitted (this was voluntarily). The models were then analysed, and we created a small taxonomy of threats, controls/barriers and consequences in order to be able to compare them. Based on this, we developed a combined bow-tie diagram, shown in Fig. 5 in Appendix A, which also indicates the frequency of the threat and consequence elements found in the models made by the students. As can be seen from the figure, the top threats were:

– *Analogue cheat sheet*, the most popular threat, appeared in 6 out of the 13 models that we collected (6/13). This is probably the most "traditional" way of cheating, and involves smuggling in and making use of some written material, e.g. paper notes hidden inside the wrapper of a candy bar or somewhere on the body of the student.
– *Access external information* (4/13) encompasses using the computer to search and access information on the Internet.
– *Another person takes exam* (4/13) is related to impersonation and not something that is unique to digital exams.
– *Digital chat with others* (3/13) is when the student computer is used to communicate with others in the same room or on the outside.
– *Hack browser* (3/13) is done by somehow modifying the source code or exploiting an existing vulnerability in the SEB software to disable the lockdown functionality.
– *Run browser in virtual machine* (3/13) was represented as a threat in two of the models, and as an escalation factor in a third. In the combined model, we represent it as an escalation factor since this is basically a way of circumventing a preventive barrier by letting the SEB software lockdown the virtual machine instead of the computer itself.
– *Digital communication with others* (3/13) covers all kinds of gadgets besides the student computer that are used for communication with others. This typically includes bluetooth devices and other radio equipment.
– *Spy on other screens* (3/13), also denoted as "shoulder surfing", is simply ways of looking at other people's answers without them noticing it.

Some additional threats can be found in Fig. 5, but these were only present in one or two of the models. Additionally, we discarded three threats that were out of scope for this top event, namely *Retrieve exam answers beforehand, Disrupt exam* and *Blackmail professor*.

On the consequence side of the diagram, *Cheater gets good results* (7/13) was most prevalent, followed by *Cheater expelled* (6/13) and *Bad publicity* (for the University). It is interesting to see that these are consequences for both successful cheating as well as consequences for the cheater if he/she gets caught.

The combined model does not show the frequency of barriers/controls because a lot of them overlap over more than one threat/consequence. We also noticed that some of the models (4/13) contained additional assets, so we added these to the combined model as well.

4.2   Models Made by Security Experts

There were three security experts participating in this experiment, resulting in three independent bow-tie models. These were analysed in the same manner as the student models and aligned using the same taxonomy. The resulting combined model from the experts is shown in Fig. 6 in Appendix A. There were only four threats that had an overlap between the expert models; *Access external information, Another person takes exam, Hack browser* and *Phone outsiders*. The three former were all present among the top threats from the student models as well, while the latter was not. We discarded one threat from the model, *Introduce vulnerability in SEB OSS project*, since this is something that must be done prior to the exam and hence out of scope for this top event. The expert and student models shared their top consequence, namely *Cheater gets good result*. Besides from that one, there was little overlap between consequences among the experts. Note that there are several threats and consequences that are without any barriers. It turned out that one of the experts forgot about adding these, and therefore spend more time on finding threats and consequences compared to the others.

Table 2 shows a numerical comparison of the models created by the two populations. The last row shows how many distinct elements that are common between the combined models from each population. Since the level of detail vary, it was not possible to always create direct mappings. Therefore, *Communicate via WiFi* and *Communication using bluetooth device* in the expert model is mapped to the single threat *Digital communication with others* in the student model. Likewise, the preventive barrier *Strong authentication* in the expert model maps towards the less strict *Authentication* in the student model.

Table 2. A numerical summary of model elements

Measurement	Experts	Students
Number of participants	3	∼30
Number of models	3	13
Total number of threats	18	49
Number of distinct threats	12	14
Average number of threats per model	6	3.8
Total number of consequences	10	27
Number of distinct consequences	8	9
Average number of consequences per model	3.3	2.1
Total number of preventive barriers	16	41
Number of distinct preventive barriers	10	9
Average number of preventive barriers per model	5.3	3.2
Total number of reactive barriers	6	6
Number of distinct reactive barriers	4	3
Average number of reactive barriers per model	2	0.5
Common threats/consequences/{preventive/reactive} barriers	7/5/3/0	

5   Discussion

5.1   Interpretation of Results

It was interesting to see how well the students were able to grasp the concepts of bow-tie modelling and apply it to the digital exam case after just a relatively short introduction. There are a few notable differences when comparing results from students with experts, such that the average numbers of threats, preventive barriers and consequences per model are all about 60% higher for the experts. This is to be expected, since the experts had a deeper security knowledge and did also have some additional time for developing their models. The number of reactive barriers was clearly higher for the experts, but this is in line with a general observation that the students tended to focus on the left side of the diagram. In fact, out the 13 models of the 13 models from the students had no elements on the right side whatsoever. Another significant difference was that two of the experts modelled two or three barriers for most of their threats, while this was not observed in any of the student models where all threats had just a single control/barrier. This can be interpreted in two ways; the students did not fully understand that the tool supported adding more than one barrier per threat, or the students did not think that it is necessary to implement more than one barrier per threat in a real system. The last experts did, as mentioned above, not model any barriers, and this skews the average barrier per threat significantly. Identifying a wide range of barriers is considered to be one of the primary advantages of bow-tie modelling, and we have made a note to encourage this a bit more in later work.

When we consider the students as a collaborative group, the numbers of the distinct threats, consequences and both types of barriers are almost identical to what the experts produced. When we look beyond these numbers and compare the type of elements in the taxonomy, there is a clear tendency for the experts to focus on technical threats and threats that are specific for digital exams, while the students have included more of the traditional ways of cheating. We believe that both of these inputs can be important, and advocate for a combination of security experts and end-users (in our case, the students) when developing these kinds of security models, and consequently defining requirement based on barriers.

Our general impression is that the students showed great creativity, covering most of the same threats and consequences as the experts identified, and discovering additional ones as well. The bow-tie notation did not seem like an obstacle for expressing this, which confirms our hypothesis that the bow-tie notation has a suitable expressiveness for security as well as safety issues. The students also identified additional elements on the consequence side that the experts had not thought of, even though it seems like the students spent most of their time on the threat side. The students seemed just as good as the experts at staying inside the scope of the top event, something we believe can be attributed to the misuse case presentation in the introduction of the experiment.

5.2   Limitations and Threat to Validity

There are several factors to consider regarding the validity of this experiment. Convenience sampling is a threat to a lot of experiments that involve a population consisting of students, as this can come at the cost of low external validity, but we argue that our sample already had taken an interest in security and represent an aspiring group of people that are likely to work with security engineering in their professional careers. According to a survey on controlled software engineering experiments by Falessi et al. [8], there are pros and cons with both the use of professionals and students, and it is impossible to state that one is always better than the other. Studies by Salman et al. [31], Svahnberg et al. [38] and Höst et al. [9] show that there is little difference in performance between these groups, especially for graduate students [30].

Though the participation was voluntarily and anonymously, the students seemed motivated and we did not see any submitted models with frivolous content. Furthermore, it was in their own interest to get some relevant experience in security modelling for their course exercises and final exam.

The time that the students had available for the analysis and modelling was very limited. In real life, a thorough analysis would include defining a series of top events within the same riskful environment, and there would be several iterations on each model to improve their coverage and quality. We have tried to address this by letting the students collaborate directly, and by spending time in the introduction on defining a narrow scope for a single top event. Alternatively, we could also have given different top events to different groups and thus have a wider analysis, but that would impose limitations to the comparison afterwards.

Another limiting factor of this study is that we did not perform any systematic user evaluation. Our evidence is thus solely based on the resulting models, aided by observations and comments received during the experiment. For future work, this can be done in several ways, e.g. with standardised usability surveys or adopt from the *Information Systems* (IS) field Moody's *Method Evaluation Model* [24] that combines measurable constructs such as effectiveness, perceived usefulness and ease of use, intention to use and actual usage. Another approach could also be to engage participants in interacting focus groups where they more freely discuss their opinions.

In our previous work [4], we have more informally evaluated situations that combine safety and security within the same bow-tie models. Though this would have been desirable to try out in this experiment as well, we chose to focus on security issues as we could not find a suitable case where the student would have enough domain knowledge to consider safety, in addition to security.

5.3 Further Research Directions

Both misuse case models and bow-tie diagrams are high-level modelling techniques, and are in their basic forms not concerned about attack sequences, relationships between threats, or attributes such as costs and likelihood. Attack(-Defense) trees [14,33] can for instance be used to further drill down the details of how the unwanted event/attacker goal can be realised, but there is a need to obtain more practical knowledge about what level of granularity and level of detail to represent with various security modelling techniques, and when we should switch between them.

In this experiment, the students and experts did not attempt to transform the barriers into well-defined security requirements. In addition, prioritisation would be the next step of this process, but that would require quantification of risk and mitigation costs. Both of these steps are natural continuations that we would like to follow up.

The bow-tie modelling tool itself was not something we set out to evaluate as a part of this study, but observations and comments suggest that the built-in support for creating and connecting the right elements together was helpful indeed. In our study, the collaborating students were sitting closely together using the same computer, but it would be interesting to see how well such a web-based tool can facilitate online collaboration. The tool has already built-in functionality for sharing models between users, as well as getting a quick start by importing templates made by others. During the analysis, it also occurred to us that an online voting mechanism could help create consensus about which threats, consequences and associated barriers should be prioritised.

6   Conclusion

Our research hypothesis has been that the bow-tie notation has a suitable expressiveness for security as well as safety, and our controlled experiment goes a long way in verifying this. One of the main strengths of bow-tie analysis is the identification of preventive and reactive barriers, which can be used as traceable sources for the following requirements elicitation process. Naïve professionals might have a tendency to focus on preventive barriers, leading to requirements for risk mitigation or avoidance, while experienced professionals seem to balance this more with reactive barriers and requirements for incident management.

Our results are useful in areas where we need to evaluate safety and security concerns together, especially for domains that have experience in HSE hazards, but now needs to expand this with cybersecurity as well. Of course, there should be further studies on a wider range of situations before this can be generalized across domains. The experiment results also advocate for a combination of people involved when creating security models. Our observations show that the security experts were better at finding technical threats and alternative barriers, while the combined mass of students found a wider range of threats (i.e. ways of cheating) and consequences that would affect individuals such as themselves.

Acknowledgment. The research leading to these results has partially been performed by the Cyber Security in Merchant Shipping (CySiMS) project, which received funding from the Research Council of Norway under Grant No. 256508. We would like to thank all participants in the experiment, as well as the group of NTNU students developing the bow-tie modelling tool that has supported our work greatly.

A   Combined Bow-Tie Diagrams

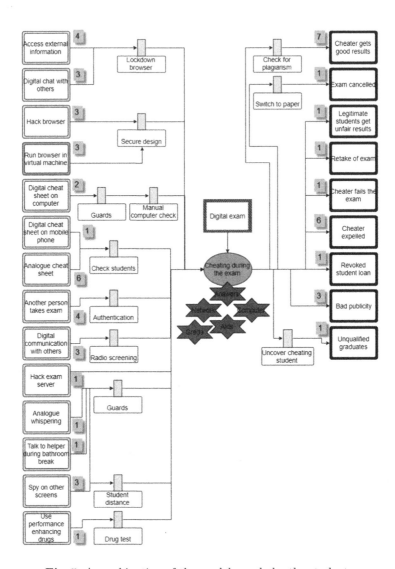

Fig. 5. A combination of the models made by the students.

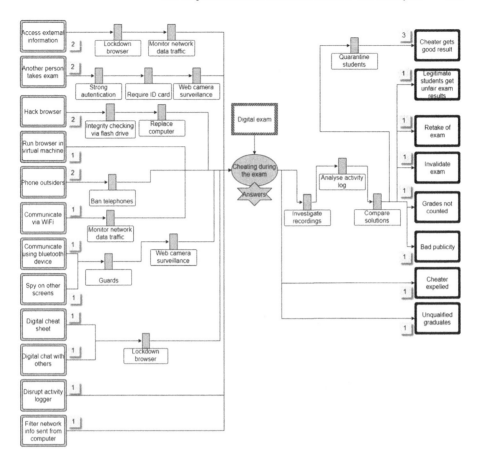

Fig. 6. A combination of the models made by the experts.

References

1. ISO/IEC 27005 Information technology - Security techniques - Information security risk management. Technical report (2008). http://www.iso.org/iso/catalogue_detail?csnumber=56742
2. Banerjee, A., Venkatasubramanian, K.K., Mukherjee, T., Gupta, S.K.S.: Ensuring safety, security, and sustainability of mission-critical cyber-physical systems. Proc. IEEE **100**(1), 283–299 (2012)
3. Bau, J., Mitchell, J.C.: Security modeling and analysis. IEEE Secur. Priv. **9**(3), 18–25 (2011)
4. Bernsmed, K., Frøystad, C., Meland, P.H., Nesheim, D.A., Rødseth, Ø.J.: Visualizing cyber security risks with bow-tie diagrams. In: Liu, P., Mauw, S., Stølen, K. (eds.) GraMSec 2017. LNCS, vol. 10744, pp. 38–56. Springer, Cham (2018). https://doi.org/10.1007/978-3-319-74860-3_3
5. Carver, J., Jaccheri, L., Morasca, S., Shull, F.: Issues in using students in empirical studies in software engineering education. In: 2003 Proceedings of the Ninth International Software Metrics Symposium, pp. 239–249. IEEE (2004)

6. Chen, Y., He, W.: Security risks and protection in online learning: a survey. Int. Rev. Res. Open Distrib. Learn. **14**(5), 108–127 (2013)
7. Chockalingam, S., Hadziosmanovic, D., Pieters, W., Teixeira, A., van Gelder, P.: Integrated safety and security risk assessment methods: a survey of key characteristics and applications. arXiv preprint arXiv:1707.02140 (2017)
8. Falessi, D., et al.: Empirical software engineering experts on the use of students and professionals in experiments. Empirical Softw. Eng. **23**(1), 452–489 (2018)
9. Höst, M., Wohlin, C., Thelin, T.: Experimental context classification: incentives and experience of subjects. In: Proceedings of the 27th International Conference on Software Engineering, pp. 470–478. ACM (2005)
10. Jacobson, I.: Object-Oriented Software Engineering: A Use Case Driven Approach. Pearson Education India, Delhi (1993)
11. Johnson, C.: Using assurance cases and Boolean logic driven Markov processes to formalise cyber security concerns for safety-critical interaction with global navigation satellite systems. Electron. Commun. EASST **45**, 1–18 (2011)
12. Khakzad, N., Khan, F., Amyotte, P.: Quantitative risk analysis of offshore drilling operations: a Bayesian approach. Saf. Sci. **57**, 108–117 (2013)
13. Kitchenham, B.A., et al.: Preliminary guidelines for empirical research in software engineering. IEEE Trans. Softw. Eng. **28**(8), 721–734 (2002)
14. Kordy, B., Mauw, S., Radomirović, S., Schweitzer, P.: Attack-defense trees. J. Log. Comput. **24**(1), 55–87 (2014)
15. Kriaa, S., Pietre-Cambacedes, L., Bouissou, M., Halgand, Y.: A survey of approaches combining safety and security for industrial control systems. Reliab. Eng. Syst. Saf. **139**, 156–178 (2015)
16. Kumar, R., Stoelinga, M.: Quantitative security and safety analysis with attack-fault trees. In: 2017 IEEE 18th International Symposium on High Assurance Systems Engineering (HASE), pp. 25–32. IEEE (2017)
17. Lewis, S., Smith, K.: Lessons learned from real world application of the bow-tie method. In: 6th Global Congress on Process Safety. American Institute of Chemical Engineers (2010)
18. London, M.: 5 ways to cheat on online exams, September 2017. https://www.insidehighered.com/digital-learning/views/2017/09/20/creative-ways-students-try-cheat-online-exams
19. Lu, L., Liang, W., Zhang, L., Zhang, H., Lu, Z., Shan, J.: A comprehensive risk evaluation method for natural gas pipelines by combining a risk matrix with a bow-tie model. J. Nat. Gas Sci. Eng. **25**, 124–133 (2015)
20. Maggi, F., Quarta, D., Pogliani, M., Polino, M., Zanchettin, A.M., Zanero, S.: Rogue robots: testing the limits of an industrial robot's security. Technical report, Trend Micro, Politecnico di Milano (2017)
21. Marsh, S.: More university students are using tech to cheat in exams, April 2017. https://www.theguardian.com/education/2017/apr/10/more-university-students-are-using-tech-to-in-exams
22. Matulevicius, R., Mayer, N., Heymans, P.: Alignment of misuse cases with security risk management. In: 2008 Third International Conference on Availability, Reliability and Security, ARES 2008, pp. 1397–1404. IEEE (2008)
23. Mokhtari, K., Ren, J., Roberts, C., Wang, J.: Application of a generic bow-tie based risk analysis framework on risk management of sea ports and offshore terminals. J. Hazard. Mater. **192**(2), 465–475 (2011)
24. Moody, D.L.: The method evaluation model: a theoretical model for validating information systems design methods. In: ECIS 2003 Proceedings, p. 79 (2003)

25. Nolan, D.P.: Safety and Security Review for the Process Industries: Application of HAZOP, PHA, What-IF and SVA Reviews. Elsevier, Amsterdam (2014)
26. Pfleeger, S.L.: Design and analysis in software engineering: the language of case studies and formal experiments. SIGSOFT Softw. Eng. Notes **19**(4), 16–20 (1994)
27. Piètre-Cambacédès, L., Bouissou, M.: Cross-fertilization between safety and security engineering. Reliab. Eng. Syst. Saf. **110**, 110–126 (2013)
28. Raspotnig, C., Karpati, P., Katta, V.: A combined process for elicitation and analysis of safety and security requirements. In: Bider, I., et al. (eds.) BPMDS/EMMSAD -2012. LNBIP, vol. 113, pp. 347–361. Springer, Heidelberg (2012). https://doi.org/10.1007/978-3-642-31072-0_24
29. Røstad, L.: An extended misuse case notation: including vulnerabilities and the insider threat. Ph.D. thesis, Access Control in Healthcare Information Systems, pp. 66–77 (2008)
30. Runeson, P.: Using students as experiment subjects-an analysis on graduate and freshmen student data. In: Proceedings of the 7th International Conference on Empirical Assessment in Software Engineering, pp. 95–102. Citeseer (2003)
31. Salman, I., Misirli, A.T., Juristo, N.: Are students representatives of professionals in software engineering experiments? In: Proceedings of the 37th International Conference on Software Engineering, vol. 1, pp. 666–676. IEEE Press (2015)
32. Schmittner, C., Ma, Z., Smith, P.: FMVEA for safety and security analysis of intelligent and cooperative vehicles. In: Bondavalli, A., Ceccarelli, A., Ortmeier, F. (eds.) SAFECOMP 2014. LNCS, vol. 8696, pp. 282–288. Springer, Cham (2014). https://doi.org/10.1007/978-3-319-10557-4_31
33. Schneier, B.: Dr. Dobb's J. Attack trees **24**(12), 21–29 (1999)
34. Shostack, A.: Experiences threat modeling at microsoft. In: Modeling Security Workshop. Department of Computing, Lancaster University, UK (2008)
35. Shostack, A.: Threat Modeling: Designing for Security. Wiley, Hoboken (2014)
36. Sindre, G., Opdahl, A.L.: Eliciting security requirements with misuse cases. Requirements Eng. **10**(1), 34–44 (2005)
37. Sjoeberg, D.I.K., Hannay, J.E., Hansen, O., Kampenes, V.B., Karahasanovic, A., Liborg, N.K., Rekdal, A.C.: A survey of controlled experiments in software engineering. IEEE Trans. Softw. Eng. **31**(9), 733–753 (2005)
38. Svahnberg, M., Aurum, A., Wohlin, C.: Using students as subjects-an empirical evaluation. In: Proceedings of the Second ACM-IEEE International Symposium on Empirical Software Engineering and Measurement, pp. 288–290. ACM (2008)
39. Tichy, W.F.: Should computer scientists experiment more? Computer **31**(5), 32–40 (1998)
40. Trbojevic, V.M., Carr, B.J.: Risk based methodology for safety improvements in ports. J. Hazard. Mater. **71**(1–3), 467–480 (2000)
41. Winther, R., Johnsen, O.-A., Gran, B.A.: Security assessments of safety critical systems using HAZOPs. In: Voges, U. (ed.) SAFECOMP 2001. LNCS, vol. 2187, pp. 14–24. Springer, Heidelberg (2001). https://doi.org/10.1007/3-540-45416-0_2
42. World Maritime News: IMB: Shipping Next Playground for Hackers (2014). http://worldmaritimenews.com/archives/134727/imb-shipping-next-playground-for-hackers/
43. Zalewski, J., Drager, S., McKeever, W., Kornecki, A.J.: Towards experimental assessment of security threats in protecting the critical infrastructure. In: Proceedings of the 7th International Conference on Evaluation of Novel Approaches to Software Engineering, ENASE 2012, Wroclaw, Poland (2012)

Towards General Scheme for Data Sharing Agreements Empowering Privacy-Preserving Data Analysis of Structured CTI

Fabio Martinelli, Oleksii Osliak[(⊠)], and Andrea Saracino[(⊠)]

Istituto di Informatica e Telematica, Consiglio Nazionale delle Ricerche, Pisa, Italy
{fabio.martinelli,oleksii.osliak,andrea.saracino}@iit.cnr.it

Abstract. This paper proposes an extension to the standard STIX representation for Cyber Threat Information (CTI) which couples specific data attributes with privacy-preserving conditions expressed through Data Sharing Agreements (DSA). The proposed scheme allows, in fact, to define sharing and anonymization policies in the form of a human-readable DSA, bound to the specific CTI. The whole scheme is designed to be completely compatible with the STIX 2.0 standard for CTI representation. The proposed scheme will be implemented in this work by defining the complete scheme for representing an email, which is more expressive than the standard one defined for STIX, designed specifically for spam email analysis. Hence, an application to an email is presented, together with DSA definition and inclusion in a STIX record. Finally, a set of experiments will show the performance improvement related to data access, brought by the adoption of the proposed scheme.

Keywords: Cyber threat intelligence · Privacy-preserving ·
Threat information sharing · Data Sharing Agreements

1 Introduction

With the huge amount of information daily collected, produced and processed by IT devices, both new opportunities and security issues are raising. (Big) Data Analytics is an extremely hot research topic and it is the enabler of a completely new business market, where collected information is extremely valuable since they can be exploited to provide services, infer customer preference, timely detect security threats, etc. However, the process of collecting and processing information for analysis brings noticeable issues on the side of security and privacy. In fact, analyzed data may contain sensitive information, whose disclosure might harm physical persons, compromise companies reputation and assets, or expose public institutions classified features. For this reason, data sharing and analysis should be done in a privacy-preserving way, i.e. according to specific policies preventing the misuse and redistribution of sensitive data.

Some frameworks have been recently proposed for secure data sharing and for privacy-preserving data analysis (PPDA) [10], which allow defining data sticky policies, by means of Data Sharing Agreements (DSA), which are enforced at the time of

© Springer Nature Switzerland AG 2019
S. K. Katsikas et al. (Eds.): CyberICPS 2018/SECPRE 2018, LNCS 11387, pp. 192–212, 2019.
https://doi.org/10.1007/978-3-030-12786-2_12

sharing data, or at analysis time. However, the main drawback of these frameworks is the difficulty to operate at the same time on data pieces coming from different domains, with a different format and semantic. Since generality is now a requirement for the existing analysis use cases, it is needed to define common formats for data representation, which also express the semantic of reported information, for allowing the definition of standardized mechanisms for data extraction and conversion from raw format, to be used as input for analysis function and as parameters for DSAs. A first significant effort in this direction is represented by the STIX[1] representation methods for CTI, which differently from other standards for CTI such as CEF, introduces CTI-related semantic to contextualize different elements of the reported information, still without being specific to the actual format and semantics of the represented piece of information.

In this paper, we propose a STIX-based data representation for privacy-preserving data analysis, to report format and semantics of specific data types, and to represent sticky policies in the format of embedded human readable DSAs. More specifically, we exploit and extend the STIX standard, to represent in a structured way analysis-ready pieces of data and the attached privacy policies. In particular, this is done by defining a JSON scheme for each information type, to be coupled with another JSON scheme used for generic DSAs. In this work, we report a novel scheme for structured representation of *e-mails*, more complete and expressive than the standard defined already for STIX[2]. The proposed scheme is specifically designed for spam email analysis, since the considered attributes have been taken from the work in [14]. The presented scheme will be detailed, with a focus on the analysis-based chosen semantic and an application will be presented with performance experiments, to show the brought improvement on the side of information handling. Furthermore, we propose a generic scheme for DSA representation, designed to easily express highly configurable privacy-preserving policies, with an attribute level of granularity. Finally, it will be shown and discussed the full compatibility with the standard STIX model, by reporting a STIX example of CTI related to a spam email, structured with the proposed method and protected through an attached DSA.

The rest of the paper is organized as follows: Sect. 2 reports background information on privacy-preserving data analysis, CTI representation standards and the concept of Data Sharing Agreement. Section 3 describes the extended scheme for email representation and reports the extension for DSA representation. Section 4 shows the application of the proposed scheme to a real email and the integration with state-of-the-art tools. Section 5 reports a small set of experiments to show the performance improvement in data access brought by the adoption of a structured data representation. Section 6 surveys a small set of related work. Finally Sect. 7 briefly concludes by proposing some future directions.

2   Background

This section reports some background concepts related to standards for CTI representation and sharing, with an emphasis on the STIX standard considered in this work.

---

[1] https://oasis-open.github.io/cti-documentation/stix/intro.

[2] https://docs.oasis-open.org/cti/stix/v2.0/stix-v2.0-part4-cyber-observable-objects.pdf.

Afterward, we will summarize some basic concepts of Privacy Preserving data Analysis and on the concept of Data Sharing Agreement.

2.1   CTI Representation

Nowadays, many organizations produce, collect and share information related to cyber threats. According to National Institute of Standards and Technology (NIST) [5], Cyber Threat Information is any information related to threats that might help organizations in protecting themselves against cyber threats or in detecting the activities of a threat agent. There are five types of threat information: Indicators, Tactics, Techniques, and Procedures (TTPs), Security Alerts, Threat intelligence reports, and Tool Configurations. Indicators as technical artifacts indicate that the attack is implementing or the system compromise has already occurred. TTPs describe the behavior of the threat agent, techniques that actor used for performing an attack (e.g., delivery mechanism, an attack tool, exploit). Security Alerts are technical notifications regarding vulnerabilities, exploits and other issues. Tool Configurations are sort of recommendations for using different mechanisms that support the automated collections, analysis, and exchange of CTI. Finally, Threat intelligence reports describe information related to the type of attacked systems, TTPs, information about the threat actor, and another CTI that provides better situational awareness to organizations.

For achieving better cyber threat situational awareness, organizations share CTI with partners, colleagues and other entities that they trust. In fact, an exchanging of CTI could help organizations in identifying potential threats, system vulnerabilities and develop a better course of actions for attack mitigation.

Several standards have been defined for CTI sharing in the last years. OpenIOC[3] is an extensible XML scheme for the description of technical characteristics that identify known threats, methodology used by the threat agent, or other evidence of compromise. This scheme can be extended as needed and free IOC editor software to create OpenIOC indicators are available. However, there is no support for describing TTPs by the OpenIOC and it has a limited commercial adoption comparing to other standards. Incident Object Description Exchange Format (IODEF) defines an XML data representation that provides the framework for sharing information commonly exchanged by Computer Security Incident Response Teams (CSIRTs) about computer security incidents. IODEF is an open standard through Internet Engineering Task Force (IETF). However, it requires other formats to describe TTPs or campaigns, and it was designed to share Incident data instead of Indicators Of Compromise. Collective Intelligence Framework (CIF)[4] is the open-source platform used to store and to share CTI. It utilize IODEF data format for sharing and storing threat-related information. The most common types of threat intelligence stored in CIF are IP addresses, domains, and URLs that are observed to be related to the malicious activity. This framework covers various data-observations from any source and creates a series of observations. Meanwhile, CIF does not provide the description of TTPs and threat actor data. Moreover, systems' vulnerabilities and

---

[3] http://www.openioc.org.

[4] http://csirtgadgets.org/.

malware information are missing. However, these approaches do not consider sensitive data protection, and they are mainly focused on collection and expression of CTI. Moreover, these standards do not utilize CTI with predefined semantics. Thus, the time needed to perform any operation on CTI is increasing.

Currently, the most widely in use standard for CTI representation is *Structured Threat Information Expression* (STIX)[5], and *Trusted Automated Exchange of Intelligence Information* (TAXII)[6] allows exchanging CTI over HTTPS. The advantage of STIX among other approaches is that this standard provides a broad and comprehensive description of CTI in a structured way.

The STIX Standard. *STIX* is a standardized language for representing and describing CTI in the structured way. The main purpose of STIX standard is to enable organizations to exchange and use CTI in the consistent and machine-readable format. The latest version - STIX 2.0 is designed using JavaScript Object Notation (JSON), which is an improvement of the previous versions which were based on XML. STIX 2.0 allows improving different capabilities, such as collaborative threat analysis, automated threat exchange, automated detection and response.

STIX 2.0 defines 14 different *objects* for describing various aspects of CTI. In particular, these objects are divided into two categories. The first category is *STIX Domain Objects* (SDOs) which contains 12 SDOs. These objects are exploited to describe observed information in a system or network, describe software used by threat actors for performing attacks, the vulnerability of a system, identify individuals, groups, or organizations which are operating with malicious purpose, etc. The second category is *STIX Relationship Objects* (SROs) and it defines 2 SROs. These objects are intended to describe the relationships between SDOs. Table 1 reports and shortly describes all STIX Objects.

STIX is able thus to assign a semantic to specific aspects of CTI, still, this is done without specifying semantic and syntactic rules for the content of every object. For example, this might lead to representation mistakes and in the end to the definition of ad-hoc event representations, which might vary for each data type and for each specific application or use case in which STIX is used. For performing a comprehensive description of specific CTI it is necessary to create the bundle with a set of SDOs and SROs for describing relationships between SDOs. Hence, having the structured representation of the cyber observable with the description of each component (e.g. malware, vulnerability, identity) and how these elements relate to each other, would strongly simplify the process of information exchange, since the standard will be given for the collection, representation, and use of structured stored information.

While STIX standard is used for describing the complete CTI, Malware Attribute Enumeration and Characterization (MAEC)[7] can provide a more detailed description of malware through five top-level objects such as *Behaviors, Malware Actions, Malware Families, Malware Instances*, and *Collections*. Moreover, STIX 2.0 is able to

---

[5] https://oasis-open.github.io/cti-documentation/stix/intro.

[6] https://oasis-open.github.io/cti-documentation/taxii/intro.

[7] https://maecproject.github.io/.

Table 1. STIX Objects

Object name	Description	Category
Observed Data	Transfers observed information on a system or network	Domain Object
Attack Pattern	Describes methods that use by threat actors for compromising targets	Domain Object
Campaign	Reports a set of malicious activities or already occurred attacks against a particular target or set of targets in a specific period	Domain Object
Course of Action	A specific action which is undertaken for prevention or responding to a cyber attack	Domain Object
Identity	Describes entity or list of entities which might be as individuals, organizations or groups	Domain Object
Indicator	Defines a pattern that can be used for detection of malicious anomalies or cyber activity	Domain Object
Intrusion Set	A set of behaviors and resources with common properties which might be utilized by a threat agent	Domain Object
Malware	A malicious code and/or malicious software, used by a threat agent to compromise data or system of victim	Domain Object
Threat Actor	Entity or list of entities that might operate with the malicious purpose	Domain Object
Tool	Software that might be used by a hacker for performing a cyber attack	Domain Object
Vulnerability	A mistake or weakness in software that might be used by a threat agent to gain illegal access to a system or network of a victim	Domain Object
Relationship	Links two different STIX Domain Objects and describes relationships between them	Relationship Object
Sighting	Denotes that an element of CTI was seen	Relationship Object
Report	A collection of cyber threat intelligence with the description of one or more subjects (e.g. malware, threat agent, vulnerability)	Domain Object

describe attack patterns by using *Common Attack Pattern Enumeration and Classification*[8] library.

2.2 Privacy Preserving Data Analysis

CTI sharing among trustful partners and customers enables collaborative analysis to identify potential cyber threats and discover unknown vulnerabilities. On the other

---

[8] https://capec.mitre.org/about/index.html.

hand, information sharing itself poses an issue for sensitive data protection during the usage by other entities [4]. In fact, different privacy-preserving techniques are exploited by data controllers to protect shared information. This operation helps to protect sensitive data from disclosure during the usage by other entities involved in the sharing process. However, by enforcing privacy mechanism on data, it may affect the accuracy of the analysis result.

As an example, let us consider the following scenario. A *data controller*[9] shares a dataset in the raw format with a data processor. This dataset includes information of emails and the sticky policy. While this information contains the number of recipients, email addresses, text, and the description of attachments, the stiky policy defines a set of requirements to be applied to dataset before sharing it with other entities. Considering, that email address is the sort of sensitive information and can be used by third parties against individuals and organizations, protecting this information is crucial for both of them. Therefore, in this scenario, the policy defined by the data owner specifies the requirement which states that email address of recipients must be encoded. However, by enforcing privacy-preserving techniques to the recipient email address, it may decrease data-utility. As the result, it affects the accuracy of different statistical data analysis such as clustering [1]. Meanwhile, in order to analyze information in a privacy-preserving way and at the same time achieve the best analysis result, entities involved in information sharing, have to define the best trade-off between data-utility and information loss [10]. Sensitive data such as email address of recipients might be used for identifying a spear phishing attack on a specific organization[10].

Since organizations can collect and share information by using different approaches and tools, the format and semantics of the shared data by one organization can be represented in the different format comparing to data provided by other entities. Thus, it could be another issue for performing a collaborative and automated data analysis of information reported in different formats because it might require the use of various tools and standards designed for analyzing data in the specific format. For this reason, organizations perform different data manipulation operations before sharing data in order to transform information from the raw format to the structured one. Together with data, organizations can provide the policy that defines a set of obligations and requirements for regulating the way of using information.

2.3 Data Sharing Agreement

Usually, organizations involved in information sharing process, apply privacy-preserving techniques to data that they share with each other in order to protect sensitive data by enforcing different policies. Such policies might be enforced directly on data before sharing, or shared together as a sticky policy [6]. The policy can be included in DSA and contain a set of requirements and obligations to be enforced on specific information.

---

[9] https://www.gdpreu.org/the-regulation/key-concepts/data-controllers-and-processors/.
[10] https://www.cpni.gov.uk/system/files/documents/87/93/spear-phishing-understanding-the-threat.pdf.

Data-Sharing Agreement (DSA) is the formal contract between one entity which has useful data *(Data Controler)* and other entities *(Data Processors)* which are seeking for data to perform analysis according to specified conditions and requirements. The main purpose of DSA is to regulate the way of data usage and sharing. DSA embeds thus the sticky policy which contains the set of requirements to be applied on specific data. These requirements specify terms and conditions of how the provided data can be shared and used by entities specified in DSA [11]. Typically, DSA describes data that is shared and it determines the list of both Data Provider and Data Consumer obligations. *Data Provider Obligations* require providing the specific data to the consumer according to the specified quality and temporal constraints, *Data Consumer Obligations* bind data consumers to protect shared information from copying, sharing with other entities which are not specified in DSA and guarantee to delete data after the defined period of usage. Obligations might be divided into two categories: conditional on events (e.g., detection of threats, a confirmation of receiving data, etc.) and state predicates [13,16].

In addition, by using DSA, the data owner can specify what type of operation should be performed (e.g., generalization, encryption) either on the dataset or a specific attribute of data and who can access to this information. Data policy can be represented in the same format as provided data or in the different one.

3   Proposed Approach

This section reports and describes our approach detailing the extended scheme for email representation and the one for DSA representation.

3.1   Email Scheme for Spam Analysis

Spam emails are still the most used attack vector for distributing malicious software and links to malicious resources among different users[11]. Thus, having an ability to analyze this information on time becomes crucial for protecting both organizations and individuals against cyber threats.

For representation and description of cyber observable events such as email messages, log files, etc., STIX 2.0 contains the Observed Data object. The data manipulation operation can be done faster and more effectively by using CTI described through the proposed model. For this work, we decided to use the spam email as a use case. For this reason, we propose the scheme for representation of emails, with more properties useful in the analysis of spam emails. To be compatible with STIX, the proposed model is based on JSON. However, unlike, the existing scheme for describing emails, we are proposing a new one, that describes email messages more widely. Instead of using referenced objects, in our scheme, we have used objects that are embedded. Table 2 reports the list of properties of the scheme and shortly describes them.

The first four properties describe information related to the sender. The sender_type property describes the type of the email sender that could be either organization or individual. The sender_ip property describes the IP address of the device

---

[11] https://www.verizonenterprise.com/verizon-insights-lab/dbir/.

Table 2. Email object properties

Property name	Type	Required	Instances
sender_type	String	Yes	Single value
sender_ip	String	Yes	Single value
sender_name	String	Yes	Single value
sender_address	String	Yes	Single value
subject	String	No	Single value
subject_language	String	No	Single value
characters	Integer	No	Multiple value
recipient	Array	Yes	Multiple value
recipient_id	Identifier	Yes	Single value
recipient_ip	String	Yes	Single value
recipient_name	String	Yes	Single value
recipient_address	String	Yes	Single value
recipient_category	String	Yes	Single value
recipient_number	Integer	Yes	Multiple value
body	String	Yes	Single value
email_id	Identifier	Yes	Multiple value
email_format	String	Yes	Multiple value
email_language	Array	Yes	Multiple value
email_size	Integer	Yes	Single value
attachment	Array	No	Multiple value
attachment_format	String	No	Single value
attachment_number	Integer	No	Single value
attachment_size	Integer	No	Single value
safety_rating	String	No	Single value
link	Array	No	Multiple value
link_number	Integer	No	Multiple value
link_ip	Integer	No	Single value
link_at	Integer	No	Single value

which was used to send the email. Under certain conditions, IP address might be used for identifying the possible location of the device. The sender_name property describes the name of the sender that might be the name of the organization or an individual person. Finally, the sender_address defines an email address from which the original email message was received. Meanwhile, it does not mean that the spammer used exactly this email address because the sender of this email might be a victim as well as recipients.

The subject of the email can be described by using three properties of the scheme. The `subject` is the single value and it defines the type and the format of the subject (e.g., digits, letters). In addition to this, the `subject_language` property defines the subject language. Finally, the `characters` property reports the type of characters used in the subject and its length.

Since the number of recipients might be more than one, the `recipient` property defines all recipients through an `array`. Moreover, each recipient defined by using the `id` which provides a unique ID number for the recipient. The `recipient_ip` property identify the IP address of the recipient. It could be used as one of the aspects for determining the recipient location. The `recipient_address` property reports the email address of the recipient, the `recipient_category` describes the category of each recipient and the possible values are `To`, `Cc`, and `Bcc`. Finally, the `recipient_number` property reports the number of all recipients specified in the email, which might vary in the interval $[1; 100]$. The part of the scheme for describing information related to the email recipient is reported in Listings 1.1.

Listing 1.1. Recipient data

```
{
"object": {
"type": "scheme",
"id": ...
...
"recipient_data" {
"recipient_number": {
"type": "array",
"minItems": "1",
"maxItems": "100",
"items": {
"recipient": {
"type": "string",
"enum": ["organization", "individual"],
"id": "string",
"ip": {
"type": ["number", "string"],
"format": ["string.string.string.string"]
},
"name": {
"firstname": "string",
"lastname": "string"
},
"address": {
"type": "email_address",
"format": [
"string.string@string.string",
"string.string@string.string.string",
"string@string.string",
"string@string.string.string"]
}
}
}
},
"recipient_category": {
"type": "string",
"enum": ["To", "Cc", "Bcc"]
}
},
...
```

The following properties of the scheme concern email format, language, size, and body. The `email_language` property is used to specify in which language the email text, if any, has been written. Since more languages can coexist in the same text, this property is described through an array. The body property reports the content of the email, which might be plain text or HTML page, including figures, and it could have both values at the same time [17].

Spammers usually use HTML-based emails in creating spam emails. For example, the message can be represented as the image with some link to the web-page of the official organization and contain the malicious code at the same time. In fact, by opening the link, the recipient can download malware or open the malicious website, which can be used by spammers for obtaining personal data. This technique was used in spreading the "Storm Worm" [2] and "VBS.Davinia.B"[12]. Moreover, by using this technique, spammers have avoided some spam filters so that the email was delivered to victims.

The format of the email and size are specified by using respectively the email_format and email_size properties of the scheme. Since different formats might coexist in the same email, the email_format property might have multiple values. The remaining part of the scheme reports the set of properties for representing attachments and links. Since the email can contain more than one attachment, the attachment property has multiple values. While the attachment_number defines the number of all attachments, attachment_size reports the size of each of them.

Spam email contains links that might be dangerous. One of the technical tricks used by spammers is link manipulation also known as URL hijacking [12]. The main idea of this engineering trick is to make the malicious link and the malicious website to which this link appears, to look like the webpage of the official organization. Thus, the victim downloads the malware or provides personal information (e.g., bank account data). Therefore, it is necessary to identify, describe and list all links contained in the email. For this reason, the scheme contains four properties which describe all necessary information about links in the text. Since the email might contain the number of links, thus the link property has multiple values. In addition to this, the link_number defines the number of all links, while link_ip reports links which appear as IP addresses and link_at determine links represented as email addresses.

3.2 Scheme Extension for DSA Representation

DSA policies express conditions on data usage and access, specifying who can access and use data, for which purpose and time extent. DSA can be written using different languages: from natural one to structured languages such as CNL, or enforceable ones, like EPAL and XACML [3]. The scheme proposed in this section aims to describe a human-readable DSA, where single pieces of data are paired with their access conditions and specific rules which report eventual Data Manipulation Operations (DMO) to be executed on data pieces in order to preserve privacy. The scheme is intended to represent DSA in a user readable format with the description of conditions and requirements for CTI sharing. Table 3 reports the list of properties for describing attributes of DSA.

The dsa_id property is intended to uniquely identify the DSA. The provided_data property reports a synthetic description of the information type object

---

[12] https://www.symantec.com/security-center/writeup/2001-020713-3220-99.

Table 3. DSA properties

Property name	Type	Required	Instances
dsa_id	Identifier	Yes	Single value
created_by_ref	Identifier	Yes	Single value
created_date	Timestamp	Yes	Single value
agreement_date	Timestamp	Yes	Single value
expiry_date	Timestamp	Yes	Single value
entities	String	Yes	Single value
data_controller	String	Yes	Single value
data_controller_id	Identifier	Yes	Single value
contact_info	String	Yes	Single value
address	String	Yes	Single value
telephone	Integer	Yes	Single value
email_address	String	Yes	Single value
data_controller_name	String	Yes	Single value
data_controller_description	String	No	Single value
data_processors	Array	Yes	Multiple value
data_processor_id	Identifier	Yes	Single value
contact_info	String	Yes	Single value
address	String	Yes	Single value
telephone	Integer	Yes	Single value
email_address	String	Yes	Single value
data_processor_name	String	Yes	Single value
data_processor_description	String	Yes	Single value
conditions	Array	Yes	Multiple value
condition	String	Yes	Single value
condition_id	Identifier	Yes	Single value
created	Timestamp	Yes	Single value
created_by_ref	Identifier	No	Single value
condition_name	String	Yes	Single value
condition_description	String	No	Single value
requirements	Array	Yes	Multiple value
requirement	String	Yes	Single value
requirement_id	Identifier	Yes	Single value
dmo	String	Yes	Single value
dmo_description	String	Yes	Single value
provided_data	String	Yes	Single value
provided_data_id	Identifier	Yes	Single value
ref	String	Yes	Single value
attributes	Array	Yes	Multiple value
attribute_name	String	Yes	Single value

of the DSA, which is uniquely identified through the `provided_data_id` property. The `created_date` property reports the date when the agreement was created, which is different from the `agreement_date` property, which describes the starting validity date of the DSA. On the contrary, the `expiry_date` property reports the end date for DSA validity.

The scheme contains information about the organization, which provides data, and information of entities that want to use this data according to the list of conditions and requirements defined in DSA. For this reason, information related to the entity that provides data is described through `data_controller` property which includes seven sub-properties. The `data_controller_id` uniquely identifies the entity with an ID-number. The `contact_info` property contains contact information of the data controller based on the `address`, `email_address`, `telephone` sub-properties. Finally, the `data_controller_name` and `data_controller_description` sub-properties define the name and shortly describe the entity.

Since, provided data by the data controller might be used by the number of various entities, the `data_processor` property has multiple value. The scheme contains `data_processor_id` property in order to uniquely identify each entity that use data. The `contact_info` sub-property describes contact information of each entity, and it is based on the `address`, `email_address`, `telephone` sub-properties. The name of the data processor might be described by `data_processor_name` sub-property, while `data_processor_description` sub-property shortly defines the description of the data processor.

The remaining part of the DSA scheme is related to `conditions`, which is a property including multiple sub-properties, duplicated for each piece of information regulated by the DSA. In particular, the `requirements` property is an array of rules which can potentially have an item for each data attribute, i.e. for each property of the data scheme. For example, supposing the DSA is related to an email, described through the scheme we proposed, a specific requirement can be defined for the *subject*, one for *recipient*, etc. For each requirement it is possible to specify the intended *party* for which is going to be valid, linked to one of the `data_processor_id`, the reference to the specific data property, represented through the `provided_data` property and the DMO to be applied, specified by the associated property. Finally, the *$ref* describes a path to the information.

It is worth noting that the proposed scheme for DSA representation can be applied to any data type, which is represented through the scheme.

4   Application

This section reports the application of the proposed scheme for the email representation, with the attached DSA used to represent anonymization conditions on some attributes of the email message.

As a use case let us consider one example, where two parties are involved in CTI sharing. In our scenario one organization [Party A] is the provider of CTI, and another

[Party B] receives and uses this information. As the part of CTI let us use one of the sanitized emails available online[13].

In the scenario, some employees of the Party A received some spam email through one of the email services. In our case, the email is in the `eml` format, while by using the proposed scheme Party A can represent it in the JSON format as the cyber observable object. Then, by using STIX 2.0 objects, Party A can create the complete bundle such as Listing 1.3, with the comprehensive description of the spam email including information of the sender, recipients, attachments, and links if they exist. The spam email in the eml format is shown in Listing 1.2.

Listing 1.2. Raw email message

```
Delivered-To: bruce@untroubled.org
Received: (fqmail 17580 invoked from network); 09 Jul 2017 20:21:44
-0000
Received: from mx04.futurequest.net
(mx04.futurequest.net [69.5.6.175])
by 10.170.1.170 ([10.170.1.170])
with FQDP via TCP; 09 Jul 2017 20:21:44 -0000
Received: (qmail 9119 invoked from network); 9 Jul 2017 20:21:44
-0000
Received: from obstacle.tynce.us (obstacle.tynce.us [79.124.56.107])
by mx04.futurequest.net ([69.5.6.175])
with ESMTP via TCP; 09 Jul 2017 20:21:43
-0000
Date: Sun, 09 Jul 2017 13:20:12 -0700
To: <bruce@untroubled.org>
Message-ID:
<f8f706c3938feec43d1f111ad3c0a047.2222...950@obstacle.tynce.us_0nh>
Mime-Version: 1.0
From: Edwin.Ponce <Edwin.Ponce@obstacle.tynce.us>
Subject: Pre-Approved Notice for up to 7250 for bruce@untroubled.org
Content-Transfer-Encoding: 8bit
Content-Type: multipart/alternative;
boundary="Section.f8f706c3938feec43d1f111
ad3c0a047"
Content-Length: 5161

—Section.f8f706c3938feec43d1f111ad3c0a047
Content-Type: text/plain

Fund Pre-Approved Notice for bruce@untroubled.org :...
```

The email message reported in Listing 1.2, contains unstructured data represented through the eml format. This data includes personal information such as email address of the recipient, IP addresses, the subject of the email with the specified recipient's email address and email address of the sender. Moreover, other information that might be useful for performing analyses contains the body of the email, its length, and links in the text.

Let us suppose that, in our scenario, according to defined DSA, Party A is obliged to inform Party B about the email in the defined period. Privacy requirements which are contained in the DSA require information of recipients to be anonymized. It is necessary to perform this operation because email addresses of recipients might be considered as sensitive information. Moreover, sender data should be protected because the sender could be a victim as well as recipients. However, in our experiment, we report an example of anonymizing recipients' information. Thus the part of the email

---

[13] http://untroubled.org/spam/.

described with the proposed scheme and reported in Listings 1.3, contains basic data about the recipient before performing policy enforcement defined in DSA. Moreover, Listings 1.3 includes a description of date when this particular email was first observed and reports a path to the proposed scheme used for representing the email.

Listing 1.3. Recipient data in STIX 2.0

```
{
"type": "observed-data",
"id": "observed-data--1a682d598fc2ea6bad8696e302b...",
"created": "2017-07-08T20:50:30Z",
"version": "3.0",
"first_observed": "2017-07-08T20:50:30Z",
"last_observed": "2017-07-08T20:50:30Z",
"number_observed": 1,
"cybox": {
"spec_version": "3.0",
"objects": {
"0": {
"type": "email",
"id": "email--a245cbd6368a7753...",
"$ref": "...\email_message_scheme.json"
}
}
}
...
"recipient_data": {
"recipient_number": 1,
"items": {
"recipient": {
"type": "individual",
"id": "individual--b45cff...",
"ip": "69.5.6.175",
"name": "bruce",
"address": "bruce@untroubled.org"
}
},
"recipient_category": {
"type": "To"
}
}
...
}
}
```

Recipient data contains unique ID number of the recipient, IP address of the recipient's device that was used for open the email message, recipient category, recipient's name and email address.

Recipients data can be considered as sensitive one. Therefore, it is necessary to have an ability to regulate the use and exchange of spam email data, in order to protect sensitive data from the disclosure. Thus, Party A can specify the type of data manipulation operation that must be applied to the specific attribute of the email. Moreover, by using DSA, the organization can list entities which can access to information about the email and how this information can be used by the parties. Listings 1.4 reports an example of applying the proposed model for describing DSA.

The part of the DSA reported in Listing 1.4 contains information related to the Party A and Party B, the condition and requirement to be fulfilled by Party B in order to use provided information. Through DSA, Party A can specify on which attribute of information, the data manipulation operation has to be performed and for whom this requirement is executed. Thus, in our example, DSA states, that for data processor with the particular ID, the recipient name and email address from shared information, has to be anonymized. However, it is worth noting, that by using the proposed model for describing DSA, organizations can specify a set of different conditions and requirements, which have to be fulfilled by various entities that want to use information provided by the organization. For example, both the recipient email address and the name must be anonymized for Party B, and Party C has access to the full dataset without any limitations.

Listing 1.4. DSA semantics

```
{
"DSA": {
"type": "DSA",
"id": "DSA--89320dbd4e0a792bc1676fde2d5bccfc"
   ...
"data_controller": "organization",
"data_controller_id": "organization--084e56ece1fa415e294f05fb...",
"contact_info": {
   ...
},
"data_controller_name": "Party A",
"data_controller_description": "Organization that provides data"
"required": ["contact_info", "data_controller_name", "type"]
}
}
   ...
"data_processor": {
"type": "organization",
"data_processor_id": "organization--0b3fd65bb847e99303e265b9fc73...",
"contact_info": {
   ...
},
"data_processor_name": "Party B",
"data_processor_description": "Organization that uses data",
"required": ["contact_info", "data_processor_name", "type"]
}
}
   ...
"conditions": {
"type": "array",
"minItems": 1,
"addItems": true,
"item": {
"type": "condition",
"condition_id": "condition--4c1a69dd6d993dbe6ce16bc2408311f5",
"created": "2018-03-23T20:50:30Z",
"requirements": {
"type": "array",
"minItems": 1,
"addItems": true,
"item": {
"type": "requirement",
"requirement_id": "requirement--89d1a82269492ea9e706f0c8f20...",
"dmo": "anonymize",
"dmo_description": "recipient address is anonymized",
"data_processor_id": "organization--0b3fd65bb847e99303e265b9fc73...",
"provided_data": {
"type": "string",
"provided_data_id": "email-message--a54b440276274e1aca51063...",
"$ref": "string",
"attributes": {
"type": "array",
"minItems": 1,
"addItems": true,
"attribute_name": "recipient_address",
```

```
"required": ["provided_data_id"]
},
"required": ["attribute_name"]
},
"required": ["data_processor_id", "DMO"]
}
},
"required": ["condition_id", "condition_name"]
...
}
}
```

Then, after performing data manipulation operation specified in the DSA, on the email, the sanitized form of the email through our model is reported in Listing 1.5.

Listing 1.5. Sanitized recipient data

```
{
"spec_version": "2.0",
"type": "bundle",
"id": "bundle --8b8ed1c1 -f01d -4393 -ac65 -97017ed15876",
"objects": [{
"type": "observed-data",
"id": "observed-data --1a682d598fc2ea6bad8696e302b...",
"created": "2017-07-08T20:50:30Z",
"version": "3.0",
"first_observed": "2017-07-08T20:50:30Z",
"last_observed": "2017-07-08T20:50:30Z",
"number_observed": 1,
"cybox": {
"spec_version": "3.0",
"objects": {
"0": {
"type": "email",
"id": "email --a245cbd6368a7753...",
"$ref": "scheme --94377c1569ac6072..."
...
}
...
"recipient_data": {
"recipient_number": 1,
"items": {
"recipient": {
"type": "individual",
"id": "individual --b45cff...",
"ip": "69.5.6.175",
"name": "HIDDEN",
"address": "HIDDEN"
}
},
"recipient_category": {
"type": "To"
}
...
}
```

The STIX 2.0 bundle reported in Listing 1.5 contains one object. The object describes the email message with anonymized recipient's data. However, more detailed information of the email with the description of the threat agent, techniques and the attack pattern used by the threat agent for performing the cyber attack and sanitized information about the recipient, can be reported in the STIX bundle, generated by using SDOs and SROs.

5   Performance Experiments

In this section, we report a set of experiments to measure the improvement brought by the proposed model to performance related to access time and anonymization operations.

To this end, we have used the dataset of emails containing more than 22k emails, extracted as the subset of the much larger spam email dataset collected through several honeypots[14]. The dataset was used for populating the database of emails attributes according to the proposed scheme for describing emails as STIX cyber-observable objects in order to compare the time needed to perform one specific operation in the database with predefined semantic and the dataset of files in the raw format.

For our experiment, we decided to anonymize all recipients' names and email-addresses in both raw dataset and database of attributes for STIX cyber-observable object. For performing our experiments, we have used the following approach.

As the first step, considering that the dataset contains thousands of emails in the raw format, we have created the parser for extracting defined CTI features from eml files. The parser uses a set of regular expressions for determining and extracting various CTI features that might be in emails. Additionally, we have used a set of Python libraries for defining the subject and text language, IP addresses of both recipient and sender, links in the email body, timestamp, etc. Then, by using this parser, we have generated the structured database with extracted emails' attributes corresponding to defined properties of the proposed scheme. In addition to that, we performed an anonymization of all recipients' names and addresses in the database by utilizing the same parser.

Naturally, an anonymization of the whole email address of a recipient decreases the data-utility. On the other hand, some K-anonymity techniques could be used for anonymizing defined parts of email addresses. For instance, the name of the recipient could be anonymized, while the domain name is accessible. In fact, such anonymization increases the data-utility so that emails could be classified according to the domain name. However, at the same time, the domain name could be recognized as sensitive data (e.g., relate to the organization) and used by an intruder. Meanwile, for this work we anonymized complete email addresses of recipients.

As the next step, we have created the second parser for anonymizing recipients' names in eml files. As well as the first parser, the second one uses the regular expression for determining all recipient addresses in both emails header and body if it exists and anonymize them according to the task that we have used in our experiment.

Finally, we have performed our experiment with three different amount of emails in both datasets.

The obtained results show that using the database with the predefined semantics for performing sanitization of CTI can be faster and more efficient with the comparison of using the dataset with files in the raw format. Thus the statistical analysis (e.g., correlation, classification) can be performed by utilizing the database which is already sanitized. Thus, sensitive information will be protected during the analysis process performed by third parties.

---

[14] untroubled.org/spam.

Table 4. Experimental results

Dataset	Raw dataset	STIX dataset
1000	3.25 s	0.015 s
10000	28.457 s	0.223 s
22485	74.866 s	1.655 s

The obtained results justify our assumption that different processes performed on the dataset with predefined semantics can be done faster with the comparison to the dataset of files in the raw format. Moreover, since the number of processes applied to data can be more than one, the time needed to perform each of them becomes critical. However, our approach can solve this issue by proposing the general model for CTI representation. Together with our model, organizations involved in collaborative CTI analysis and sharing can achieve several benefits such as analyze more information at the same time, predict the bigger number of possible cyber threats, detect new vulnerabilities faster and conserve resources needed to perform operations.

6 Related Work

This section reports some works related to CTI sharing. Our work aims to fulfill the lack of the general CTI representation for privacy-preserving data analysis, by proposing the new model for standard CTI and DSA expression.

The approach proposed in [7] deals with correlation analysis of cyber threat incidents using CTI. The proposed framework utilizes an Event Relation Tree (ERT) to store relationships between events and Event Transition Graph (ETG) to represent the temporal transition of characteristics of the event. Meanwhile, the proposed work does not take into account sensitive data protection during the analysis. For instance, the experiment was done by utilizing spear-phishing emails without applying privacy-preserving techniques before performing data analysis. Thus, sensitive information (e.g., emails addresses, IP-addresses) can be illegally used by third parties during the data analysis. However, our approach aims to protect private and/or confidential information during analysis of structured CTI by applying privacy-preserving techniques with the best trade-off defined in [10].

The proposed model in [8] aims to share security information between organizations in one or several countries to improve cyber situational awareness. CTI is described by utilizing STIX standard, while for automated and secure CTI sharing, model uses TAXII protocol. Meanwhile, the proposed model deals with the scenario where communities involved in sharing process, are trustful. It could be an issue for protecting sensitive data such as system type, vulnerability, the name of the victim organization, etc. To achieve trust could be used a trust negotiation framework. However, to minimize the risk of sensitive data leakage, this information, as well as the way of using it, must be protected. Therefore, our work aims to regulate data usage according to DSA.

The approach proposed in [18] reports the framework for collaborative information sharing for community cybersecurity. The framework based on g-SIS model [9] and by using it organizations can share both routine and cyber incident information in the secure way. However, the format of shared information is not defined, and organizations share information only about cyber incidents instead of complete cyber threat intelligence. Moreover, privacy-preserving did not consider during the research, and it can affect both data utility and data leakage.

The framework proposed in [10] deals with secure collaborative information sharing for data analysis. The framework consists of Information Sharing Infrastructure (ISI) and Information Analysis Infrastructure (IAI). It could utilize different types of information provided by data consumers to analyze and share this data according to defined DSA. However, our work aims to speed up the process of applying privacy-preserving techniques, by adopting predefined semantics of both CTI and DSA.

There are many works done related to Data Sharing Agreements (DSAs). For instance, the proposed model in [15] designed with XML language. This model might be useful for applying it together with STIX 1.4. However, our work deals with the latest version of STIX. Thus, the proposed model is inapplicable for our research.

In [16], the proposed model of the data sharing agreement framework was designed with Cω programming language[15]. However, this model is not compatible with STIX 2.0, while DSA model proposed in this work utilizes JSON scheme, which is also used by STIX objects.

7   Conclusion and Future Work

Timely CTI analysis is a task required to infer relevant information to tackle or mitigate new and upcoming security threats in IT systems. To simplify the task of information analysis, common standards for CTI semantic representation enable simplified development of tools for automated analysis, which can rely on a standardized format for specific CTI types. In this paper we have presented a preliminary effort in this direction, to represent the semantic of STIX cyber-observables by defining a general JSON scheme, applied to email for spam analysis. The second proposed general scheme allows to include in the same STIX record privacy policies for privacy-preserving data analysis, in the form of a DSA.

As future work we are planning to extend the methodology by abstracting it to represent attributes common to a wider set of CTI, defining relation and derivation properties for CTI specific attributes. Furthermore, the model will be validated by being applied to other relevant CTI and other properties of the STIX 2.0 standard. Furthermore, we plan to define additional conditions to be included in the proposed DSA scheme, to represent complex policies.

Moreover, for further research, we are planning to use machine learning techniques for automated preprocessing of data in order to extract all necessary CTI features. Finally, we will test both our models by using them together in an automatic way.

Acknowledgments. This work has been partially funded by EU Funded project H2020 NeCS, GA #675320 and H2020 C3ISP, GA #700294 and EIT Digital Trusted Cloud and Internet of Things.

---

[15] https://msdn.microsoft.com/en-us/library/ms974195.aspx.

References

1. Diday, E., Simon, J.C.: Clustering analysis. In: Fu, K.S. (ed.) Digital Pattern Recognition, pp. 47–94. Springer, Heideberg (1980). https://doi.org/10.1007/978-3-642-67740-3_3
2. Genes, R., Arrott, A., Sancho, D.: Stormy weather: a quantitative assessment of the storm web threat in 2007 (2011)
3. Han, W., Lei, C.: A survey on policy languages in network and security management. Comput. Netw. **56**(1), 477–489 (2012)
4. Johnson, C., Badger, L., Waltermire, D., Snyder, J., Skorupka, C.: Guide to cyber threat information sharing. NIST Spec. Publ. **800**, 150 (2016)
5. Johnson, C.S., Feldman, L., Witte, G.A.: Cyber threat intelligence and information sharing. Technical report (2017)
6. Karjoth, G., Schunter, M., Waidner, M.: Platform for enterprise privacy practices: privacy-enabled management of customer data. In: Dingledine, R., Syverson, P. (eds.) PET 2002. LNCS, vol. 2482, pp. 69–84. Springer, Heidelberg (2003). https://doi.org/10.1007/3-540-36467-6_6
7. Kim, D., Woo, J.Y., Kim, H.K.: I know what you did before: general framework for correlation analysis of cyber threat incidents. In: IEEE Military Communications Conference, MILCOM 2016–2016, pp. 782–787. IEEE (2016)
8. Kokkonen, T., Hautamäki, J., Siltanen, J., Hämäläinen, T.: Model for sharing the information of cyber security situation awareness between organizations. In: 2016 23rd International Conference on Telecommunications (ICT), pp. 1–5. IEEE (2016)
9. Krishnan, R., Sandhu, R., Niu, J., Winsborough, W.H.: A conceptual framework for group-centric secure information sharing. In: Proceedings of the 4th International Symposium on Information, Computer, and Communications Security, pp. 384–387. ACM (2009)
10. Martinelli, F., Saracino, A., Sheikhalishahi, M.: Modeling privacy aware information sharing systems: a formal and general approach. In: 2016 IEEE Trustcom/BigDataSE/I SPA, pp. 767–774. IEEE (2016)
11. Matteucci, I., Petrocchi, M., Sbodio, M.L., Wiegand, L.: A design phase for data sharing agreements. In: Garcia-Alfaro, J., Navarro-Arribas, G., Cuppens-Boulahia, N., de Capitani di Vimercati, S. (eds.) DPM/SETOP -2011. LNCS, vol. 7122, pp. 25–41. Springer, Heidelberg (2012). https://doi.org/10.1007/978-3-642-28879-1_3
12. McAfee: What is Typosquatting? https://securingtomorrow.mcafee.com/
13. Seligman, L., Rosenthal, A., Caverlee, J.: Data service agreements: toward a data supply chain. In: Proceedings of the Information Integration on the Web workshop at the Very Large Database Conference, Toronto (2004)
14. Sheikhalishahi, M., Saracino, A., Mejri, M., Tawbi, N., Martinelli, F.: Fast and effective clustering of spam emails based on structural similarity. In: Garcia-Alfaro, J., Kranakis, E., Bonfante, G. (eds.) FPS 2015. LNCS, vol. 9482, pp. 195–211. Springer, Cham (2016). https://doi.org/10.1007/978-3-319-30303-1_12
15. Swamp, V., Seligman, L., Rosenthal, A.: Specifying data sharing agreements. In: Seventh IEEE International Workshop on Policies for Distributed Systems and Networks, Policy 2006, 4-p. IEEE (2006)
16. Swarup, V., Seligman, L., Rosenthal, A.: A data sharing agreement framework. In: Bagchi, A., Atluri, V. (eds.) ICISS 2006. LNCS, vol. 4332, pp. 22–36. Springer, Heidelberg (2006). https://doi.org/10.1007/11961635_2

17. Wang, J., Herath, T., Chen, R., Vishwanath, A., Rao, H.R.: Research article phishing suscep-
tibility: an investigation into the processing of a targeted spear phishing email. IEEE Trans.
Prof. Commun. **55**(4), 345–362 (2012)
18. Zhao, W., White, G.: A collaborative information sharing framework for community cyber
security. In: 2012 IEEE Conference on Technologies for Homeland Security (HST), pp. 457–
462. IEEE (2012)

Run-Time Monitoring of Data-Handling Violations

Jassim Happa$^{(\boxtimes)}$, Nick Moffat, Michael Goldsmith, and Sadie Creese

Department of Computer Science, University of Oxford, Oxford, UK
{jassim.happa,michael.goldsmith,sadie.creese}@cs.ox.ac.uk,
nick@sysverity.com

Abstract. Organisations are coming under increasing pressure to respect and protect personal data privacy, especially with the European Union's General Data Protection Regulation (GDPR) now in effect. As legislation and regulation evolve to incentivise such data-handling protection, so too does the business case for demonstrating compliance both in spirit and to the letter. Compliance will require ongoing checks as modern systems are constantly changing in terms of digital infrastructure services and business offerings, and the interaction between human and machine. Therefore, monitoring for compliance during run-time is likely to be required. There has been limited research into how to monitor how well a system respects consents given, and withheld, pertaining to handling and onward sharing. This paper proposes a finite-state-machine method for detecting violations of preferences (consents and revocations) expressed by Data Subjects regarding use of their personal data, and also violations of any related obligations that might be placed upon data handlers (data controllers and processors). Our approach seeks to enable detection of both accidental and malicious compromises of privacy properties. We also present a concept demonstrator to show the feasibility of our approach and discuss its design and technical implementation.

Keywords: Privacy · Run-time monitoring ·
Policy-violation checking

1 Introduction

As legislation and regulation evolve to incentivise protection of personal data, so too does the business case for demonstrating compliance to the privacy requirements of "Data Subject" (DS). Some believe there is also an ethical obligation on enterprises to consider how to enable individuals to take better, more informed responsibility for the sharing of their personal data, and to support consent and revocation. Whether driven by law, ethics or competitive advantage, we expect demonstration of compliance will become a necessary component of future security and privacy governance and operations. Indeed this is sign-posted clearly by the General Data Protection Regulation (GDPR) [12], and GDPR impacts organisations that handle EU citizens' personal data beyond EU boarders.

© Springer Nature Switzerland AG 2019
S. K. Katsikas et al. (Eds.): CyberICPS 2018/SECPRE 2018, LNCS 11387, pp. 213–232, 2019.
https://doi.org/10.1007/978-3-030-12786-2_13

It is necessary to evolve the risk-management methods employed by enterprises to ensure that they can manage their own risks associated with personal-data handling whilst also supporting enhanced individual-centric controls. Personal data (e.g. date of birth, address, name, likes, photos, etc.) can be thought of as a commodity with service providers holding a licence to use it, but usually not to use it without the express consent of the person who is the subject of the data, the DS. An important enabler for compliance will be to monitor for compliance violations, enabling organisations to detect and analyse violations and so understand how they occur and how to prevent them recurring.

1.1 Contributions of the Paper

We base our work on objectives from the EnCoRe project [11]. This paper considers the challenge of **designing a compliance-monitoring framework for detection of data-handling violations in real time**. Specifically, our focus is on violations of the personal-data use preferences (consents and revocations) expressed by DSs, and also violations of any related obligations that might be placed upon data handlers. To the best of our knowledge, the work in this space is in designing policy and policy languages for data handling against criteria, but not in detecting where these policies and supporting technologies have failed. Our approach is loosely inspired by Intrusion Detection Systems (IDSs) [26], and adds a finite-state machine to identify potential misuses of personal data. From a concept demonstrator, we outline how false positives and false negatives may occur as well as mitigation strategies to minimise them.

2 Related Work

Standards bodies, legislation and regulation have ruled that organisations must respect the privacy of individuals. Examples include OECD [21], EU [19], UK DPA [4]. Updates to the EU regulations regarding are making this requirement more explicit, particularly with the enforcement of the General Data Protection Regulation (GDPR) in 2018. The GDPR embraced 'data protection by design and default' without detailing technical specifications on how it can or should be applied [16].

We believe that what is required is a run-time monitoring approach that if designed into systems handling personal data would provide a genuine data protection by design and default feature capable of taking account of all systems and service evolutions – which supports data usage as opposed to preventing it, and will continue to work no matter how the system changes. This is a property not achievable through verification of system-component integrity and their behaviours alone.

Many commercial products exist, but these are mainly focused on compliance with information-security regulation and standards such as Sarbanes-Oxley [24] and ISO27001. There are no equivalent products focused on privacy and particularly compliance with consents given regarding data handling. This is likely to be because the common practice is to seek blanket consents with limited ability for change (by users or DSs).

The EU project COMPAS has developed a business compliance framework for *Service-Oriented Architectures* (SOAs), specifically for process-driven SOAs [9,27]. It uses *Complex Event Processing* (CEP), achieved using state machines, to recognise patterns of 'low level' events performed by the monitored system [18]; low level events are system-level events that have significance for compliance. A pattern captures one way the system might violate a specific compliance requirement. CEP signals the occurrence of any such pattern using a corresponding 'high level' event. In particular, Mulo [20] describes how to map business activities to so-called 'event trails' and thence to CEP queries/rules. It is a model-aware approach in the sense that monitors have run-time access to models of correct behaviour. Monitors designed using the COMPAS approach aim to check compliance to particular business processes. In contrast, we seek monitors that check for satisfaction of particular 'compliance criteria' (which we will define) concerning the efficacy of controls made available to DSs in relation to the privacy of their data. Our approach is also based on state machines.

Liu et al. [17] describe a static compliance-checking framework targeted at showing that executing business processes satisfy certain specifications. This involves transformation of *Business Process Execution Language* (BPEL) models to pi-calculus processes, and model checking of these processes against LTL models derived from BPSL (a specification language for business processes). The work focuses on business process compliance and not on monitoring actual data-flow compliance as we concern ourselves with here. Garg et al. [15] present an algorithm called: *"reduce"*, that checks audit logs for compliance with privacy and security policies. The paper proves correctness, termination, time and space complexity results of reduce. Chowdhury et al. [8] outlines an approach to temporal mode-checking for run-time monitoring of privacy policies by checking online event trace compliance from caching satisfying instances when it can and fall back to brute force checking when it cannot.

Basin et al. [3] states that existing logic-based policy monitoring is currently limited in their support for aggregations. They take inspiration from aggregation operators found in database query languages like SQL develop a monitoring algorithm for this language. Basin et al. [2] proposes an approach to identify a purpose (of data) with a business process, and show how formal models of interprocess communication can be used to audit or even derive privacy policies. From this assumption, they then propose a methodology for auditing GDPR compliance from a interprocess dataflow model, aspects of GDPR compliance can be determined algorithmically. They also highlight aspects that cannot become GDPR compliant by algorithmic means (i.e. where human action is required). This is an interesting complementary work to ours, which assumes one can design and implement a correct run-time monitor (such as might be achieved using our method) and then investigates efficiency in features.

Other related work that is not aimed at similar run-time monitor designs include: Soto-Mendoza et al. [25] proposed a mechanism to compose privacy policies based on semantic-web technologies. Their composition of rules is based on the data usage context and deduces implicit terms. Their approach uses basic operators and ontology-based rules to consider data-usage context. The authors point out that inconsistencies can be minimised with contextual rules that incorporate priorities. Barth et al. [1] explore contextual integrity by proposing a conceptual framework for understanding privacy expectations and their implications. They formalise a logical framework for expressing and reasoning about norms of transmission of personal information. Datta et al. [10] describe a semantic model that is designed with the goal of enabling specification and enforcement of practical privacy policies. The model consists of a set of interacting agents in roles who perform actions involving personal information in a given context. It is then possible to use traces where each trace is an alternating sequence of states and actions performed by agents that update state.

Privacy-by-design is an approach to systems engineering with seven key principles aimed at taking human values, such as privacy into account in a system's design [6]. The Privacy Management Reference Model (PMRM) [7] is one example of a methodology for understanding and analysing privacy policies and their privacy management requirements in defined use cases. The National Institute of Standards and Technology (NIST) [5] discusses the concepts of privacy engineering and risk management for federal systems and aims to establish the basis for a common vocabulary to facilitate better understanding and communication of privacy risk within federal systems. Fisk et al. [14] define three engineering privacy principles that guide sharing security information across organisations: Least Disclosure, Qualitative Evaluation, and Forward Progress.

3   Establishing Monitoring Requirements

3.1   Assumptions

We assume the system being monitored provides DSs with an ability to express constraints on the handling of their personal data via *Consent and Revocation* (C&R) controls [11]. We say a DS chooses (or makes) particular 'C&R choices' from among available 'C&R options' presented by the monitored system (as dictated by the enterprise and service being operated), where data includes all 'personally identifiable information' pertaining to the DS. We assume enterprises seek to respect the C&R choices made by each DS, within the bounds of the law (i.e. unless a legal warrant will make an enterprise overlook a DS's preference *"not-to-share"*). We allow for the possibility that certain obligations are placed on data handlers regarding how revocation functionality is delivered, whether onward sharing of data is permitted (and to what degree), and how the DS must be kept informed of any data handling.

Our particular focus is on monitors that signal violations of specific types of C&R choice, rather than all types of choice that might arise. We define the control flows related to particular forms of data sharing, parametrized by variables capturing specific instances. The monitors we design then detect in real time any relevant data flows that might violate the wishes of the individual. We recognise that latency within the system could result in false positives, and have developed a strategy for reducing them. In this way we seek to enable detection of accidental or malicious compromises of privacy properties. We describe a concept demonstrator that shows the potential capability of such a system.

We consider how a specific monitor to be deployed must be informed by the data available for collection on a system, and present a general architecture for sensor placement which can be mapped easily onto multiple conforming architectures. The service principles we use are a subset of those adopted by the EnCoRe project [11, 22] (a research project that focused on establishing a logic for how to handle consent and revocation of data from data subjects), which are designed to meet privacy law and regulation.

3.2   Service Principles and Compliance Criteria

Relevant guiding principles to monitor privacy-compliant systems are given below. We consider these to be key to best practice and highly relevant to the satisfaction of privacy regulations in general:

- **Revocation Management:** DSs must be able to revoke previously given consents (explicit or otherwise). Service providers must provide a declared minimal revocation functionality, and respect and act upon all revocation requests except to the extent that the law mandates otherwise.
- **Service Responsiveness:** Clear commitments must be made with regard to availability of service and the speed with which changes in preferences (new consents and revocations) will be implemented. DSs must be offered the facility to be informed whenever the service does not meet pre-specified commitment levels, and of the nature of any resulting non-consented data exposure.
- **Choice Flow-Down:** Data passed between systems will be protected such that the DS's consent and revocation choices are respected by the receiving party. Projected choices at least as restrictive will be respected as the DS's will accompany the data[1].

These principles can be satisfied by a number of criteria that should be met by compliant systems, and which can be used to determine events to monitor. These criteria are generic in the sense that they are independent of the nature of the service or any particular technology platform:

1. Where neither explicit nor implicit consent has been given for storage/processing/sharing of particular personal data, the data should not be used in this way. All revocations of consent must be supported and respected by the system (except where not permitted by law).

---

[1] For the types of CR considered in this paper, projection amounts to removal of 1-step sharing consents. This enables their interpretation at receiving systems without regard for where the data and choices came from. If, on the other hand, projection is trivial (the identity function) then only original choices are ever communicated, which would mean they must be interpreted according to whether the data was received directly from the DS or instead from an upstream system.

2. A published commitment to service performance must be made, specifically including speed of response in acting fully on new choices and changes in choices, in both cases for explicit choices and implicit choices. Furthermore, the speed-of-response commitment must be reasonable, actual service performance relative to commitments must be monitored, and DSs. must from the outset be given the option to be notified when violations occur.

3. When service providers pass personal data to third parties, they must ensure that DSs' consent and revocation choices are passed on with the data and they must seek to protect the data in accordance with these choices. Forwarding of projected choices should be mandatory, which for us are original choices strengthened by removal of 1-step sharing consents.

3.3   A Simple Architecture

Suppose there are some systems, such as the one to be monitored, that are joined together in a chain. We focus on personal data pertaining to a particular DS, and suppose for simplicity that this data may be passed unchanged from a DS to one or more systems in turn, one of which is the monitored system. Personal data that originates from a DS may pass along a chain of systems. This is depicted in Fig. 1 with DS on the left and data passing only left-to-right. The analysis extends straightforwardly to trees. Suppose a DS makes some choices about how his provided data may be processed and/or shared – C&R choices – and that any such choices pertaining to particular data should be passed on faithfully whenever the data is passed between systems (where no explicit choices have been made we suppose default choices have been presented to a DS and he/she has accepted them.) We allow the DS to provide new data and choices at any time, or new choices pertaining to data provided previously. We suppose the architecture of the monitored system is as shown in Fig. 2. This architecture contains three components:

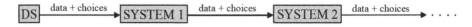

Fig. 1. A system of systems that may pass a particular DS's data and choices along a chain of systems, where one particular system is to be monitored.

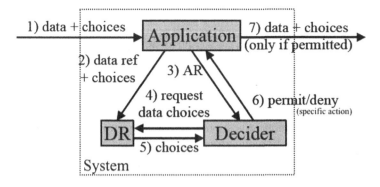

Fig. 2. Architecture of the monitored system, with an intended sequence of messages.

- **"Application"** represents the essential functionality provided by the system, though unconstrained by any Consent and Revocation (C&R) choices that arrive.
- **"DR"** stands for Data Registry and represents a store for C&R choices.
- **"Decider"** represents a component that decides whether to permit or deny requests to process or share particular data (access requests).

The application could be a legacy system onto which are added C&R controls implemented using the Data Registry and Decider. The arrow numbering shows the intended sequence of messages. First, some data and associated choices arrive at the Application component from upstream (either the DS or the closest upstream system). Then a reference to the data is passed, along with the choices, to the DR for storage. Some time later the Application generates an Access Request (AR) to request permission to handle the data in a certain way, and sends this AR to the Decider, which then requests the relevant choices from the DR. On receiving the response, the Decider decides whether to allow the requested access, sending either a permit message or a deny message to the Application. Finally, if the request was to share the data and a suitable permit message was received, the data and associated C&R choices may be passed downstream. Note that we could alternatively assume that data and choices are passed directly to the Data Registry. This would require only small changes to the analysis presented here.

3.4   Sensor Locations

Naturally a monitor for checking end-to-end behaviour of the system would monitor system inputs (message 1 in Fig. 2) and outputs (message 7) and compare the two, looking for unacceptable patterns of these events over time. We call this a "*1:7 monitor*". In the case of the monitors developed here, 'unacceptable patterns of events' means behaviour in violation of C&R choices. Given in-depth knowledge of a system's architecture, it becomes feasible to define further monitors, each corresponding to a particular choice of events to monitor.

Any such choice determines the types of sensors needed and the locations at which to place them. In the following we will focus on specifying "*1:6 monitors*", i.e. monitors that look for violations of C&R choices as evidenced by patterns of system inputs and messages from the Decider to the Application that permit or deny individual data handling requests.

A 1:6 monitor alone gives only partial protection because the Application might misbehave by releasing data when not permitted by the Decider. However, it is fair to expect non-malicious service providers to take steps to avoid Application misbehaviour, by implementing the Application to respect the Decider's decision (using a simple 'final-gate' check, probably easier to assure than the full Application) and/or by using a separate 6:7 monitor. A separate 6:7 monitor may also be suitable in the case of a malicious service provider, or simply a single 1:7 monitor (not relying on the Application respecting the Decider's decision, or even on the system being architected as supposed above). Suitable placement and configuration of monitor components would of course be required for any monitoring solution to be certified as acceptable.

The system handles each DS's personal data, and gives permission for its handling by the operational environment only as allowed by the current records pertaining to that data. The run-time monitoring requirement is to monitor system data-flows at the point decisions are communicated internally (output of the Decider component) and at the point of interface with third parties to check onward sharing, and to compare such flows with the choices retrieved from the repository.

4   Defining Individual Monitors

Individual monitors focus on particular types of data handling: *processing, sharing one step*, and sharing in a way that allows *sharing 'downstream'* (see respective sections below). These notions are explained in the following subsections. C&R choices available to a DS amount to his consenting to certain types of data handling (for particular data) or his revoking of such consents.

4.1   Data Processing

The state machine in Fig. 3(a) specifies a very simple data processing monitor. It is only concerned about processing of a particular datum (item of data) d. The initial state is at the top left of the figure. The state machine observes (events denoting) consent and revocation actions pertaining to processing of d and also to the monitored system giving permission to process d. Events are written using a CSP[2]-like notation [23]. These forms of event are involved:

- **consent.Process.b.d** = the DS gives consent for b to process d;
- **revoke.Process.b.d** = the DS revokes this consent;

---

[2] Communicating Sequential Processes.

- **permit.Process.b.d** = the monitored system gives local permission for b to process d;
- **violation.Process.b.d** = the monitor raises an alert reporting that b has incorrectly given permission to process d.

Here b, c = identifiers for individuals, while d, d' = identifier for datum. The dots ("·") within an event separate it into distinct fields, where the first field is known as the channel. So the events of this state machine occur on the channels consent, revoke, permit and violation. Notice that events on the consent channel denote giving of consent to the monitored system, whereas those on the permit channel denote the monitored system giving local permission for a particular instance of processing. The two states at the top of Fig. 3(a) keep track of whether or not permission to process (given locally by the system) is acceptable given the earlier consents and revocations; the intention is to raise an alert when the system incorrectly gives permission to process d. Both top states allow the permission to be given, but the monitor reacts differently according to its state at the time: if in the right-hand state it simply performs a self-loop (silently accepting the giving of permission); if in the left-hand state it moves to the bottom state and can then only report violation.

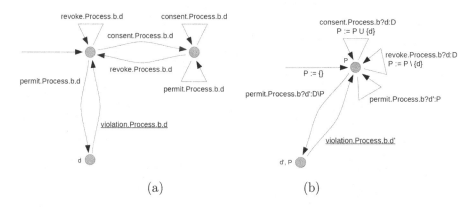

Fig. 3. (a) ProcessDatum (b, d) models compliance monitoring of principal b for processing of a single item of data d. (b) ProcessData (b, D) models compliance monitoring of principal b for processing any elements of a data set D. Underlining in figures denotes an output event; the rest are inputs events to it ('output by'/'internal to' the system).

Figure 3(b) extends the previous state machine to one specifying a monitor for processing any data in a given data set D. This machine uses state variables (sometimes called parameters) to capture some aspects of state. In particular, it maintains a state variable P, which records the set of data items for which local permission to process is acceptable. The bottom node also uses state variable d', which records the data for which permission was (erroneously) given. Each state of this machine is represented partly by an explicit node of the machine and partly by the values of any state variables that annotate the node.

The same forms of event are involved in this machine as in that of Fig. 3(a), though the transition label notation now involves question marks ("?") to denote input of a value from a specified set of values, in particular "*?d:D*" denotes input of the datum d from the data set D. Transitions with labels involving "?" are shorthand for multiple transitions, each labelled by a particular event where the input variable (d or d' in Fig. 3(b)) has been replaced by a particular value from the selection set (D, D\P, or P in the figure) where '\' is setminus.

By maintaining the variable P the machine in Fig. 3(b) avoids having to move between explicit nodes to keep track of when particular local permissions are acceptable. P is always a subset of D. It is initialised to the empty set, as shown in this Figure by the action "$P := \{\}$". P expands and contracts as actions are performed that correspond to consents and revocations. Occurrence of any unacceptable permission event moves the machine to a state in which an alarm is then raised; these about-to-alarm states are all represented by the bottom node. (State variable d' is used in these alarms and promptly forgotten, while P is maintained at all nodes.)

Machines with at least one state variable are known as symbolic and those without are known as explicit. Use of state variables does not increase expressiveness but is a notational convenience that enables a much more succinct graphical representation than would be possible with explicit state machines.

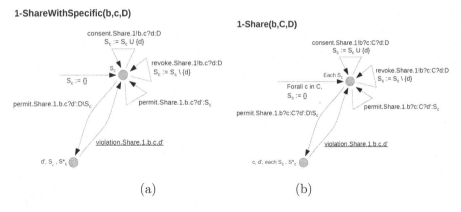

Fig. 4. Monitoring single-step sharing of elements of a data set D (a) with a specific third party c, or (b) with elements of a fixed set C of third parties.

4.2   Data Sharing: One Step

By consenting to one-step sharing the DS permits the recipient to process the data locally and to share it just a single step (in such a way that the next recipient down the chain is permitted to process the data but not to share it). The following new forms of event are involved:

- **consent.Share.1.b.c.d** = the DS gives consent for b to share d with c;
- **revoke.Share.1.b.c.d** = the DS revokes this consent;
- **permit.Share.1.b.c.d** = the monitored system gives local permission for b to share d with c;
- **violation.Share.1.b.c.d** = the monitor raises an alarm reporting that b has incorrectly given permission to share d with c.

Figure 4(a) specifies a monitor for b's one-step sharing of data in D with a specific third party c. Exclamation marks ("!") in the transition labels indicate output of some data. In the state machines shown they are equivalent to dots. Figure 4(b) extends this machine to one for sharing with third parties chosen from a fixed set C.

4.3 Data Sharing: Multiple Step

Figure 5 specifies a monitor for sharing transitively with any third party in C, where "transitive sharing" means enabling the recipient to process the data locally and to share it onward just a single step (if he so chooses) or transitively (enabling the next recipient in the chain to share similarly). Although transitive sharing enables multi-step sharing, it is a consent action between only two principals: the data owner and b here, though in a next step b and a principal with whom b chooses to share transitively.

ShareWithSpecific(b,c,D)

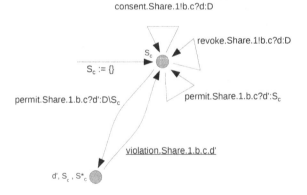

Fig. 5. Monitoring transitive sharing of elements of a data set D with elements of a set C of third parties.

5 Composing Monitor Specifications

The individual monitors of Sect. 4 (or variants of them) can be composed together to yield a monitor capable of reporting any and all of the violations addressed by the individual monitors. Individual monitors described thus far use sets P, S_c and S_c^* having simple interpretations: at all times these sets contain exactly those data items d that the monitored system has permission to process, to share one step (only) or to share transitively. In our discussion we omit subscript c, supposing a particular third-party c is understood.

In many situations it is possible to view consenting to transitive sharing as also consenting implicitly to one-step sharing and processing, and consenting to one-step sharing as also consenting implicitly to processing. It is reasonable to view revoking consent to process as also revoking consent to share one step and revoking consent to share transitively, and to view revoking consent to share one step as also revoking consent to share transitively.

There is thus a natural subset ordering between the sets P, S_c and S_c^* if we continue to use these sets to record precisely when the monitored system has permission to process (in the case of set P), to share one step (in the case of set S), or to share transitively (in the case of set S^*): i.e., $S^* \subseteq S \subseteq P$. Unfortunately this simple interpretation of the sets P, S_c and S_c^* would require each monitor to observe all those consents relevant to these conditions, e.g. the monitor that maintains set P would have to observe all consent events for data sharing, whether one step or transitively (since these are taken to imply consent to process). Similarly, the monitor that maintains set S would have to observe consents to share transitively and also revocations of processing permissions.

We choose to adjust the meaning of the sets P, S_c and S_c^* to reduce the complications needed when composing monitors: we continue to specify that the individual monitors observe precisely those consents and revocations pertaining directly to processing, to one-step sharing, or to transitive sharing, but now interpret the sets as recording whether the corresponding individual monitor would report a violation from its perspective. With this interpretation, after any sequence of Cs and Rs the composite monitor will report a violation if any individual monitor does so. This can be achieved by synchronizing individual monitors on permit events and leaving them to interleave on all others.

6   Accounting for Delays

The simple monitors discussed thus far make no allowance for system latencies. Consequently they can generate false positives (raising alarms when not appropriate due) and false negatives (failing to raise alarms when alarms should be raised) – in both cases because the monitors may judge acceptability of processing/sharing according to out-of-date C&R choices. We now study this issue and attempt to extend the monitors to cope better. Recall that we suppose the monitored system to be architected, see Fig. 2. Each component and each communication path will introduce some delays into the system, causing system latency. Communication delays in the type of system we consider are likely to be very small compared with delays across components, so they may be expected to contribute relatively little to system latency. So for a first approximation we may reasonably disregard the communication delays, or include them in the component delays. For example, in Fig. 6 any delay between the Application sending message 2 and that message being received at DR will be treated as part of the Application's delay.

Recall further that we assume the existence of a published commitment to service performance. It would be sensible for the organisation to allow in this commitment for reasonable delays in processing and communication. We accept the possibility that a change of C&R choices may be implemented in a staged fashion – it would be quite demanding to insist that all changes received together are implemented together simultaneously – but we insist that all data is handled at all times according to at least some complete set of choices expressed by the DS up to some reasonably recent time. Accordingly we propose the notion of 'recent snapshots', where a 'snapshot' captures all the latest choices at some time and a snapshot is 'recent' if its time is at least as recent as necessary to satisfy the service performance commitment. A recent snapshot need not be the most recent snapshot, but it must not be too old (we call any that are too old 'stale'). The service performance agreement should make clear exactly when snapshots would become stale, and we would expect a service provider to offer commitments to service levels according to their understanding of likely system latency, and to propose a notion of "recent" which they intend to deliver against.

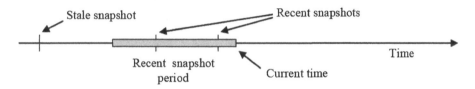

Fig. 6. A recent snapshot is a complete record of a DS's latest C&R choices up to a recent point in time; the time period is chosen to satisfy the service performance agreement. This Figure shows three points at which snapshots were taken, but only the later two are considered to be recent snapshots.

We call the monitors defined in earlier sections "latest-choice monitors" as they work w.r.t. the most recently made relevant C&R choices. Let "recent-choice monitor" mean a monitor that judges action events ("permit" decisions in the case of 1:6 monitors) in accordance with at least one recent snapshot, so requiring a relevant consent EITHER within the "recent snapshot period" OR before it and with no revocation occurring after it. We anticipate that recent-choice monitors can be obtained from corresponding latest-choice monitors by:

1. (additionally) maintaining certain state information that enables recently-consented-to activities (processing or sharing) to be determined even when these are not permitted by the most recent snapshot (i.e. the latest complete set of C&R choices);
2. using this extra state information, not the most recent snapshot, to judge acceptability of action events.

7   Concept Demonstrator

We built a concept demonstrator with an analyst in mind who is responsible for reporting consent and revocation violations. These reports are intended to be used to incentivise protection of DS personal data, but also for demonstrating compliance. Our standalone application assumes an analyst monitors all DS permissions on a service. Implementing our method requires a staged process using the following steps. It is necessary to:

1. determine types of system events relevant to the privacy properties addressed;
2. use generic privacy monitors that notice the occurrence of these events and announce violations deemed to have occurred;
3. choose particular architectural locations at which to place sensors to detect these events;
4. implement a generic monitor fed by sensors placed at the chosen locations.

Any particular choice of locations yields a monitor for the generic property but specialised to these locations. Multiple monitors could be deployed simultaneously. The choice of which monitors to deploy, and at what locations, should be driven by risk assessments.

The tool was built in Java using Swing, JFreeChart and JUNG libraries to handle GUI components. The tool has four main components: the data parsers, the monitors themselves, the archiver and a visual dashboard. The monitors check for violations from parsed events, the archiver stores the outcome of the monitor checks for archiving purposes and finally the dashboard presents the output of the monitors. The monitor creates violation logs that the visualizations make use of. In the future, we envisage monitors could accommodate for enhanced understanding and investigative purposes. The tool parses log files as they appear in a folder, sends the content of these assumed to be in the correct order to a data handler. The data handler stores a current set of actions, whether these be permission changes or requests to read, write or share personal data, and passes them to monitors. Once the monitors raise violations, these are both written to a file for archiving purposes, but also passed to a manager that sends content to its relevant visualization panes and presented to the end-user individual, either the DS or an analyst. For our demonstrator, we ran simulations to synthesize EnCoRe events by maintaining a list of permissions per DS and created a list of how permissions had been handled by an existing data-handling system. Our implementation then checked that list of actions against a DSs permission profile using our method. We ran several simulations on our concept demonstrator to show a proof of concept with several thousand permission requests with a handful of DSs (including groups of DSs). Our simulation did not take delays into account.

We built a state machine to check for read, write and share violations monitors. (Note: this is share once, we do not control for whether data that has been shared once and reached outside our system is shared further). At the simplest level, we check if the Access Subject [11] exists, then check the action intended to be performed, then check purpose of said action, then check the parameter of the purpose and action. If all these access request checks report non-violation, the monitor assumes there to be no violations of the event. The states we can return are akin to those described by Fawcett [13]. However, instead of reporting False Positive, False Negative, True Positive and True Negative, our monitors check events to be **GOOD PERMIT, BAD PERMIT, GOOD DENY, BAD DENY** (see Fig. 7), and finally **MAINTAIN** when no event is occurring.

Monitor Entry #	Log Type	Permit/Deny	Conse...	Violations	Action	ASGroup Term	Violation Time	Log Time
1	AR	BAD_PERMIT;		SHARE;	Share	ASGroup	25/Apr/2012 17:00:07.045	07/Sep/2015 15:0
2	AR	BAD_PERMIT;		SHARE;	Share	ASGroup	25/Apr/2012 17:00:11.081	07/Sep/2015 15:0
3	AR	GOOD_PERMIT;			Write	ASGroup	25/Apr/2012 17:00:12.010	07/Sep/2015 15:0
4	AR	GOOD_PERMIT;			Read	ASGroup	25/Apr/2012 17:00:12.080	07/Sep/2015 15:0
5	AR	GOOD_PERMIT;			Read	ASGroup	25/Apr/2012 17:00:17.074	07/Sep/2015 15:0
6	AR	BAD_PERMIT;		WRITE;	Write	Herbert Smith	25/Apr/2012 17:00:24.094	07/Sep/2015 15:0
7	AR	GOOD_PERMIT;			Read	ASGroup	25/Apr/2012 17:00:26.098	07/Sep/2015 15:0
8	updateSM						25/Apr/2012 17:00:28.446	07/Sep/2015 15:0
9	AR	GOOD_PERMIT;			Read	ASGroup	25/Apr/2012 17:00:30.034	07/Sep/2015 15:0
10	updateDRM		CONSENT		Read	ASGroup	25/Apr/2012 17:00:31.478	07/Sep/2015 15:0
11	AR	BAD_PERMIT;		SHARE;	Share	ASGroup	25/Apr/2012 17:00:35.005	07/Sep/2015 15:0
12	AR	BAD_PERMIT;		SHARE;	Share	ASGroup	25/Apr/2012 17:00:43.075	07/Sep/2015 15:0
13	AR	BAD_PERMIT;		WRITE;	Write	HR	25/Apr/2012 17:00:46.090	07/Sep/2015 15:0
14	AR	GOOD_PERMIT;			Read	ASGroup	25/Apr/2012 17:00:52.034	07/Sep/2015 15:0
15	AR	BAD_PERMIT;		SHARE;	Share	ASGroup	25/Apr/2012 17:00:55.067	07/Sep/2015 15:0
16	updateSM						25/Apr/2012 17:01:02.446	07/Sep/2015 15:0
17	AR	GOOD_DENY;			Share	ASGroup	25/Apr/2012 17:01:04.033	07/Sep/2015 15:0
18	AR	BAD_PERMIT;		SHARE;	Share	ASGroup	25/Apr/2012 17:01:11.013	07/Sep/2015 15:0
19	AR	GOOD_PERMIT;			Read	ASGroup	25/Apr/2012 17:01:14.068	07/Sep/2015 15:0
20	AR	GOOD_PERMIT;			Read	ASGroup	25/Apr/2012 17:01:22.002	07/Sep/2015 15:0
21	AR	GOOD_PERMIT;			Write	ASGroup	25/Apr/2012 17:01:27.003	07/Sep/2015 15:0
22	AR	GOOD_PERMIT;			Read	ASGroup	25/Apr/2012 17:01:31.017	07/Sep/2015 15:0
23	AR	GOOD_PERMIT;			Read	ASGroup	25/Apr/2012 17:01:36.008	07/Sep/2015 15:0

Fig. 7. Monitoring log input/output as shown in the visualization dashboard.

Figure 8 shows the dashboard. Its aim is to show where are violations happening, the health status of the system, what violations relate to particular DSs (Lists), what is the distribution of violations is over time, and finally, what is the network of total violations is. Figure 8 shows the default visualizations: Architecture, Lists, Plot and Graphs. These have been selected for the purpose of communicating the key questions relevant to understand violations, including: "Where are violations happening (on the Architecture)?", "What violations relate to particular DSs (Lists)?", "What is the distribution of violations over time (Plot)?" and "What is the network of total violations (Graph)?"

To the left of the diagram, there is the Tool Bar. The Tool Bar contain various configuration buttons such as refresh/play button (refresh a data capture or continue data input), stop button (stop the intake of new events), zoom-in button (let the last clicked visualization occupy the whole visualization space (as opposed to a quadrant)), zoom out button (show four visualizations), snapshot dump button (create a screen shot and a textual dump of the current state of the visualization), and an exit button (quits the tool). The Menu Bar (top of the screen) contains the same options as the Tool Bar.

These have been added for the purpose of communicating the key questions deemed relevant for understanding violations, including: Where are viola-

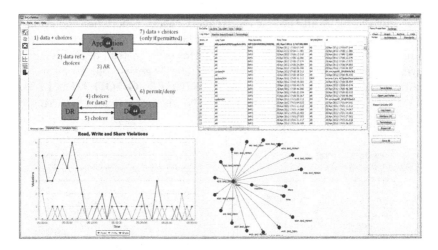

Fig. 8. Screenshot of concept demonstrator.

tions happening (on the Architecture)? What violations relate to particular DSs (Lists)? What is the distribution of violations over time (Plot)? What is the network of total violations (Graph)? To the left of the diagram, there is the Tool Bar. The Tool Bar contain various configuration buttons such as refresh/play button (refresh a data capture or continue data input), stop button (stop the intake of new events), zoom-in button (let the last clicked visualization occupy the whole visualization space (as opposed to a quadrant)), zoom out button (show four visualizations), snapshot dump button (create a screen shot and a textual dump of the current state of the visualization), and an exit button (quits the tool). The Menu Bar (top of the screen) contains the same options as the Tool Bar. The Control Panel (right-hand side) contains the parameters for each visualization, but also the program as a whole. The Control Panel also has the ability to export notes that analysts and DSs make during usage of the tool. Each of visualization pane inherits from a generic pane that describes the basic aspects of what a visualization has to contain, such as listeners from the control panel and monitor, tool bar and menu bar input.

8   Discussion and Future Work

Privacy Impact Assessments presently mostly take no account of run-time performance or the evolution of systems between assessment periods. We believe our method can supplement the existing frameworks of principles by adding to engineering approaches. We believe this engineering space will eventually coalesce to three key ideas:

– **creating and maintaining company policies** that adhere to legislative frameworks and non-disclosure agreements. These policies should allow for developers to understand what data inputs go into a system in the first place, and how the data is handled at the business-decision level. E.g. GDPR and purpose limitation of data collection – data should not be collected for any other purpose than its original intention, and certainly not behind the scenes with the data owner not knowing.

– **creating and maintaining software that adheres to privacy by design principles**, with both the design and implementation of any system being developed with privacy as a *feature*, and *not as a limitation* of new and existing systems.

– **creating and maintaining run-time monitoring systems** that provide added levels of assurance to *document how data has been handled*, but also *enforce data-handling rules* in the interest of DSs as well as the business. Run-time monitoring of compliance to data-handling requirements of DSs may help organisations manage the risk they are exposed to should they act contrary to requirements of any system.

One may consider our approach to be privacy monitoring, as the particular properties we aim to detect would be risks for the privacy of personal data that indicate violations of associated preferences. We observe that there are necessarily performance limitations associated with such a monitoring approach, as system latency can introduce false positive alerts and create situations where violations are missed. However, we demonstrate that our method can be evolved to develop a sensor system that can take account of expected latency and in particular the service performance commitments, which should be developed in a manner cognisant of any expected latencies. Future work will include a detailed design for obligation monitoring, including extensions which allow us to detect violations of time-triggered notification requirements.

– **Information Sharing Enforcement.** In our approach we describe the detection process of permission violations. This is akin to an IDS, whereas there may be cases in which driving the monitors akin to an Intrusion Prevention System (IPS) may be more desirable. In such a system, we envisage key GDPR actions such as anonymisation, pseudonomisation, aggregation of data, but also simply dropping data will play vital roles moving forward to preserve privacy of DSs. We are currently exploring this in the PROTECTIVE project[3] for Cyber Threat Intelligence.

– **Scalability.** Our implementation focused on a locally-hosted solution, in which throughput performance concerns would unlikely be observed. We tested the system with several thousand actions on a handful of DSs as well as a handful of group DSs [11]. We synthesized test data by maintaining a list of permissions per DS and created a list of how permissions had been handled by an existing data-handling system. Naturally, performance will greatly depend on implementation decisions. In production environments: volume, throughput and permission-checking capabilities of permission requests are essential to building a platform that is scalable, specifically: throughput performance, latency and utility.

---

[3] https://protective-h2020.eu/.

- **More Detailed Sensor Architectures.** For any given system, further architectural details could be used to decide on further locations at which to place sensors, and the method described below could then be used to design corresponding monitors. For example, what we call the Decider is implemented in the EnCoRe technical architecture [22] using a set of *Privacy Enforcement Points* (PEPs) and a single *Privacy Decision Point* (PDP). PEPs act as gatekeepers: wherever data handling might occur they request permission to do it from the PDP. This strongly suggests placement of sensors within, or at the interfaces to, the PEPs and PDP when such an architecture is used. In principle it is possible to have sensors detect any intrasystem communications (even distinguishing between sends and receives) or internal processing (notably C&R choice storage or retrieval), and to define monitors that consume these sensor outputs.
- **Monitor Extensions.** *Strict Monitors* – The monitor represented by the state machine can be strict in the sense that it makes no allowance for delays within the system. Such delays are inevitable and could lead to false positives and false negatives. We should ensure the logged data appears (or at least is processed) in suitable order, i.e. ordered according to the right timestamps. *Lenient Monitors* – Conversely, the monitor represented by the state machine can lenient in the sense that it makes allowance for delays within the system. A tock for instance represents the passing of a unit of time, which may for example be a second. The tock can be used as a control self-loop i.e. it leaves the state machine in its current control state but has an associated action that has the effect of dropping any choices (consents, revocations) made since the start of the time window, and taking of account of them in a maintained 'Start of window Snapshot'. The test to decide whether to report a violation is replaced by a test for some suitable consent in the snapshot so consenting. We suspect it will also be necessary to consider consent periods, i.e. timeouts.
- **Usability Considerations.** Our framework assumes the DS is able to understand all of the access and sharing details and consequences and knows when to consent and revoke their consent, which may not always be the case. Future work should assess the usability of any implementation in order to propose best practices, including new visualization methods.

9   Conclusion

In this paper we have presented a novel approach to designing run-time privacy-compliance monitors using a simple finite-state machine to check for permission violations of the various preferences expressed by DSs. We also check for violations of any related obligations that might be placed upon data handlers. We used the EnCoRe [11] policy framework as the basis of method. We designed and implemented a demonstrator intended to be used similarly to IDS tools by analysts and outlined some of the benefits and remaining challenges in implementation. Finally, we also provided a discussion on the broader topic of run-time monitoring and its role moving forward. We believe monitoring of privacy preserving mechanisms will be vital in the years ahead to feasibly demonstrate that 'privacy by design' is designed and implemented in digital systems both in spirit and to the letter, through appropriate documentation of permission violations (that can be reported to DSs more straightforwardly), but also through information sharing compliance enforcement.

Acknowledgement. This research was conducted as a part of the PROTECTIVE project. This project has received funding from the European Union's Horizon 2020 research and innovation program under grant agreement No. 700071. This output reflects the views only of the author(s), and the European Union cannot be held responsible for any use which may be made of the information contained therein.

The EnCoRe project [11] was an interdisciplinary research project, a collaboration between UK industry and academia, partially funded by the UK Technology Strategy Board (TP/12/NS/P0501A), the UK Engineering and Physical Sciences Research Council and the UK Economic and Social Research Council (EP/G002541/1).

References

1. Barth, A., Datta, A., Mitchell, J.C., Nissenbaum, H.: Privacy and contextual integrity: framework and applications. In: 2006 IEEE Symposium on Security and Privacy, 15-p. IEEE (2006)
2. Basin, D., Debois, S.: and Thomas Hildebrandt. Compliance under the GDPR, On purpose and by necessity (2018)
3. Basin, D., Klaedtke, F., Marinovic, S., Zălinescu, E.: Monitoring of temporal first-order properties with aggregations. Form. Methods Syst. Des. **46**(3), 262–285 (2015)
4. British Parliament. Data Protection Act. London Stationery Office (1998)
5. Brooks, S., Brooks, S., Garcia, M., Lefkovitz, N., Lightman, S., Nadeau, E.: An Introduction to Privacy Engineering and Risk Management in Federal Systems. US Department of Commerce, National Institute of Standards and Technology (2017)
6. Cavoukian, A.: Privacy by design. 7 foundational principles (2011). www.ipc.on. ca/wp-content/uploads/Resources/7foundationalprinciples.pdf
7. Cavoukian, A., et al.: Privacy by design documentation for software engineers version 1.0. (PbD-SE). Organization for the Advancement of Structured Information Standards (OASIS), Burlington (2014)
8. Chowdhury, O., Jia, L., Garg, D., Datta, A.: Temporal mode-checking for runtime monitoring of privacy policies. In: Biere, A., Bloem, R. (eds.) CAV 2014. LNCS, vol. 8559, pp. 131–149. Springer, Cham (2014). https://doi.org/10.1007/978-3-319-08867-9_9
9. Daniel, F., et al.: Business compliance governance in service-oriented architectures. In: International Conference on Advanced Information Networking and Applications, AINA 2009, pp. 113–120. IEEE (2009)
10. Datta, A., et al.: Understanding and protecting privacy: formal semantics and principled audit mechanisms. In: Jajodia, S., Mazumdar, C. (eds.) ICISS 2011. LNCS, vol. 7093, pp. 1–27. Springer, Heidelberg (2011). https://doi.org/10.1007/978-3-642-25560-1_1
11. EnCoRe project partners. Encore: Ensuring consent and revocation (2008). http://www.hpl.hp.com/breweb/encoreproject/index.html

12. European Commission. General Data Protection Regulation (2018). https://ec.europa.eu/commission/priorities/justice-and-fundamental-rights/data-protection/2018-reform-eu-data-protection-rules_en

13. Fawcett, T.: An introduction to ROC analysis. Pattern Recognit. Lett. **27**(8), 861–874 (2006)

14. Fisk, G., Ardi, C., Pickett, N., Heidemann, J., Fisk, M., Papadopoulos, C.: Privacy principles for sharing cyber security data. In: 2015 IEEE Security and Privacy Workshops (SPW), pp. 193–197. IEEE (2015)

15. Garg, D., Jia, L., Datta, A.: Policy auditing over incomplete logs: theory, implementation and applications. In: Proceedings of the 18th ACM Conference on Computer and Communications Security, pp. 151–162. ACM (2011)

16. Koops, B.-J., Leenes, R.: Privacy regulation cannot be hardcoded. A critical comment on the 'privacy by design' provision in data-protection law. International Review of Law, Computers & Technology 28(2), 159–171 (2014)

17. Liu, Y., Muller, S., Ke, X.: A static compliance-checking framework for business process models. IBM Syst. J. **46**(2), 335–361 (2007)

18. Luckham, D.: The power of events: an introduction to complex event processing in distributed enterprise systems. In: Bassiliades, N., Governatori, G., Paschke, A. (eds.) RuleML 2008. LNCS, vol. 5321, p. 3. Springer, Heidelberg (2008). https://doi.org/10.1007/978-3-540-88808-6_2

19. Movius, L.B., Krup, N.: US and EU privacy policy: comparison of regulatory approaches. Int. J. Commun. **3**, 19 (2009)

20. Mulo, E., Zdun, U., Dustdar, S.: Monitoring web service event trails for business compliance. In: 2009 IEEE International Conference on Service-oriented Computing and Applications (SOCA), pp. 1–8. IEEE (2009)

21. O'Leary, D.E., Bonorris, S., Klosgen, W., Khaw, Y.-T., Lee, H.-Y., Ziarko, W.: Some privacy issues in knowledge discovery: the OECD personal privacy guidelines. IEEE Expert **10**(2), 48–59 (1995)

22. Papanikolaou, N., Creese, S., Goldsmith, M., Mont, M.C., Pearson, S.: Encore: towards a holistic approach to privacy. In: Proceedings of the 2010 International Conference on Security and Cryptography (SECRYPT), pp. 1–6. IEEE (2010)

23. Roscoe, B.: The theory and practice of concurrency (1998)

24. Sarbanes-Oxley Act. Sarbanes-oxley act of 2002. Public Law (107–204) (2002)

25. Soto-Mendoza, V., Serrano-Alvarado, P., Desmontils, E., Garcia-Macias, J.A.: Policies composition based on data usage context. In: Sixth International Workshop on Consuming Linked Data (COLD 2015) at ISWC (2015)

26. Sundaram, A.: An introduction to intrusion detection. Crossroads **2**(4), 3–7 (1996)

27. Tran, H., et al.: An end-to-end framework for business compliance in process-driven SOAs. In: 2010 12th International Symposium on Symbolic and Numeric Algorithms for Scientific Computing (SYNASC), pp. 407–414. IEEE (2010)

Author Index

Printed in the United States
By Bookmasters